JOHN WESLEY

AND

CHRISTIAN ANTIQUITY

JOHN WESLEY

AND

CHRISTIAN ANTIQUITY

RELIGIOUS VISION AND CULTURAL CHANGE

Ted A. Campbell

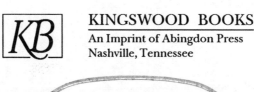

KINGSWOOD BOOKS
An Imprint of Abingdon Press
Nashville, Tennessee

JOHN WESLEY AND CHRISTIAN ANTIQUITY
RELIGIOUS VISION AND CULTURAL CHANGE
Copyright © 1991 by Abingdon Press

Library of Congress Cataloging-in-Publication Data

Campbell, Ted A.
    John Wesley and Christian antiquity: religious vision and cultural change/ Ted A. Campbell
        p.   cm.
    Revision of the author's thesis (Ph.D.)—Southern Methodist University, 1984.
    Includes bibliographical references and index.
    ISBN 0-687-20432-1 (alk. paper)
    1. Wesley, John, 1703-1791.   2. Christianity—Early church, ca. 30-600.   3. Fathers of the Church.   I. Title.
BX8495.W5C25   287'.092—dc20   91-12718

ISBN 0-687-20432-1

Printed in the United States of America
on acid-free paper

In Memoriam
Albert C. Outler

Contents

Preface

This is a study of a religious vision for the renewal of the church, and arises very much out of my own involvement in the quest for renewal. Following a Lay Witness Mission in 1970, the small suburban congregation of which I was a part was captivated by a vision of renewal. The congregation no longer exists, but the quest for Christian renewal has become a central facet of my own life. It is hardly a dispassionate quest on my own part, and the research which this book represents flows immediately from it. If I remark in the course of this book that at points John Wesley's historical understanding was shaped by his own vision for renewal, I do not mean to exclude myself from similar predicaments. History, for me as for Wesley, is tied up with "present politics."[1]

I am indebted to a number of persons and institutions who made this study possible. This book originated as a doctoral dissertation (1984) at Southern Methodist University under the direction of Professor Richard P. Heitzenrater. Not only his critical acumen as an historian, but also his gentle ways with students and his own witness of faith helped to guide this project in its earliest years. Professors John Deschner and William Babcock of Southern Methodist University also served on my dissertation committee and gave valuable guidance to this project. A Foundation for Theological Education in Marshall, Texas, provided a scholarship for the first three years of my doctoral training, and I am very grateful indeed for their continuing support. Dr. Leighton Farrell and the congregation of Highland Park United Methodist Church in Dallas found ways in which I could complete my doctoral work while serving their church. Finally, my friend and companion (and wife), Dale Marie, offered the gifts of time and encouragement and practical wisdom and happiness. To each of these, then, I express my profound gratitude. I also want to express a debt of gratitude to the individual who inspired this study.

In February of 1974, a group of about twenty pre-ministerial students from Lon Morris College traveled north to Dallas to attend a day of Ministers' Week at Perkins School of Theology. We arrived in time to hear an intolerably dull lecture by a representative of the World Council of Churches on "Contemporary Crises in Education." All but two of our company then parted after lunch to take in *The Exorcist*, which had recently made it to Dallas and was very much the topic of conversation among pre-ministerial students.

The two of us who remained were treated to one of Dr. Albert C. Outler's spellbinding lectures on "Theology in the Wesleyan Spirit." It was a kind of intellectual awakening for me; an occasion I shall not soon forget. I wandered the surface of this planet until the autumn of 1979 when I returned to Dallas to begin a doctoral program in religious studies. One evening that fall Professor and Mrs. Outler invited us to their home, and at some point in the evening Albert brought out his massive volumes of William Cave's *Synodikon*, a scholarly treatise on ancient Christian canons, a copy of which John Wesley had taken to Georgia in 1735. We tried to imagine Wesley in the wilds of colonial Georgia with these erudite tomes and their Latin, Greek, and Syriac texts.

If it was Professor Outler's lectures that inspired my initial interest in Wesley Studies as a critical, intellectual enterprise, it was his personal interest in Wesley's vision of "Christian antiquity" that suggested what became the topic of my dissertation and now forms the subject of this book. Dr. Outler served as an *amicus curiae* (that was his description) to my dissertation committee. I fear that my research disappointed him in some ways: he had hoped, in particular, that it would confirm his suspicion that Wesley's doctrine of sanctification was in essence that of ancient Eastern Christian asceticism, which came to Wesley from Gregory of Nyssa by way of the so-called "Macarian" homilies.[2] Although my researches have indeed shown that Wesley was attracted to the doctrine of sanctification expressed in the *Spiritual Homilies* attributed to Macarius, they also show that Wesley consistently omitted references to ascetic life and to the notion of *theiosis*—"divinization" or "deification"—perhaps the most distinctively Eastern note in the Macarian literature.

If I have differed in my particular findings, however, I shared with Dr. Outler his passion to "place" Wesley in an ecumenical framework. In my own case, this passion arises from my heritage in Evangelical Christianity and the quest for a self-critical Evangelicalism in which I am engaged. Those of us who face the challenge of ecumenical thought from the perspective of the Evangelical inheritance are deeply indebted to Dr. Outler, who in his later years befriended so many of us, and offered us both rebuke and encouragement in our quest. I want to honor him by dedicating *John Wesley and Christian Antiquity* to his memory.

Chapter 1

INTRODUCTION

To understand a person deeply is to understand not only how she imagines the world to be, but also to understand how she *wishes* the world to be: one must understand, we might say, her *vision* of how the world should be. But this is not only true of individuals: it is true as well of human communities, since to understand a culture involves understanding a people's hopes and aspirations, understanding their vision of the *ought*, as well as their conception of what is. We live not only by our understandings of reality, but also by our dreams of what reality may become.

The historian, it may be objected, has enough difficulty describing how individuals and cultures imagine the world as it is, without pursuing the will-o'-the-wisp of their hopes and visions. But if we are to understand deeply, we are bound to inquire about hopes and visions. Sometimes a person's vision is so striking, and so fluently expressed, that in fact we can know more about it than we can know about her sense of reality; sometimes a people's aspirations are so vividly displayed that their vision is plain for all to see.

Even the casual observer of eighteenth-century British culture will be struck by its pervasive vision of classical antiquity. The architectural monuments of "Augustan" England (England in the late-seventeenth and eighteenth centuries) stand as perennial reminders of an age obsessed with the revival of ancient ideals. From as early as the Queen's House in Greenwich (1616) through the age of such landmarks as the Sheldonian Theatre in Oxford (1664–1669), St. Paul's Cathedral in London (1673–1711), and even the Royal Crescent in Bath (ca. 1767), these edifices display the perfect symmetry, geometrical regularity, and simple decorum that recall the architecture of ancient Greece and Rome. The Augustan age, an age in which education largely meant education in classical history, languages, literature, and philosophy, saw the revival of classical forms of prose and poetry in

1

the essays of Steele and the verse of Alexander Pope. The enlightened *philosophes* of this age turned naturally to Lucretius and Cicero for models of unsuperstitious morality. If there was, then, a consistent cultural vision in this age, it was the vision of a culture purified by the return to ancient models.

The vision of "reviving" a pure, ancient culture had its religious counterpart as well. English theologians of this period stressed the revival of "classical" early Christian practices and theology. Conservative Anglicans claimed to have revived the polity of ancient episcopalianism and the theology of the earliest ecumenical councils. Latitudinarians appealed to early Christianity for models of diversity in religious establishments. Neo-Arians and Deists tried to show that the most primitive Christians either regarded Jesus as a lesser divine figure, or as a merely human teacher.

I offer, then, a study of an eighteenth-century vision: the religious vision of John Wesley (1703–1791), and in particular his understanding of "Christian antiquity," not only as a historical period, but also as a model or vision for what Christian individuals and communities in his age could become. His was, I have found, an intricately complex vision. It was complicated, in the first place, by the fact that his understanding of a historical period was utilized as a vision or model for contemporary culture. It was complicated, further, by the fact that the boundary between reality and hope was frequently blurred in Wesley's understanding, with ancient Christian institutions reborn in the Methodist movement, and with Methodist teachings sometimes rewritten into the story of ancient Christianity. It was complicated even further because Wesley's own vision was further transmitted to the Methodist people, and thus a cultural vision was transformed in an individual's understanding and it in turn became the basis for a new cultural vision.

Wesley's vision was even further complicated by the fact that ancient Christianity was but one, however prominent, of the sources for his vision of true Christian faith. Looking back over four decades of the Evangelical Revival, Wesley could make the high-flown claim that Methodism was nothing less than "the old religion, the religion of the Bible, the religion of the primitive Church," and "the religion of the Church of England."[1] Although Wesley's claims to be "a man of one book"[2] (the Bible), and his claim to be a faithful priest of the Church of England have been explored to some degree,[3] his understanding of "the religion of the primitive Church,"[4] that is, his religious vision informed by the ideal of a pristine, ancient Christianity to be revived in his own age, needs to be studied critically.

Since John Wesley's time, questions about "patristic influences" on his life and thought have been raised, especially since late in the nineteenth century when Anglican, Methodist, and Catholic scholars, influenced by the Tractarian movement, attempted to demonstrate Wesley's "catholicity" by showing his reverence for ancient Christianity.[5] Similar concerns have surfaced in recent years, especially in the context of ecumenical contacts between Methodists, Anglicans, Roman Catholics, and Eastern Orthodox Christians.[6] Common to these investigations into Wesley's relationship to early Christianity has been an attempt to show how early Christian doctrines and church practices were passed down through the tradition to Wesley, and so influenced him.

There are, however, some critical problems with attempts to show how Wesley was influenced by early Christianity. The attempt to trace influences across fourteen to sixteen hundred years of Christian history involves formidable methodological difficulties. To take an example, the similarities between Wesley's view of Christian love and that of Clement of Alexandria do not themselves prove that it was Clement's view that influenced Wesley, for the other possibilities for influence are almost innumerable. Wesley might have derived his view of Christian love from a number of other sources: the Bible, the Caroline divines, Roman Catholic mystics, Puritan divines, or Pietists, just to name a few. It is possible that Wesley's view may have come from a more immediate source which was in turn influenced by Clement's view. It is even possible that Wesley came to his views on his own. The demonstration of specific influences of early Christian beliefs or practices on Wesley, then, requires far more than simple comparisons between early Christian writers and his writings: it requires a systematic consideration of all the likely sources for such an influence.

Even when specific influences of early Christian beliefs or practices on John Wesley can be demonstrated (and sometimes they can), conclusions about Wesley's own understanding of ancient Christianity, or about Wesley's own uses of ancient traditions, do not always follow, because so many ancient Christian ideas and practices came to Wesley in mediated, or indirect, fashion. Conclusions about the influence of ancient Christian ideas or practices on Wesley tell us more about the environment in which Wesley lived, and learned, and worked, than about Wesley himself.

The quest for ancient *influences* on Wesley, then, is methodologically perilous, and likely to shed relatively little light on Wesley himself. Nevertheless, there is much to be gained by considering how Wesley himself conceived of ancient Christianity as a motivating vision for the Evangelical Revival. The fact that Wesley *thought of* his treatise on "The Character of a Methodist" as being derived from Clement of Alexandria reveals a great deal about how Wesley saw the continuity between the Methodism of his age and early Christianity. It will be fruitful, then, to consider how Wesley's vision of Christian antiquity reflects both the stable structures of eighteenth-century British religious culture, and also what one social scientist has called the "anti-structures" by which conceptions of ideal states are opposed to existing cultural structures.[7] To utilize the same example, Wesley's "Character of a Methodist" bears critical value as revealing his critique of British Christianity in the eighteenth century and his historicized vision of the Christian ideal.

Beyond examining the influence of ancient Christian ideas and practices on Wesley, then, this study will focus on the ways in which Wesley himself *conceived* of ancient Christianity, and the manners in which he *utilized* his conceptions of Christian antiquity as a vision for culture change. This approach has the advantage of dealing directly with Wesley's own thought and practice, and reveals much about his ideals of individual and communal life.

The question of Wesley's "conceptions" of Christian antiquity asks how Wesley *understood* events, beliefs, and ideals of virtue in the period of Christian antiquity,[8] and (moreover) how Wesley *evaluated* Christian antiquity, especially concerning its fidelity to the Christian message. Having this focus on Wesley's own understanding, our concern is not so much with the historical *accuracy* of Wesley's conceptions, nor with the *sources* from which Wesley derived his conceptions of Christian antiquity. Wesley's notions of early Christianity were frequently incorrect both in detail (he thought of the "Spiritual Homilies" as actually being the work of the fourth-century Egyptian monk Macarius) and in general (throughout much of his career he held an exaggerated view of the unity and the holiness of the ancient church). Nevertheless, even the distortions or exaggerations of Wesley's conceptions of ancient Christianity reveal the tendencies of the critique of the contemporary church and the delineation of a vision of the Christian ideal that was developing among early Evangelicals.

The question of Wesley's "uses" of Christian antiquity asks how Wesley used or *applied* his conceptions of Christian antiquity as a vision for the Evangelical Revival, both in supporting and in challenging the culture of his age. Wesley's interests in ancient Christianity were not merely antiquarian: beneath almost every discussion of the ancient church there was lurking a vital issue in eighteenth-century religious culture. What authority did bishops have in the ancient church? (And were Methodists obliged to obey Anglican bishops?)

Did the ancient Christians claim direct divine inspiration? (And was it mere "enthusiasm" for eighteenth-century Christians to claim a direct, divine "assurance of pardon"?) What virtues characterized the ancient saints? (And what virtues were lacking in eighteenth-century "professors" of Christian faith?) The study of Wesley's uses of Christian antiquity reveals most clearly this interplay between ancient and eighteenth-century religious ideals.

I have found that John Wesley conceived of Christian antiquity as a period in which an ideal of Christian individual and community life was realized. The "ideal" Wesley believed to have been realized in Christian antiquity was that to which he referred as "true" or "genuine Christianity," and whose paradigm he found in Christ and in the Christianity of the New Testament.[9] Nevertheless, as Wesley saw it, this religious ideal was "realized" in post-canonical Christianity, especially in the ante-Nicene period, and thus he could call upon Christianity in the first three centuries as a vision for the renewal of "true" Christianity.

This is a study of religious vision and culture change.[10] It examines the ways in which a cultural system was challenged and changed by a particular religious vision. Wesley's understanding of Christian antiquity was part of an alternative vision of Christianity which he held up against the traditions he had received—an alternative vision that became part of a new cultural system. Both British and American cultures in the nineteenth and twentieth centuries have been shaped by the shifts in cultural patterns that the Evangelical Revival brought about. What we have to examine, then, is a particular religious vision that empowered this cultural change.[11]

5

Chapter 2

THE REVIVAL OF ANTIQUITY:
CLASSICAL AND CHRISTIAN REVIVAL
IN JOHN WESLEY'S AGE

John Wesley's life spanned the eighteenth century, from 1703 to 1791. Born in a Lincolnshire rectory to staunch Anglican parents—both of them converted from the Dissenting faith of their own parents—Wesley attended Charterhouse, a prominent "public" school in London, and Oxford University, where he became a fellow of Lincoln College in 1726. He spent nearly two years (1736 and 1737) in North America as an agent of the Society for the Propagation of the Gospel. After a vivid religious experience shortly after his return to England in 1738, he entered a career of itinerant preaching (1739) which characterized the remainder of his life. Working from bases in London, Bristol, and Newcastle-upon-Tyne, he taught, organized, and preached among the working-class people who came to be known as "Methodists."

Wesley was in no sense isolated from the cultural currents of his time, and his vision of Christian antiquity reflects the very broad current of eighteenth century culture that found in the distant past a vision for shaping the present.[1] To understand his conceptions of Christian antiquity in their own context, then, it is important to know how "antiquity" in general, and "Christian antiquity" in particular, had become critical cultural themes in his age.

Classical Revival

If the architecture of Augustan England serves as the most impressive reminder of the emphasis that Wesley's age placed on the restoration of ancient culture,[2] the literature of the age reflects a similar vision, a vision shared by a wide spectrum of eighteenth-century authors, from the most conservative to the most progressive. Cultural conservatives of the late sixteenth and early seventeenth centuries tended to regard the writings of Greece and Rome as the only proper models for literature. The so-called "struggle of ancients and moderns" (*querelle des anciens et des modernes*) of seventeenth-century France had pitted conservatives against more progressive writers and educators who wanted to use Romance legends as literary models. This "struggle" had an English parallel in which Sir William Temple represented the "classical" position. His "Essay upon the Ancient and Modern Learning" (1672) argued that the French, Italian, and Spanish languages were barbaric corruptions of their pure Latin original. Young persons, Temple insisted, should be instructed in the Latin and Greek paradigms, not in their latter-day corruptions.[3] His essay concluded with the staunch observation,

> That among so many things as are by men possessed or pursued, in the course of their lives, all the rest are baubles, besides old wood to burn, old wine to drink, old friends to converse with, and old books to read.[4]

Since the study of ancient Greek had been introduced into the English universities in the early sixteenth century, studies in classical literature had replaced a good deal of their medieval, scholastic regimen. The literature that flowed from these sources, including the poetry of Alexander Pope, has been called "Augustan," a term that itself recalls the height of ancient Roman literary accomplishment.

The appreciation of classical languages and literature had come to be shared by nearly all educated persons in the seventeenth and eighteenth centuries, conservatives and progressives alike. The progressive thinkers who contributed to the rise of Enlightenment culture tended to see history as oscillating between ages of faith and superstition and ages of science and reason. Many had come to regard ancient Greece and Rome as scientific and rational societies whose accomplishments had been lost in the Middle Ages and reappropriated since the European Renaissance. Lucretius's *De Rerum Natura* and Cicero's *De Natura Deorum* were especially valued by Enlightenment *philosophes* (such as Hume and Voltaire) as casting off the superstitions of the past and striving toward a scientific view of the world. Thus "history became not past, but present politics" in what one scholar has termed "the rise of modern paganism."[5]

If John Wesley (and his brother Charles) did not use classical authors to the same ends as Hume and Voltaire, the point should not be lost that, like their Enlightenment counterparts, their educations stressed the purity of classical models, and their love for classical literature was not abated after decades of the Evangelical revival. John

Wesley read Horace and Juvenal (and considered editing a collection of Horace's works) as he walked the gardens and paths of Oxford, and also as he traveled his itinerant course, preaching through the countryside later in life. Charles Wesley's hymns would reflect the influence of classical verse. When John prepared educational materials for his relatively poor schoolchildren, he personally wrote out Latin and Greek grammars for them. The revival of classical antiquity, then, was a pervasive, eighteenth-century theme that deeply influenced John and Charles Wesley.[6]

Revival of Early Christian Studies

Christian leaders of the late seventeenth and early eighteenth centuries also venerated antiquity—"Christian antiquity," in their case—and called upon it in refuting their opponents, in defending their own beliefs and practices, and sometimes in challenging the culture of their age. A popular Anglican exposition of the Apostles' Creed expressed their vision of pristine antiquity in its claim that "in Christianity there can be no concerning truth which is not ancient; and whatsoever is truly new, is certainly false."[7] Christian leaders disagreed on the standard of "antiquity": those of a more radical Protestant persuasion tended to regard all developments beyond the New Testament canon as corruptions; Anglicans in the "middle of the road" differed among themselves about the limits and usefulness of post-canonical antiquity; Catholics tended to revere antiquity as the first stage in an unbroken tradition of Christian belief and practice. In each case, though, visions of Christian antiquity affected "present" church "politics," and "present politics" entered deeply into the presuppositions of the study of Christian antiquity.

"Christian antiquity" was in fact the focus of intense study and debate in the British Christianity of John Wesley's age, and had been for at least a century. By the time Wesley arrived in Oxford in 1720, the University's libraries were replete with scholarly editions of ancient Christian works, learned histories of the early Christian centuries, and a host of tracts and books claiming "Christian antiquity" and "the Church Fathers" to be on their sides in the many-faceted inter-Christian polemics of that age.

Although British scholars published few early Christian materials prior to 1600, they produced a steady stream of books on the subject after that year, and even more so after the English Revolution. British scholars showed a particular concern in this age for the history of the church in the first three centuries. At least sixty-nine editions and

9

translations of ante-Nicene Christian works were published in the seventeenth and eighteenth centuries, most coming from presses in London or Oxford.[8] British scholars Joseph Bingham and William Cave wrote general histories of the early Christian centuries.[9] Other writers such as John Pearson and James Ussher took up textual criticism of early Christian works, concerning themselves especially with the authenticity of the corpus of epistles attributed to Ignatius of Antioch in the early second century.[10]

These advances in the publication of early Christian texts and in the study of the early Christian centuries arose out of a century or more of conflicts within British Christianity, in which conceptions of Christian antiquity had played a central role. Dissension over these issues, in fact, reached back as far as the Protestant and Catholic Reformations. Although the Protestant Reformers took scripture to be the primary norm of the church's teaching and practice, they often utilized church history in order to show how the church had deviated from its scriptural norm. Most Reformation groups had some conception of the continuity of post-canonical Christianity with scriptural Christianity. "Magisterial" Reformers, for instance, showed respect for the teachings of the early Christian writers, especially Augustine. They affirmed that a faithful remnant, the "invisible church," had persisted through the centuries, not to be identified with heretical groups. "Radical" Reformers stressed the fall of the church in the age of Constantine, and identified themselves with the continuing tradition of those who had been called heretics.[11] The insistence on the unique authority of scripture characteristic of Protestant groups, however, eventually led some Protestants to reject the authority of any post-canonical sources for Christian teaching and practice, except in cases where the teachings and practices they affirmed could be grounded in an explicit warrant of scripture.[12] The issue of the authority of Christian tradition over against that of scripture was a major point of contention between Protestants and Catholics, as the decrees on Holy Scripture promulgated by the Council of Trent indicate. [13]

Rejection of the Authority of Christian Antiquity

As a result of these controversies, a variety of attitudes toward Christian antiquity emerged in the sixteenth through eighteenth centuries. British Christians of Puritan leanings rejected the authority of post-canonical sources for Christian doctrine and practice, except where confirmed by explicit grounds in scripture. The sixteenth-century Cambridge divine Thomas Cartwright, for instance, insisted that the authority of the early Christian writers should be strictly subject to the authority of scripture. For him, this meant that early Christian writers could be used only to substantiate doctrines and practices that had a clear scriptural warrant. He insisted, moreover, that any appeal to Christian antiquity should be made to the consensus of writers from the first five centuries, during which period he envisioned a gradual deterioration of the church's life.[14]

Considerable controversy over the authority of antiquity was precipitated in 1632 with the publication of a *Traicté sur l'Employ des saincts Pères* ("A Treatise on the Use of the Holy Fathers") by the Huguenot divine Jean Daillé. Daillé's work rejected the authority of post-canonical antiquity for determining contemporary religious controversies, and was taken as a manifesto by many Anglicans, such as those of the so-called "Tew Circle." This group, one of the earliest to explore the use of reason in theology and to advocate toleration in religious establishments, sponsored a translation of Daillé's work, *A Treatise of the Right Use of the Fathers* (1651), which included a list of approbations by influential Anglicans. Daillé's work thus represented the views of an important segment of British as well as Continental Protestantism, and the seriousness with which Anglicans responded to Daillé's charges also indicates the importance of this outlook.[15]

There was, then, a strong current in Protestantism, well represented in England, which questioned whether post-canonical sources for Christian teaching and practice could be granted any credence unless they had explicit warrants in scripture. Persons who took this point of view, it should be noted, did refer to ancient Christian sources. Cartwright and the Anglicans of the Tew Circle quoted liberally from the early Christian writers, but only in cases where they felt that ancient Christian views were substantiated by warrants of scripture. Such persons felt a special freedom in using the early Christian writers to refute their opponents' views and practices, as Cartwright did against Richard Hooker. Daillé himself called upon early Christian writings in order to question the authority of early Christian writings! Nevertheless, the central religious vision of these Protestants was dominated by the image of the church in the New Testament to such an extent that Christian antiquity (beyond the New Testament age) played only a trivial role in it.

Conservative Uses of Christian Antiquity

Cartwright, Daillé, and Tew-Circle Anglicans had reacted against those Christians of both Catholic and moderate Protestant leanings who maintained, in one way or another, that the early Christian writings could serve as authoritative sources for Christian faith and practice in areas where scripture was either silent or unclear. Conservative Anglican leaders called upon Christian antiquity in this manner in order to defend their church's polity and doctrine, and thus developed a vision of Christian antiquity more or less consonant with their own church's teachings and practices.

Characteristic Anglican uses of Christian antiquity as an authoritative source of the church's doctrine and practice had roots in the theological and practical formulations of the English Reformation. Bishop John Jewel of Salisbury, who figured prominently in the Elizabethan Settlement, asserted the use of the ancient Christian writers as "interpreters" of scripture:

> But what shall we say of the fathers, Augustine, Ambrose, Hierome, Cyprian, etc.? What shall we think of them, or what account may we make of them? They be interpreters of the word of God.[16]

Jewel's pupil Richard Hooker further developed Anglican views of theological authority in his *Laws of Ecclesiastical Polity* (1594–1597). Hooker's views of the authority of Christian antiquity may be contrasted with those of his contemporary, Thomas Cartwright, whose opinions have been noted above. Countering Puritan objections to Anglican practices and teachings, Hooker insisted that, after scripture, the church's practices and teachings should be subject to the criteria of reasonableness, the judgment of antiquity and the continuing tradition of the church, and the authority of the contemporary church. Hooker stressed that the *consensus* of ancient Christian doctrine and practice was to be regarded as authoritative, as opposed to the teachings of any particular writers. He asserted that ecclesiastical practices could be grounded in ancient Christian teachings so far as these did not *contradict* scriptural teachings, and this contrasts with Cartwright's insistence on a positive warrant of scripture for church practices. He denied Cartwright's doctrine of the deterioration and fall of the church, conceding that this doctrine would indeed vitiate any authoritative use of the early Christian writers. As Hooker saw it, the church had never utterly fallen.[17] Bishop Lancelot Andrewes of Winchester carried the English Reformers' insistence on the authority of Christian antiquity to an even higher degree in his assertion that the beliefs and practices of the early Christian communion ought to determine the beliefs and practices of Anglicans: ". . . one canon . . . two testaments, three creeds, four general councils, five centuries, and the series of Fathers in that period," wrote Andrewes, "determine our faith."[18]

In general, the English Reformers and subsequent Anglicans viewed the early Christian centuries as having authority for the church in later ages because they thought that the church had remained in a pristine or unspoiled condition for several centuries after the New Testament canon was complete. Archbishop William Laud referred to the first four or five centuries as the time when "the church was at the best."[19] There appears to have been a general agreement among these early Anglican leaders as to the length of this "primitive" period of the church's life: to Laud's "four or five centuries" one may compare the definitions of Christian antiquity as inclusive of five centuries given by Lancelot Andrewes, and by the Westminster Conference of 1559, which held the first five centuries to be an authoritative period for Christian faith and practice. John Jewel stands out in his extension of this period to six centuries.[20]

If Anglicanism never developed an official theological perspective, it did develop in the seventeenth century a characteristic *method* of theological reflection, in which their vision of Christian antiquity figured prominently in demonstrating the continuity of Anglicanism with the ethos of the church in its pure, "primitive" state. Following the precedents set by the English Reformers, the "classical" conservative Anglican divines of the seventeenth century (often identified as "Caroline" divines) utilized the teachings of the first four or five Christian centuries in order to vindicate their claims against those of both Roman Catholics and Puritans.[21]

The conservative Anglican leaders of the seventeenth and eighteenth centuries frequently expressed their high approbation of Christian antiquity. It was bishop John Pearson, whose *Exposition of the Creed* (1659) became a standard work of Anglican divinity, who remarked that "in Christianity there can be no concerning truth which is not ancient; and whatsoever is truly new, is certainly false."[22] The dedication to his *Exposition* states, "my design aimeth at nothing else but that the primitive faith may be revived."[23] Similarly, Archbishop William Wake reflected a lofty vision of the early post-canonical period, as the following comments from his introduction to the Apostolic Fathers indicate:

> We cannot doubt but what was universally approved of and allow'd, not by a few Learned Men but by the whole Church in those days; what was permitted to be publicly read to the Faithful for their Comfort and Instruction; must by this means have received a more than Humane Approbation; and ought to be look'd upon by us, tho' not of Equal Authority with those books which they have deliver'd to us as strictly Canonical, yet as standing in the first Rank of Ecclesiastical Writings, and as containing the pure Faith of Christ, without the least Error intermix'd with it.[24]

William Reeves's "Prefatory Dissertation about the Right Use of the Fathers" attached to the first volume of his edition of *The Apologies of Justin Martyr, Tertullian, and Minucius Felix in Defence of the Christian Religion* (1709) defended the use of the early Christian writers as religious authorities against the claims of Daillé and others. In Reeves's own words, his purpose was

> to lay before the People in the most instructing view we can, that *Primitive Form and Power of Godliness*, that Strength of Reason and Beauty of Example, whereby the old suffering *Heroes* Apologiz'd and Liv'd the *Gentiles* into *Christians*, in an Age when Wit and Wickedness, with all the *Kingdom* of *Darkness*, were at the highest Elevation, and in Confederacy against them.[25]

Reeves held that the works of "the Catholick Writers of the first Three or Four Centuries" were "the next valuable Writings" after the scriptures themselves.[26]

Conservative Anglicans, holding such a high regard for Christian antiquity, characteristically used their vision of Christian antiquity in apologetic works that defended their church's polity and doctrine. A great deal of effort was expended by the Anglicans in defense of their church's polity, against Roman Catholic claims of papal supremacy and Puritan objections to episcopal church government. Anglicans wanted to show that their episcopal polity was most consonant with the government of the church in antiquity. It is not surprising to find that the supporters of the authenticity of the Ignatian epistles, which inculcate obedience to bishops, were often bishops. William Ussher, whose *Ignatii Epistolae* defended the corpus, was Archbishop of Armagh, and John Pearson was Bishop of Chester when he wrote his *Vindiciae Epistolarum S. Ignatii* (1672). Their opponents, such as Daillé, who himself produced a treatise *De Scripturis quae sub Dionysii Areopagitae et Ignatii Antiocheni nominibus circumferuntur* (1666), tended to favor presbyterian church government. Pearson's *Vindiciae* attempted to prove, on the basis of the Ignatian correspondence, that episcopacy was an institution essential to the church. In doing so, he had to defend a second-century dating of the epistles in opposition to Daillé, who held them to be post-Constantinian.[27] Similarly, William Reeves's "Dissertation" devoted a great deal of space to defending the threefold orders of deacons, presbyters, and bishops by appeal to the Apologists of the second century. "*Bishop, Presbyter*, and *Deacon*," wrote Reeves, "were the Three Orders of the Church from the beginning to the Days of John Calvin, who was a wise and learned Man, but he was a *Man*. . . ."[28]

On the other front, Anglicans were concerned to refute Roman Catholic claims. Reeves noted that the study of the early Christian writers was especially crucial,

> since the *Papists* make such a noise in vulgar Heads, with the cry of *the Fathers, the Fathers*, as if all the *Saints* and *Martyrs* in *Christendom* had been *Romanists*. . . .[29]

14

On the issue of papal supremacy, the works of Cyprian became a focal point. Protestants pointed to letter seventy-five of the Cyprianic correspondence, in which Cyprian condemned Pope Stephen, as evidence against claims of papal supremacy. Catholics referred to the Cyprianic "primacy text" in order to substantiate their claims. The primacy text, however, did not appear in all editions of Cyprian's works; thus John Fell's edition of the works of Cyprian (1688) argued that the primacy text had been interpolated into the Cyprianic corpus by secondary editors wishing to vindicate Roman claims.[30] Here again, scholarship on ancient Christian life was employed in defense of the Anglican polity.

Anglicans also defended their church's liturgical practices and doctrinal teachings by the appeal to Christian antiquity. Non-Juror Robert Nelson's *Companion to the Festivals and Fasts of the Church of England* (1704) utilized ancient Christian resources to defend the Anglican observances of Lent, Easter, and other seasons, and to vindicate such practices as observation of weekly fasts (prescribed for every Friday by the Prayer Book).[31] Similarly, William Reeves defended the practices of infant baptism and frequent communion by appeal to Christian antiquity.[32]

Bishop George Bull echoed the opinions of conservative Anglicans who defended conciliar doctrine (especially the Niceno-Constantinopolitan doctrine of the Trinity) against those progressive Protestants who had come to raise serious doubts about the harmony of conciliar expressions of orthodoxy with the criteria of scripture, reason, and even the pre-conciliar Christian writers.[33]

There was, then, from the seventeenth-century a well-defined, conservative Anglican use of the ancient Christian sources. Identified in general with the "Caroline" Anglicanism that had defined itself against Puritanism on one side, and Roman Catholicism on the other, this use of Christian antiquity held up the vision of the ancient church as a test of ecclesiastical polity and doctrine; a test which, as the Caroline divines saw it, the Church of England passed with honors.

Programmatic Uses of Christian Antiquity

Conservative Anglican divines agreed in affirming the consensus of Christian antiquity as normative for the church's doctrine and practice, and in defending Anglicanism as truly replicating ancient Christian doctrine and practice. There was, however, another group of Anglicans of the late seventeenth and early eighteenth centuries who also affirmed Christian antiquity as an authority for Christian doctrine and practice, but differed from the former group in that they viewed

the Church of England more as the best possible setting for the realiza-
tion of the primitive Christian ethos, than as fully realizing that ethos
in its present life. This group's uses of Christian antiquity may be referred to as "programmatic," to distinguish them from the
"conservative" uses of Christian antiquity of the Anglicans considered
above. Conservative uses of Christian antiquity viewed the ancient
church's life as a pattern realized in the faith and practice of Anglicans; programmatic uses of Christian antiquity viewed the ancient
church's life as a model yet to be reinstituted (or renewed, or revived)
in the Church of England.

The emergence of various programmatic uses of Christian antiquity in the late seventeenth century in England should be seen against
the background of the cultural upheaval that had occurred during the
English Revolution. Although the Anglican party had appealed to
scripture and Christian antiquity in support of its polity and doctrine,
revolutionary thinkers (such as "Levellers" and "Diggers") tended to
appeal to scripture alone as an authoritative basis for their challenges
to the existing culture and society.[34] After the Revolution, however,
there emerged less radical forms of culture change which appealed to
Christian antiquity in support of their alternative cultural patterns.

Latitudinarian Uses of Christian Antiquity. Latitudinarians
appealed to a vision of Christian antiquity in their attempts to find a
broader church establishment that would embrace both conservative
Anglicans and Dissenters. Their work offers a parallel to that of the
Continental Protestant divine Georg Calixtus, who in 1650 had
proposed a union of Protestants and Roman Catholics on the basis of
the *traditio quinsecularis*, the consensus of teachings and practices of
the first five Christian centuries, interpreted in the light of the
Commonitorium of Vincent of Lérins.[35]

Latitudinarian Bishop Edward Stillingfleet proposed in his
Irenicum (1659) that episcopalians and presbyterians might be united
on the basis of early Christian practice in church government. Stillingfleet argued that there never was a rigidly set form of ecclesiastical
government in the ancient church, but that there were numerous local
variations. Ordination by presbyters was sometimes regarded as valid,
he maintained, and bishops acted in consultation with the presbyteries
of their dioceses.[36]

Peter King's *Enquiry into the Constitution, Discipline, Unity, and
Worship of the Primitive Church* (1712) offered a similar attempt to bring
Dissenters into the religious establishment. King based his account on
"the genuine and unquestionably authentic writings" of the first three
centuries, as well as portions of Eusebius relating to those centuries.[37]
King cited Ignatius of Antioch, the Epistle of Barnabus, I and II

Clement, Irenaeus, Pliny's letter to Trajan regarding the Christians, Justin Martyr, Clement of Alexandria, Tertullian, Novatian, Cyprian, Minucius Felix, Origen, and Eusebius. He attempted to demonstrate that there were but two orders (*ordines*) of ministers in the ancient church, deacons and elders, and that bishops were a higher degree (*gradus*) of elders.[38] His account of the *Primitive Church* thus differed from Stillingfleet's, in that it affirmed a common structure of church government among the early congregations. The two concurred, however, in attenuating the High Anglican view of episcopacy by reference to ancient Christian precedents.

Protestant Free-Thinkers. The spirit of free inquiry associated with the Enlightenment stimulated many religious thinkers to question whether teachings of the church long held to be orthodox could be reconciled with reason, scripture, or even early Christian teachings. Certain Protestant divines, in particular, questioned whether the doctrines of the ecumenical councils reflected the teachings of scripture and Christian antiquity. Those who challenged traditional christological and trinitarian formulations found some encouragement in the scholarly works of the French Jesuit Denis Pétau, who had suggested early in the seventeenth century that the ancient conciliar formulations did not reflect the views of earlier Christian writers, whose thought he believed to have been more similar to Arianism.[39]

British anti-trinitarian thought came to clear expression in the later years of the seventeenth, and early years of the eighteenth, centuries. William Whiston, a Cambridge mathematician noted for his translation of Josephus, published in 1711 a work entitled *Primitive Christianity Reviv'd*, in which he argued that the Arians' teachings were in harmony with earlier Christian teachings, and suggested that Athanasius was a perverter of Christian truth. In the year after Whiston's manifesto appeared, Samuel Clarke published *The Scripture Doctrine of the Trinity*, which argued that God the Father is alone eternal and worthy of worship, that the Son is worthy of worship only as a mediator to the Father, and that the Holy Spirit is not to be accorded worship. Clarke based his arguments on scripture alone, without reference to later traditions, although his work was understood as supporting the Neo-Arianism that Whiston and others had advocated.[40] To Anglicans committed to conciliar expressions of orthodoxy, these theologies posed a serious, alternative vision of religious belief.

Revival of Ancient Christian Liturgy and Discipline. Some Anglicans who maintained orthodox theological outlooks nevertheless called on their vision of Christian antiquity in proposing revivals of ancient Christian liturgical or disciplinary practices. An outstanding example of this category is Bishop William Beveridge, an eccentric High-Church Anglican who accepted a Calvinistic doctrine of predestination. In 1672 Beveridge published two massive folio volumes of conciliar canons accepted in the Eastern churches, entitled *Synodikon, sive Pandectae Canonum SS. Apostolorum et Conciliorum Ecclesia Graeca Receptorum* ("Synodikon, or, Summaries of the Apostolic Canons and Councils Received in the Greek Church"). Beveridge gave the texts of these canons in Greek and Syriac, with Latin translations. At the beginning of the collection he placed the so-called Apostolic Canons, eighty-five canons which deal with ordination and the official responsibilities and moral conduct of the clergy.[41] Beveridge went on to defend the authenticity of these canons in his *Codex Canonum Ecclesiae Primitivae Vindicatus ac Illustratus* ("The Book of Canons of the Primitive Church Vindicated and Illustrated," 1678), in which he attempted to show that the Apostolic Canons reflect the practice of the church in the second and third centuries. The work was specifically directed against attacks on the authenticity of the ancient Canons leveled by Jean Daillé and others. In it, Beveridge relied heavily on citations from early church writers and historians.[42] He insisted that it is the duty of all particular churches to observe what is agreed upon by the consensus of the universal church. The early church provided the paradigm for the universal church, since the church was undivided in its early ages and "maintained its primitive vigor and virginity for two or three centuries." Failure to conform to this standard, Beveridge reasoned, amounts to schism.[43] Thus, for Beveridge, the primitive nature of the Apostolic Canons itself justified their application in the Church of England, as one of the particular churches obliged to follow the consensus of the universal, primitive church.

A similar, programmatic use of Christian antiquity was offered by Nathaniel Marshall in *The Penitential Discipline of the Primitive Church* (1714). Originally written as a proposal to Convocation (the governing body of the Church of England), the *Penitential Discipline* argues that for the first four Christian centuries penance was a public act, involving separation from the rest of the congregation and episcopal absolution. It then shows that public penance was replaced by private confession after the fourth century. The book ends with a series of specific proposals for reintroducing public penance into the Church of England, including segregation of catechumens and penitents in church and the addition of a public penitential office to the Prayer Book.[44]

Renewal of Moral and Spiritual Life. Meanwhile, a different group of writers held up the ancient Christians as models for the moral and spiritual lives of contemporary Christians. There is a certain parallel between their activities and the activities of the Jansenists in France and elsewhere, who, (in Yves Congar's words) "went one better" than the Gallicans in their appeal to Augustine as the grounds for their challenging views of human nature and grace.[45] William Cave, whose historical works have been noted above, and who was a contemporary of Beveridge at St. John's, Cambridge, gave a general and idealized portrait of the life of the early church in his first work, *Primitive Christianity* (1672). The three main parts of *Primitive Christianity* describe charges brought against the early Christians and their religious customs, their virtues in relation to God, and their virtues in relation to other persons. Cave contrasted the ancient ideal of Christian conduct with Christianity in his own age:

> I had not been long an observer of the manners of men, but I found them generally so debauched and vicious, so corrupt and contrary to the rules of this holy religion, that if a modest and honest heathen was to estimate Christianity by the lives of its professors, he would certainly proscribe it as the vilest religion in the world.[46]

Cave noted in *Primitive Christianity* that he placed special authority in the church of the first three or four centuries.[47] The idealized biographies of early Christians which Cave produced in *Primitive Christianity* led to the accusation of Jean LeClerc that he was "writing panegyrics rather than lives."[48] A similar work was produced by the Catholic scholar Claude Fleury in 1682. Fleury's *Moeurs des Chrétiens* described the life of the Christian community from the first century through the seventh century, dwelling especially upon its ritual and disciplinary practices. An English translation appeared in 1698 as *An Historical Account of the Manners and Behaviour of the Christians*.[49]

The range of theologians who called upon Christian antiquity as a model for moral reform in the late seventeenth and early eighteenth centuries is remarkable; for not only staunch Anglicans (such as Cave), and Roman Catholics (such as Fleury), but Continental Pietists also called upon Christian antiquity as a pattern for moral reform, and their work, in turn, would influence British Christianity. The second part of Philipp Jakob Spener's *Pia Desideria* (1675) quoted extensively from ancient Christian writers in order to show that the Christian church could attain to a high degree of purity and moral perfection in post-biblical times. Spener especially cited ante-Nicene authors (Tertullian, Ignatius of Antioch, Eusebius, Justin Martyr, Tatian, Origen, and even Pliny's letter to Trajan), but also referred to later Eastern Christian writers (Basil, Gregory of Nazianzen, Chrysostom, and Ephraem Syrus).[50] Among other Pietist writers the "Spiritual Homilies" attributed to Macarius of Egypt were held in high esteem. Johann Arndt was said to have known all fifty of the homilies by heart. Ernst

Benz has examined the reception of the Macarian literature among Pietist groups, and has concluded that "in Macarius the Pietistic renewal movement found the model and example for its struggle for holiness and perfection."[51]

The rise of Anglican "religious societies" late in the seventeenth century reflected the spirit of moral reformism of their age. Anthony Horneck, the instigator of the London Religious Societies, noted in the "Epistle Dedicatory" to his *Happy Ascetick* (1681) his view of the Church of England as a promising setting for a revival of the primitive Christian ethos:

> We are happy in this Church, that we have so many Prelates who are bent upon reviving the strictness of the Primitive Church, excellent Patterns for us the inferiour Clergy to imitate. . . . [52]

Horneck attached to this work "A Letter to a Person of Quality, concerning the Heavenly Lives of the Primitive Christians," a summary of a work by the Chancellor of the University of Paris, Jean Fronteau, published in Latin in 1660, which itself was an encomium upon the virtues and good works of Christians in the early church. The work closes by recommending to the reader the works of Ignatius of Antioch, Polycarp, Minucius Felix, Tertullian, Clement of Alexandria, Cyprian, and Origen (all ante-Nicene Christian writers).[53]

These programmatic uses of Christian antiquity should alert us to the fact that the mere appeal to Christian antiquity does not identify an author or church leader of this period with any particular theological position. In particular, the bare fact that John Wesley admired and appealed to Christian antiquity does not in itself demonstrate that Wesley conformed to the conservative Anglicanism of his day; he may, indeed, have begun his life (through the influence of his parents) with a devotion to Caroline Anglicanism and the conservative uses of Christian antiquity that they supported, but there is much evidence (as the next chapter will show) that even from his Oxford years his uses of Christian antiquity were more programmatic than conservative.

But, before we consider the development of Wesley's own views and uses of Christian antiquity, an important qualification must be made: these three uses of the vision of Christian antiquity were not mutually exclusive. Some Christian leaders, such as Jean Daillé and the Tew Circle, did use their conceptions of Christian antiquity in an almost exclusively polemical manner, since their views of scriptural authority made a positive appeal to Christian antiquity (either apologetic or programmatic) unnecessary. Those who used their conceptions of Christian antiquity in a culturally conservative manner to defend their own church's teachings and practices, however, also cited ancient Christian authorities in a polemical manner in order to refute their opponents. Those who used their conceptions of Christian antiquity in a culturally programmatic manner might also use those conceptions to refute their opponents, and to defend institutions or teachings they believed to be appropriate. William Cave, for instance, whose *Primitive Christianity* called upon ancient Christian sources in order to renew ancient standards of conduct and piety, also called upon Christian antiquity to defend the Anglican episcopate.

Thus one may distinguish three "configurations" of uses of Christian antiquity, each of which is characterized by a particular one of the three uses of Christian antiquity. These configurations might be represented as follows:

Polemical Configuration	Conservative Configuration	Programmatic Configuration
Polemical Use	Polemical Use Conservative Use	Polemical Use Conservative Use Programmatic Use

The uses of Christian antiquity tend to build upon one another, with polemical uses being the most common, conservative uses somewhat more distinctive, and programmatic uses the most distinctive of all.

John Wesley was born into an age in which Christian antiquity, far from being a subject of merely historical interest, had been a focal point for theological, ecclesiastical, and moral discourse for more than a century. As the next chapter considers the development of Wesley's own notions of Christian antiquity, it will be important to hold in mind the uses (and configurations of uses) of Christian antiquity that were developing in the decades before his birth.

21

Chapter 3

PRIMITIVE CHRISTIANITY IN THE WILDERNESS: THE DEVELOPMENT OF JOHN WESLEY'S VISION OF CHRISTIAN ANTIQUITY

John Wesley's early life exposed him to the cultural patterns of his age, with their reverence for classical and Christian antiquity. These patterns impinged upon Wesley in his home, in his School, in his University, and in the new relationships he forged with Continental Pietists in his venture to Georgia in 1735. In each of these settings, and beyond the beginnings of the Methodist Revival in 1739, his views of the early Christian centuries continued to develop, and his vision of the ancient church inspired his revivalistic efforts.

To understand how Wesley's vision of Christian antiquity could function in tension with his culture, it is important to observe how his ideas of Christian antiquity actually emerged, since in almost every case his interests in Christian antiquity were inspired by programmatic concerns about the reform of the church. His vision for the reform of the church, however, and his correlated vision of ancient Christianity, shifted significantly throughout his career. The account that follows attempts to describe Wesley's developing conceptions of Christian antiquity in some detail.

His Father's Advice

Samuel Wesley functioned as a sort of funnel through which the Anglican culture of the late seventeenth and early eighteenth centuries flowed into the rectory at Epworth and saturated its inhabitants. He was familiar with several ancient languages, and devoted his scholarly abilities to the production of a massive Latin exposition of the book of Job, *Dissertationes in Librum Jobi*, published in the year of his death

(1735). The book contains references to the intertestamental and early Christian literature on Job, and shows Samuel's familiarity with Hebrew, Greek, Latin, Syriac, and other ancient languages.[1]

Two documents from Samuel Wesley, both read by John, illustrate his interest in ancient Christianity. The first is a pamphlet entitled *The Young Student's Library* (1692), attributed to Samuel Wesley as Secretary of the Athenian Society. This work contains a list of books in various fields recommended to students by the Society. Among other books in divinity, it advises students to read Eusebius's *Ecclesiastical History*, *The History of the General Councils*, a *Summa Conciliorum* ("Summary of the Councils"), William Beveridge's *Synodikon*, Cotelier's *Ecclesiae graecae Monumenta* ("Documents of the Greek Church"), and finally, "All the Fathers, as St. Ambrose, etc."[2] Striking in this list are the prominence of works on conciliar (that is, post-Nicene) theology, the blank reference to "All the Fathers," of whom the only one listed is from the later fourth century, and the inclusion of two works on Greek Christianity (those of Beveridge and Cotelier). The conception of Christian antiquity one would gather from these works would be that of a Christian church established under the Roman Empire with a highly-developed system of ecclesiastical offices, institutions, dogmas, laws, and the like; but not "Roman," in the sense of yielding to papal supremacy.

Samuel Wesley passed on a more extensive prospectus of his recommended readings in ancient Christianity in his *Advice to a Young Clergyman* (1735), written to Mr. Hoole, his curate at Epworth and Wroote, and published by John Wesley in the year that Samuel died. The *Advice* deals with the clergy's "intention, converse and demeanour, reading prayers, studies, preaching and catechising, administrating the sacraments, and discipline." Thirty-four of the sixty-nine pages of this work are dedicated to a discussion of the clergy's studies. Samuel urged the candidate for orders to study Latin, Greek, and, if at all possible, Hebrew. Ten pages are specifically concerned with early Christian studies. In an early section, he recommended the New Testament Apocryphal works and the Apostolic Fathers. He took up post-Nicene Christian antiquity later in the book, noting that the fourth century marked the church's conflicts with Sabellianism and Arianism. He defended Eusebius's orthodoxy by noting Eusebius's assent to the Nicene Creed and its formulation of the *homoousion*. Samuel insisted that the teachings of Nicea were consistent with those of the ante-Nicene Christian writers, and on this subject he recommended the *History of the Council of Nice*, Eusebius, Athanasius, Basil, conciliar documents themselves, Chrysostom, and modern works by Tillemont, Dupin, Pearson, and Bull. Samuel added a final paragraph in his consideration of patristic studies in which he recommended some fifth-century and later writers, "if you have a mind to step a little lower." These are Augustine, Jerome, Ambrose, Boethius, Cassiodore, Gildas, Bede, and the Saxon Councils and Homilies.[3] Among modern works in divinity, Samuel recommended some works concerned with early Christianity, including books by Stillingfleet and Grotius (although he acknowledged some errors in them), Pearson's *Exposition of the Creed* and *"Critique on Ignatius"* (this must refer to the *Vindiciae*), Bull (again), Beveridge's sermons, William Cave's *Primitive Christianity*, LeClerc ("has more wit than learning"), Bingham, and Nelson.[4] In his comments on preaching, Samuel suggested that his curate refer to the ancient Christian writers "for Illustration, and Probable, not Infallible, Interpretation."[5]

Some indications of Samuel Wesley's estimate of Christian antiquity arise from these parts of his *Advice* and his *Young Student's Library*. Throughout both one sees the high approbation of Christian antiquity characteristic of the conservative Anglicanism of the late seventeenth and early eighteenth centuries. The *Advice* shows more regard for the first three Christian centuries, but gives its approval to fourth- and fifth-century works, especially the Nicene formulation of Trinitarian dogma. Although Samuel was familiar with Beveridge and Cave, his defence of the Nicene formulations as consistent with ante-Nicene and scriptural teachings, his references to Bull, Pearson, and Wake, and his general appreciation for post-Nicene Christianity in the *Young Student's Library* and the *Advice* suggest that, among the various positions outlined in the previous chapter, his vision of Christian antiquity approximated that of such Anglican apologists as Bull, Pearson, and Wake. This apologetic outlook would be consistent with the fact that Samuel had converted to Anglicanism on dogmatic grounds.

In the winter of 1724–1725, John Wesley, still a scholar of Christ Church, decided to seek ordination as a priest of the Church of England. On the twenty-sixth of January, 1725, Samuel Wesley wrote him and promised to send the manuscript of his advice to Mr. Hoole (that is, the *Advice to a Young Clergyman*). In this and two subsequent letters in 1725, Samuel urged John to read Chrysostom's work *De Sacerdotio* ("On the Priesthood"). "Master it," he urged, "digest it."[6]

From his father, then, John Wesley received the impetus to study Christian antiquity in the context of Anglican writers who had appealed to Christian antiquity in order to vindicate the doctrines and practices of the Church of England. If John Wesley had followed his father's prescription, his vision of ancient Christianity would have been tied to the culturally conservative Anglicanism of the seventeenth century which Samuel represented, but there is very little evidence that John took up his program. Instead, he soon turned in another direction.

Oxford and the Manchester Non-Jurors

John Wesley's alma mater functioned in much the same manner as his father had done for him: it supplied a channel through which Anglican culture engaged him in the formative period of his life between 1720 and 1735. At Oxford, however, Wesley encountered a sort of Anglican subculture whose distinctive vision of Christian antiquity would send Wesley on quite a different trajectory than his father had envisioned. Oxford had been a center for patristic studies as well as a stronghold of the conservative Anglicanism which employed the early Christian writers in its defense. Johann Ernst Grabe had been chaplain of Christ Church early in the century; George Bull had been a member of the same College as Wesley's father; William Wake had been a scholar, then a canon, of Christ Church before his election as Archbishop of Canterbury. If Wesley had followed in the train of these Oxford scholars, again, his uses of Christian antiquity might have conformed to what we have described as the "conservative" configuration; but this was not to be the case.

There is, in fact, little evidence that Wesley followed the program of ancient Christian studies outlined by his father or that had been favored by conservative Oxford scholars. His diaries record his readings in only a few patristic works in the years between 1725 and 1730. He read mostly in Augustine and Justin Martyr, naming only Augustine's *Confessions* and the supposititious work *De Meditatione* (attributed to the Bishop of Hippo). Wesley also noted in his diary that he had translated Justin Martyr's *Apology*.[7]

Almost every indication from his Oxford years suggests that even then Wesley's vision of Christian antiquity was used more in what we have called a programmatic manner than a conservative one. The first suggestion of a more intense interest in early Christianity on Wesley's part appears in a letter from one of his companions, Mary Pendarves (the sister of his friend Robert Kirkham), addressed to her sister and dated 4 April 1730. Pendarves wrote, "I honour *Primitive Christianity*, and desire you will let him know as much when you next meet him."[8] The circle of John and Charles Wesley, Robert Kirkham, and Kirkham's three sisters had affected the custom of referring to one another by classical nicknames, "Cyrus," "Varanese," "Aspasia," and others. The name *Primitive Christianity* in the letter from Mary Pendarves is thought to refer to John Wesley, an indication of his interest in the ethos of the early church.

By 1730, however, Wesley had become involved in an Oxford society, his association with which appears to have led to a more intense interest in ancient Christianity on his part. Originally intended as a fellowship for the study of the New Testament and classical literature, the interests of the group shifted towards the cultivation of piety. In the spring of 1732, they began to observe fasts on Wednesdays and Fridays in imitation of the practice of the early church.[9] The group may have known of this practice from Robert Nelson's *Companion to the Festivals and Fasts of the Church of England*, which Wesley had read as early as 1731. Nelson was a friend of the Wesley family, whose book observed that

> The ancient Christians were very exact, both in their weekly and annual fasts. Their weekly fasts were kept on Wednesdays and Fridays, because on the one our Lord was betrayed, and on the other crucified. These fasts were called their stations, from the military word of keeping their guard as Tertullian observes. . . . For these fasts usually lasted till after three in the afternoon, as did their public assemblies.[10]

In June of 1732 Wesley resolved "To abstain from food till 3 on 16th, Wednesdays, Fridays, and Fasts appointed by the Church," and from this date his diaries note his regular observance of these fasts.[11]

The weekly fasts became a particularly serious matter with Wesley, and he attempted to convince his students to observe them. This brought accusations that the group's asceticism was extreme.[12] An attack on the Oxford Methodists in *Fog's Weekly Journal* for Saturday, 9 December 1732, accused the group of taking Origen as their pattern in an attempt to rise to the contemplation of spiritual things and to divest their senses of attachments to earthly objects by means of ascetic practices.[13] There is no evidence that the Oxford group had actually espoused Origen's asceticism, although the account in *Fog's* may reflect a garbled rumor that the group's practices were supposed to have been grounded in patristic teachings.

Wesley's readings beginning in the middle of 1732 show a vigorous interest in the early church: between June and December of that year he read in the Apostolic Constitutions, the Apostolic Canons, William Cave's *Primitive Christianity*, and Ephraem Syrus.[14] The so-called Apostolic Constitutions, a collection of church law from the second half of the fourth century, were attributed to Clement of Rome by some seventeenth and eighteenth century scholars. The compiler of the Constitutions is thought to have had Arian sympathies (Samuel Wesley had suspected this himself).[15] Ephraem Syrus was a Syrian hermit, biblical exegete, and spiritual writer of the fourth century. A

27

list of Wesley's anticipated reading from the same period includes the *Decreta Conciliorum*, and under "desiderata" lists "Patres Apost." and "translate the Fathers till 350."[16]

John Wesley acknowledged that the suggestion of observing the weekly fasts came from his friend John Clayton, and his diaries note that his study of the Apostolic Constitutions and Canons in August of 1732 was carried on in Clayton's company.[17] John Clayton was a native of Manchester and a member of Brasenose College (across from the back of Lincoln) who had been admitted to the Oxford Methodist society in 1732. The fact that Clayton identified himself with a group of Non-Jurors who laid an extraordinary stress on the writings of the early church most adequately explains the renewal of interest in early Christian life and thought which appears in Wesley after 1732. The Non-Jurors, in general, were those members of the Church of England who refused to take Oaths of Allegiance and Supremacy to William and Mary, on the grounds that their so doing would violate their previous oaths to James II. Because of their loyalty to James, they were sometimes referred to as "Jacobites," and were suspected of "popish" inclinations, since the Stuart monarch had found asylum in France and had converted to Roman Catholicism. The nine Anglican bishops and approximately four hundred clergy who adhered to Non-Juring principles were deprived of their livings.[18] The Non-Jurors were strongly attached to the Anglican reverence for Christian antiquity, and in 1716 their bishops had promulgated "A Proposal for a concordate betwixt the orthodox and catholic remnant of the British churches, and the Catholic and Apostolic Oriental Churches" based on adherence to the ecumenical councils.[19] Oxford, it may be noted, was a center of Jacobite sympathies in the early eighteenth century.[20] John Wesley himself had been exposed to the Non-Jurors' opinions early in his life; his mother, prior to John's birth, had refused to say "amen" to Samuel's prayers for William and Mary. Wesley was impressed by an Oxford sermon of Dr. George Coningsby in 1727 which, according to V. H. H. Green, "fringed on treason" in its praise for Charles I, and for which Coningsby was forbidden from preaching before the University. Wesley was also familiar with other Non-Jurors, such as Robert Nelson and William Law.[21]

The particular circle of Non-Jurors to which John Clayton was attached, and into which John Wesley was drawn, differed in some respects from the majority of Non-Jurors. Whereas most Non-Jurors were willing to use the Book of Common Prayer, only omitting the name of the sovereign in their prayers, a schismatic faction led by Bishop Archibald Campbell and later by Dr. Thomas Deacon of Manchester (who was irregularly consecrated bishop by Campbell in

1733) insisted on the use of the 1549 Prayer Book of Edward VI, which advocated mixture of water and wine, prayers for the dead, an epiclesis (prayer for the descent of the Holy Spirit on the eucharistic elements), and an oblatory prayer in the eucharist. The Manchester group came later to use Deacon's *Compleat Collection of Devotions* (1734), which also insisted on these practices. The Manchester group was also referred to as the "Usagers" because of their advocacy of these particular "usages" from the 1549 Prayer Book.[22] John Wesley himself referred to them as the "Essentialist" Non-Jurors.[23] The "usages" had been defended by Jeremy Collier in his tract, *Reasons for Restoring Some Prayers, Etc.* (1717), who, in the case of each of the usages, attempted to show that the practice in question was not Papist, but grounded in the "constant usage of the Primitive Church." In his defence of the usages Collier cited Tertullian, Cyprian, Cyril of Alexandria, Ambrose, Epiphanius, Chrysostom, Augustine, the Apostolic Constitutions, Justin Martyr, Clement of Alexandria, and Irenaeus.[24]

Thomas Deacon, in particular, laid a peculiar stress on the Apostolic Constitutions and Canons in his defence of the usages, as well as other ancient Christian practices such as trine immersion, the allowance of public baptism only between Easter and Pentecost, the rule that baptisms must be performed by members of one's own sex (and thus by deaconesses for women), and the inclusion of a form of exorcism to be used at baptism.[25] The Deacon-Clayton circle may not have been innocent of Arian leanings, since Deacon, like Whiston, was an ardent advocate of the Apostolic Constitutions, and since at a later date Clayton sent Wesley a copy of Whiston's catechism to take to Georgia.[26]

John Wesley met Thomas Deacon in June 1733 when Wesley traveled with John Clayton to Manchester. Clayton had already convinced Wesley of the importance of the "stationary" fasts, and had led Wesley to study the Apostolic Constitutions and Canons. Their correspondence after the trip to Manchester reveals a continuing interest in the customs of the ancient church. In July 1733 Clayton responded to a question from Wesley about the Christian observance of Saturday. Clayton recommended keeping "both the sabbath and the Lord's Day" as separate festivals, with prayers at the "primitive hours" and also morning and evening prayers taken from the Apostolic Constitutions, with Friday as a (fast) day of preparation for both festivals. Clayton also noted in this letter that Dr. Deacon's studies in "the worship and discipline of the Primitive Church" had so taken up his time that he had not read the ancient Christian writers with an eye to their moral doctrines, about which Wesley had inquired.[27] In September Clayton responded to a question of Wesley's about "reading the ancients," and recommended Cotelier's edition of the Apostolic Fathers, and Beveridge on the Apostolic Canons, which Clayton regarded as "vindicated" along with the Apostolic Constitutions.[28] Similarly, in a letter of August 1734, Clayton wrote,

> Fit books for you and every Christian priest are all the Fathers of the first three centuries, whereby you may be enabled both to know and profess the faith once delivered to the saints, and to steer your course in the due medium between the monkish mysticism of the fourth century and the lukewarm indifference of the present age.[29]

Clayton stated further in this letter that the stationary fasts were to be replaced by festivals in the fifty days of Eastertide, according to the Apostolic Constitutions.[30]

Further evidence of the impact of the Manchester Non-Jurors on Wesley in this period appears in an undated manuscript in Wesley's hand on a single leaf of paper taken from a notebook. Along with notes on the Apostolic Canons and Constitutions there appear the following comments:

> I believe *myself* it a duty to observe, so far as I can *without breaking communion with my own church*:
> 1. To baptize by immersion.
> 2. To use Water, oblation of elements [and] alms, invocation and a prothesis, in the eucharist.
> 3. To pray for the faithful departed.
> 4. To pray standing on Sunday and in Pentecost.
> 5. To observe Saturday, Sunday and Pentecost as Festival.
> 6. To abstain from blood and things strangled.
>
> I think it prudent (our own church not considered):
> 1. To observe the stations.
> 2. Lent, especially the Holy Week.
> 3. To turn to the east at the Creed.[31]

Items two and three of the "duties" listed above will be seen to correspond to the "usages" of the Manchester Non-Jurors. Items one and five of the "duties," and item one of those considered "prudent," have been noted above as encouraged by either Deacon or Clayton. Frank Baker has shown, moreover, that each of the items on this list has a direct parallel in the Apostolic Constitutions or Canons.[32]

Wesley's readings in works on early Christianity in 1733 and 1734 show the continuing influence of the Manchester Non-Jurors. He read Horneck's *Happy Ascetick* and Marshall's *Penitential Discipline of the Primitive Church*. His reading of the *Commonitorium* of Vincent of Lérins exposed him to the "Vincentian Canon," the claim that Christian doctrines and practices are to be judged by that which has been accepted "every, always, and by all." The Vincentian canon was understood by Beveridge, Deacon, and others as reinforcing the authority of the post-canonical church. He read Wake's translation of the Apostolic Fathers, and Lactantius's *De Mortibus Persecutorum*, which described in grisly detail the deaths of those who had persecuted ancient Christians.[33] In 1734 and early 1735 he read I Clement, William Reeves's translation of the second-century Apologists, Clement of Alexandria, Beveridge's *Codex Canonum*, and the "Shepherd" of Hermas.[34]

Thomas Deacon was impressed with Wesley, for in the September following their meeting he sent word through Clayton that he would appreciate Wesley's advice on a collection of Psalms Deacon was preparing for publication.[35] Although it is not known what advice Wesley may have afforded Deacon on this matter, Wesley did submit to the Non-Juring bishop an "Essay upon the Stationary Fasts," of which Deacon published an excerpt in his *Compleat Collection of Devotions* the next year. Wesley must have been at work on this essay prior to his trip to Manchester, for he read and "collected" (wrote out summaries of and quotations from) Beveridge on the Wednesday fasts in April of 1733, and read Gunning and Hooper on the "stations" in July of that same year.[36] As noted above, his regular observation of the stations had begun in the preceding year.

Although Wesley's "Essay" has not come down to us in complete form, there exist at least two portions of it, both of which shed light on Wesley's view of the authority of Christian antiquity at this time. The first is a manuscript in Wesley's hand entitled "Of the Weekly Fasts of the Church" which appears in a notebook later used for his third Georgia diary. This manuscript appears to date from the period 1732–1734 when Wesley was under the influence of the Manchester Non-Jurors. The essay begun in it is incomplete, but an outline given in the second paragraph shows the following structure (my summary):

1. It is the duty of all Christians to obey the ancient injunctions of the universal church;

2. the ancient church universally enjoined fasting on Wednesdays and Fridays; therefore

3. it is our duty as Christians to fast on Wednesdays and Fridays.

The remainder of the manuscript gives the text of the first point of the essay as given in this outline. The entire segment is translated from a comment on I Corinthians 11:16 in William Beveridge's *Thesaurus Theologicus*. Wesley evidently gave full approval to Beveridge's argument that practices which were universally observed in the ancient church are binding upon all modern churches, and, moreover, that a church is schismatic if it fails to observe customs universally observed by the church in antiquity.[37]

The other extant portion of Wesley's essay is that which was published by Deacon in *A Compleat Collection of Devotions* (1734). Wesley's essay appears in "An Appendix in Justification of this Undertaking, consisting of *Extracts* and *Observations* taken from the Writings of very eminent and learned Divines of different Communions."[38] The selection from Wesley purports to show "That the stations were instituted by the Apostles," which Wesley would demonstrate from the universality and antiquity of the practice, and from the express testimony of ancient writers concerning the practice. This may correspond to point two of the outline given in the manuscript portion of the essay. Only the first demonstration (from the universality and antiquity of the practice) is included in the published extract. Wesley quoted Augustine and Vincent of Lérins to the effect that whatever customs were universally observed in ancient Christianity must have had an apostolic origin. He then quoted Bishop Gunning, who asserted that not to follow scripture "as we find it interpreted by the Holy Fathers and Doctors of the Church, as they received it from those before them" amounts to allowing every person to form his or her own opinion of the meaning of scripture, and this would inevitably lead to heretical opinions. Because the practice of observing the stationary fasts was universally observed in Christian antiquity, Wesley argued, and because there is a dominical warrant for fasting in general, the practice must be binding upon Christians of every particular ecclesiastical communion.[39]

A fragment of another manuscript bears resemblances to these portions of Wesley's "Essay upon the Stationary Fasts" and suggests Wesley's developing concern with ancient Christian liturgical practices. This manuscript is of an "Essay on Water Baptism" dated December 1733, in which Wesley argued for the use of "water baptism" (presumably this refers to baptism by immersion, upon which Clayton and Deacon insisted), on the basis of the usage of Christ, the apostles, and "the Catholic Churches . . . after them."[40]

Further evidence of the view of Christian antiquity which Wesley was developing at this time comes from Benjamin Ingham's diary. Ingham was one of the Oxford Methodists who began observing Saturday-evening watches on 4 May 1734 after reading of the practice in Horneck's *Happy Ascetick*.[41] After John Wesley arrived in Oxford from a trip to Epworth, the two men had breakfast together, where they discussed the Saturday watches. Ingham's record of the conversation is as follows:

> Religious Talk of the Obligations of the Apostolic Church; every particular Church may conform to it entirely; every Member of any particular Church may conform to it so far as he is at Liberty; in particular instances we must consider their nature and necessity;

> Standing on Sundays only decency; religious talk of Watching, acceptable, but not necessary for all.[42]

Although the verb "may" seems inappropriate for a discussion of "Obligations," it seems clear that Ingham's and Wesley's thoughts on watches and other customs were guided by the criterion of conformity to the consensus of teaching in the ancient church. In this respect, the ideas expressed in this conversation parallel very nearly those enunciated in Wesley's "Essay upon the Stationary Fasts."

Wesley's concern with the ancient church in general, and with its fasts in particular, continued through his departure for Georgia. As he sat on board the *Simmonds* awaiting his departure in September 1735, he received a letter from Clayton, promising to send him William Whiston's "catechesis," and admonishing him to "Be sure remember [*sic*] to dip when you baptize, if it can be possibly done, according to the church's direction."[43] Wesley wrote Richard Morgan, Jr., expressing a doubt about whether the Wednesday fast was "strictly obligatory; though," he continued, "I believe it very ancient, if not apostolical."[44]

What all of this shows is that in Wesley's later years in Oxford (1732 through 1735), the cultural and religious forces operative on him were not those of the conservative Anglicanism recommended to John Wesley by his father. Rather, they were almost uniformly what we have called "programmatic," that is, they were directed toward the reinstitution of early Christian practices and the renewal of the ancient Christians' moral and spiritual character. Wesley's extensive readings in Beveridge, Marshall, Cave, and Horneck in this period, as well as his exposure to the programmatic intentions of the Manchester Non-Jurors, would have mediated this programmatic concern to him. Wesley's conceptions of Christian antiquity in this period seem to have been dominated by an interest in ancient liturgical and disciplinary practices, such as the ancient weekly fasts. Given the concern for just these matters in the Apostolic Canons and Constitutions, one can understand the prominence these works held in Wesley's conceptions of Christian antiquity in this period. Wesley's "Essay upon the Stationary Fasts" and the record of his conversation with Benjamin Ingham show that by 1734 Wesley had made this programmatic intent his own, and was anxious to see his own church conform in detail to practices he believed to have been universally observed in Christian antiquity.

Primitive Christianity in the Wilderness

Under the influence of the Manchester Non-Jurors, and immediately after the death of his father, John Wesley decided to go to North America as a missionary of the Society for the Propagation of the Gospel. His readings, writings, and practices in this period show that he originally saw the Georgia mission as an opportunity to restore ancient Christian disciplinary and liturgical customs in an environment similar to that of the ancient Church. On board the *Simmonds* he resolved with his brother Charles and with his friends Benjamin Ingham and Charles Delamotte to rise early every morning for prayers, an hour of Bible study, and an hour of reading "something relating to the primitive church."[45] During the voyage, he read from Deacon's *Compleat Collection of Devotions* and Nelson's *Companion to the Festivals and Fasts of the Church of England.*[46]

Wesley's intentions for the Georgia mission appear prominently in a record of a conversation between him and Moravian leader August Gottlieb Spangenberg, recorded in the diary of the latter during the Atlantic crossing. Martin Schmidt summarizes Spangenberg's earliest impressions of Wesley in the following terms:

> [Wesley] had stressed his plan for evangelizing the Indians and the fact that he desired to carry this through in the manner of the early church. He thought that one of the brethren from Herrnhut might go with him, but there ought to be also ordained deaconesses in order to be able to conform to the early Christian practice of baptism by immersion for women. His standard for primitive Christianity in general was the consensus of opinion from the Fathers of the first three centuries.[47]

Here one may note the emphasis on the consensus of patristic teaching, as well as Deacon's belief in baptism by immersion, to be performed by members of the catechumen's own sex. Here also one may see most clearly Wesley's vision of evangelization on the pattern of the early church.

In a further conversation, Spangenberg again noted Wesley's preoccupation with Christian antiquity:

> [Wesley] has moreover several quite special principles, which he still holds strongly, since he drank them in with his mother's milk. He thinks that an ordination not performed by a bishop in the apostolic succession is invalid. Therefore he believes that neither Calvinists nor Lutherans have *legitimos doctores* and *pastores*. From this it follows that the sacraments administered by such teachers are not valid: this also he maintains.[48]

Spangenberg went on to explain that Wesley refused to share in the eucharist with, or accept the baptisms of, persons from traditions where the apostolic succession of bishops was not maintained. Wesley acknowledged, Spangenberg stated, that the Moravians did have a valid claim to the apostolic succession. (In fact, the British Parliament recognized the Moravian *Unitas Fratrum* as "an ancient Protestant Episcopal Church" in 1749.)[49] Spangenberg then explained the authority which Wesley claimed for his views,

> All these doctrines derive from the view of the episcopacy which is held in the Papist and English churches and which rests upon the authority of the Fathers. Above all he believes that all references in Scripture of doubtful interpretation must be decided not by reason, but from the writings of the first three centuries, e.g., infant baptism, footwashing, fast days, celibacy and many others.[50]

The contrast expressed in the phrase "not by reason but from the writings of the first three centuries" shows the distinction Spangenberg must have seen between a conventional Protestant view of the interpretation of scripture, which would have stressed the use of reason and the integrity of the scriptural text itself, and the view of Anglicans who had stressed the importance of Christian antiquity in interpreting scripture. Spangenberg's references to "footwashing, fast days, celibacy and many others" suggests Wesley's concern for reinstituting ancient customs which had fallen into disuse.

Wesley's readings throughout his stay in Georgia illustrate his continuing interest in the ancient church. Between 16 March and 2 April 1736 he was involved in reading Laurence Echard's *General Ecclesiastical History* (1702), a chronological history of Christianity from the birth of Christ until the establishment of the church under Constantine. Echard's work acknowledged its debt to Cave, Dupin, Tillemont, Fleury, Pearson, Stillingfleet, and Wake, among others. It is interesting to observe (in light of Wesley's changing views noted below) that this work rejected the theory of early authorship of the Apostolic Canons.[51] Later that year Wesley read in Ephraem Syrus and studied Cotelier's Greek edition of the Apostolic Fathers with the Moravians. He read in the works of William Cave (probably *Primitive Christianity*), in the "Spiritual Homilies" attributed to Macarius of Egypt, and in numerous works of French Bishop Claude Fleury, many of which treated the early Christian church.[52] In his second year in Georgia, he was involved in the study of Wake's translation of the Apostolic Fathers, mentioning specifically I Clement and the Epistle of Polycarp in his diaries. Along with these he read Irenaeus and Stillingfleet.[53]

During his stay in Georgia John Wesley produced a manuscript abridgement of Claude Fleury's *Moeurs des Chrétiens* which illuminates the conceptions of Christian antiquity which he held at that time. His

Journal and diaries indicate his frequent study in Fleury's works, and manuscripts of Wesley's versions of *Moeurs des Chrétiens* and Fleury's *Catéchisme historique,* written in notebooks bound in the same manner as the Georgia diaries, have survived. Wesley's manuscript originally entitled "An Abridgement of Fleury's Manners of the Christians" displays significant alterations of Fleury's text. Whereas Fleury's work treated the life of the church through the seventh century, Wesley's abridgement included only those parts of the work concerned with the first three centuries, ending with the age of Constantine. Even within the parts of Fleury's work he included, Wesley omitted chapters dealing with the eucharistic mysteries, relics of martyrs, confessors, excommunication, and ascetic orders. Of the chapters Wesley included, he omitted considerable detail, and almost all of the numerous references to patristic sources which Fleury had given. Wesley replaced Fleury's chapter on penance with a chapter abridging Marshall's *Penitential Discipline of the Primitive Church,* and replaced Fleury's chapter on the clergy with a short chapter, perhaps of Wesley's own devising, explaining the orders of bishop, priest, deacon, and deaconess in the early church.[54]

The result of this labor of excision, abridgement, and addition is a compressed portrait of Wesley's vision of Christianity in the ante-Nicene period: a Christianity having its perfection in Christ, whose example the apostles and their disciples in turn imitated. It is a vision of a Christian community holding its possessions in common, exercising a strict discipline over its catechumens, worshiping together at daily canonical hours, observing Wednesdays and Fridays as fasts, celebrating the eucharist weekly, and expressing its faith in its ordinary meals and even its modes of dress. It is a vision of a church that disciplines with excommunication its offenders, and receives them again, only once, and only upon their temporary segregation from the community, their public confession of sin, and their formal absolution by the bishop. It is a vision of an orderly communion, governed by bishops in succession to the apostles, ministered to by its priests, and served by its deacons and deaconesses. It is a vision of a community suffering under persecutions, providing for the needs of its own constituents, first, then for the rest of humankind so far as it is able. In some points of detail, Wesley's version of "The Manners of the Christians" affirmed chrismation as the appropriate mode of confirmation, prayer facing the east, the frequent use of the sign of the cross, elaborate penitential discipline including public confession and segregation from the church, and trine immersion as the normative mode of baptism.[55]

Wesley's practices in Georgia illustrate further his intentions for a renewal of the life of ancient Christianity. Twenty days after arriving in the colony, Wesley baptized an infant "according to the custom of the first church, and the rule of the church of England, by immersion." "The child was ill then," Wesley wrote, "but recovered from that hour."[56] This practice reflects not only the views of Deacon, Clayton, and Fleury, noted above, but also the instructions in the 1549 Prayer Book, to which the Manchester Non-Jurors were attached. Two weeks later, Wesley informed his congregation of his intention to "divide the morning service on Sundays in compliance with the first design of the church."[57] This, too, reflects the 1549 Prayer Book's separation of the office for morning prayer from the eucharistic liturgy, which might be justified on the basis of the ancient distinction between the *missa cate-chumenorum* and the *missa fidelium*, as Cave and others had described it.

What emerges from a close examination of John Wesley's study and work in Georgia, then, is that his original inspiration for the mission was a religious vision of the renewal of ancient Christian practices and institutions in the primitive North American environment. His vision, at this point, was colored by his encounter with the Manchester sect, and by their stress upon the Apostolic Canons and Constitutions and the consensus of ancient conciliar teachings.

His experience in Georgia, however, led him to alter some of his conceptions of the ancient church. There can be little doubt that these changes were due to his encounter with Continental Pietists, who had their own ideas about Christian antiquity. Wesley's approval of the Moravians, in particular, may be seen in his comments on a Moravian episcopal election and consecration which he attended three weeks after arriving in America:

> After several hours spent in conference and prayer, they proceeded to the election and ordination of a Bishop. The great simplicity, as well as solemnity, of the whole, made me forget the seventeen hundred years between, and imagine myself in one of those assemblies where form and state were not; but Paul the tent-maker, or Peter the fisherman presided; yet with the demonstration of the Spirit and Power.[58]

The "great simplicity" of the Moravian service would have contrasted with an Anglican episcopal ordination. Secular occupations of bishops were maintained by the Moravians. This contrasts with the Anglican pattern as well, although it may be noted that Thomas Deacon was a physician who maintained his medical practice after his episcopal ordination.[59]

In the autumn of 1736 Wesley was engaged in the study of early Christian texts in the company of the Moravians. On the thirteenth of

September, according to the account in his *Journal*, Wesley took up William Beveridge's *Synodikon* (subtitled *Pandectae*), a collection of conciliar canons including the Apostolic Canons, with Charles Delamotte. His entry in the *Journal* for this date reflects an uneasiness over the authority of ancient church councils:

> *Mon.* 13.—I began reading, with Mr. Delamotte, Bishop Beveridge's *Pandectae Canonum Conciliorum.* Nothing could so effectually have convinced us, both that Particular and 'General Councils may err and have erred'; [and of the infinite difference there is between the decisions of the wisest men and those of the Holy Ghost recorded in his Word;] and that things ordained by Councils as necessary to salvation have neither strength, nor authority unless they be taken out of Holy Scripture.[60]

This passage reflects an alteration of the high approbation of conciliar orthodoxy expressed by Wesley's father and such Anglican apologists as George Bull and John Pearson. Because the *Synodikon* contained the Apostolic Canons, this comment must be taken as referring to them as well. There is a discrepancy between this passage and Wesley's diary for this date, which observes that he began the *Codex Canonum*, Beveridge's defence of the Apostolic Canons, with Delamotte on this date.[61] This suggests that Wesley's subsequent recollection of the events, when he composed his *Journal* account, may have been in error; although the diary shows Wesley as reading the "Councils" a week later. It is probable that Wesley had taken up both of Beveridge's works during this period.[62]

The Apostolic Canons are the subject of a further observation in the *Journal* a week later that shows the same tone of disappointment:

> *Mon.* 20.—We ended the *Apostolical Canons*, of which I must confess I once thought more highly than I ought to think. Of them Bishop Beveridge observes that they are the decrees of the several Synods, which met at several places, and on several occasions, in the second and third age after Christ; and therefore called Apostolical, because partly grounded upon, partly agreeing with, the traditions delivered down from the Apostles. He farther observes ['That as they were enacted by different Synods, so they were collected by different persons; till, about A.D. 500, John, Bishop of Constantinople, placed them at the head of the Canons, which he then collected into one code; since which time they have been in force in the Eastern Church. But then' he adds] (*Codex Canonum Ecclesiae Primitivae*, p. 159; and why did he not observe it in the first page of the book?), 'they contain the discipline used in the church at the time when they were collected; not when the Council of Nice met, for then many parts of it were useless and obsolete.'[63]

On the page referred to in the parenthetical comment, Beveridge is responding to a challenge against the authority of the Apostolic

Canons raised by Jean Daillé. Daillé asked why, if the Apostolic Canons had been acknowledged to have been of apostolic origin, or even of venerable antiquity, they had not been inserted in the most prominent position among other collections of ancient canons, such as those of the Council of Nicea. Beveridge responded that very often later councils did not include in their own lists of canons such canons as had been in effect earlier in their own provinces, since earlier canons might not be relevant at the time of the later Council. Beveridge gave as an example the fact that the code of canons of the ancient African church did not include the canons which had been promulgated under Cyprian, or by earlier African councils. Beveridge suggested, further, that the suspension of persecutions by Constantine may have made some second- and third-century canons obsolete by the time of the Council of Nicea.[64] Wesley's objection to the Apostolic Canons, then, was not that they were post-Nicene, for he seizes upon Beveridge's observation that some of them were obsolete by the time of Nicea. Rather, Wesley finally realized at this point that the Apostolic Canons could not have expressed the consensus of early Christian practice if in fact some of them were not in use in some areas by A.D. 325.

A similar pattern of criticism may be observed in a manuscript in Wesley's hand containing notes on the Apostolic Constitutions. Wesley's diaries show that he was studying the Constitutions, sometimes with Delamotte, sometimes with "the Germans," in late September and early October 1736.[65] One item in this manuscript has the note "therefore S. Hilary knew not these Constitutions, for he calls Philemon a layman." Wesley questioned whether other parts of the Constitutions were extant before the Council of Nicea, but dated some parts from the third century.[66] The remark about Hilary not knowing the Constitutions would have conveyed an important objection to any theory, such as that of Deacon, that the Constitutions reflected the consensus of ancient Christian practice.

A clearer statement of Wesley's changing evaluation of Christian antiquity appears in a manuscript dated 25 January 1738. At this time, Wesley was on board ship, returning to England. After explaining some earlier phases of his theological development, Wesley noted his attachment to the Vincentian canon, and problems he had begun to perceive with it:

> 5. But it was not long before Providence brought me to those who showed me a sure rule of interpreting Scripture, viz.: *Consensus veterum: quod ab omnibus, quod ubique, quod semper creditum.* At the same time they sufficiently insisted upon a due regard to the one Church at all times and in all places. Nor was it long before I bent the bow too far the other way:

1. By making antiquity a co-ordinate rather than a subordinate rule with Scripture.

2. By admitting several doubtful writings, as undoubted evidences of antiquity.

3. By extending antiquity too far, even to the middle or end of the fourth century.

4. By believing more practices to have been universal in the ancient church than ever were so.

5. By not considering that the decrees of one provincial synod could bind only that province; and that the decrees of a general synod bound only those provinces whose representatives met therein.

6. By not considering that the most of these decrees were adapted to particular times and occasions; and, consequently, when these occasions ceased, must cease to bind even those provinces.[67]

This passage suggests that Wesley continued to regard the consensus of teachings and practices in the ancient church (hence his citation of the Vincentian Canon) as "a sure rule of interpreting Scripture," brought to his attention—providentially, in his own view—by the Manchester Non-Jurors.

He also acknowledged, however, that he had come to recognize errors in their views of Christian antiquity. The errors listed are of two sorts. First, there were excesses in the application of this principle, as noted in items one and three. In this document, Wesley himself takes responsibility for these errors, and does not attribute them to the Manchester Non-Jurors. Second, there were errors of scholarly judgment involved in the application of this principle, as items two, four, five, and six note. The "doubtful writings" referred to in item two would be the Apostolic Canons and Constitutions; the "practices" in item four would be the "usages" and other practices emphasized by the Manchester Non-Jurors; and the attenuations of the rule noted in items five and six correspond to the criticisms raised about the Apostolic Canons and Constitutions in his studies in the autumn of 1736, that is, the criticisms that these documents, of whatever antiquity, did not reflect the consensus of ancient Christian teachings and practices.

In 1737, then, John Wesley had come to hold a different vision of Christian antiquity than he had held before. Having come to question the authenticity of the Apostolic Canons and Constitutions, he would have had much less support for the views of ancient liturgical and disciplinary practices he had espoused before. Having recognized the eccentricity of his earlier uses of Christian antiquity, he would try in the future to see antiquity as a supplement to the authority of scripture; but his religious vision, in fact, would still rely upon his sense of the purity of the ancient church.

Evangelical Revival and Christian Antiquity

A series of events between 1738 and 1740 propelled John Wesley into the evangelistic ministry that characterized the rest of his life. Late in the spring of 1738 he experienced the "assurance of pardon" stressed by Continental Pietists. He traveled to Germany in mid-summer of the same year in order to explore Pietism more directly. Late in the autumn he spent some time in Oxford considering the Church of England's Articles and *Homilies* on faith and justification. He found himself engaged in field-preaching in the spring of 1739, and began to organize societies later in that year. His exclusion from the partly-Moravian Fetter Lane Society in 1740 marked the independence of his own branch of the revival movement.[68]

Although some have represented Wesley as losing his earlier interests in early Christianity after the beginning of the revival, he continued to study and refer to ancient Christian writings, and to call upon them in the work of the revival movement itself.[69] Over one hundred and fifty references to early Christian works can be found in Wesley's writings after 1737, including references to all of the following ancient Christian authors or writings:

Arnobius	Ephraem Syrus
Augustine	Epiphanius
the Athanasian Creed	Eusebius
Athanasius	Ignatius of Antioch
Athenagoras	Jerome
Basil	Justin Martyr
Chrysostom	Macarius of Egypt
Clement of Alexandria	Origen
Clement of Rome	Polycarp
Cyprian	Tertullian
Dionysius of Alexandria	Theophilus of Antioch[70]
Dionysius the Pseudo-Areopagite	

Notably lacking in this period are references to the Apostolic Constitutions or Apostolic Canons. Wesley's readings throughout this period, recorded in his diaries and sometimes in the *Journal* and letters, show a continuing interest in early Christian life and thought.[71] On board ship returning from North America, Wesley turned to the works of Cyprian, and found encouragement in them. At the request of a friend in 1740, he read in the *Mystical Theology* of Dionysius the Pseudo-Areopagite, and reacted strongly against what he perceived as its quietism. In November of the next year, he was engaged in reading Eusebius's *Ecclesiastical History* and the *Historiae Ecclesiasticae Compendium* ("Compendium of Ecclesiastical History") of Jean Alphonse

Turrettini, a Genevan theologian who had rejected the reactionary Calvinism of the Synod of Dort.[72]

Two works appeared quite early in the years of the revival that indicate Wesley's fondness for the Christian Platonism of Clement of Alexandria. A poem, "On Clemens Alexandrinus's Description of a Perfect Christian," appeared in John and Charles Wesley's *Hymns and Sacred Poems*, published in 1739. The poem describes the distance between the state of a human being in pilgrimage and the state of a perfect Christian, then, the power of God to bring human beings to the perfect state. It reflects Clement's description of the Christian "Gnostic" in book seven of his *Stromateis*, although it does not reproduce exactly any specific parts of the *Stromateis* passage.[73] It is unclear whether the poem is to be attributed to John or Charles Wesley, or perhaps even to John Gambold, an Oxford Methodist (and later a Moravian bishop) who wrote some of the poems in the collection and who was attracted to ancient Christian mysticism.[74]

John Wesley's continuing appreciation for Clement's description of the Christian ideal appears in a tract entitled "The Character of a Methodist," published in 1742 in responses to queries about the meaning of the term "Methodist." The tract was intended to display the Methodist *ideal* (the inscription "Not as though I had already attained" appears below its title) and Wesley acknowledged twenty-five years after its publication that it was based on "the character of a perfect Christian drawn by Clemens Alexandrinus."[75] Wesley's "Character of a Methodist" and the passage from book seven of Clement's *Stromateis* share some common elements: both stress the hope of immortality, prayer without ceasing, love of one's neighbor, obedience to God's commandments, and freedom from worldly desires as characteristics of the ideal Christian (Gnostic or Methodist!). Nevertheless, Wesley's delineation of the model Christian neither follows the order of Clement's, nor uses Clement's precise words to any obvious degree, and Wesley's concern to avoid doctrinal disputation in this treatise stands in contrast to Clement's insistence that the perfection of *gnosis* included adherence to particular doctrinal assertions. Also, characteristically Clementine emphases such as the Christian's passionlessness and contemplation of the divine find no place in Wesley's work.[76] But even though Wesley's delineation of "The Character of a Methodist" does not follow Clement's *Stromateis* precisely, it nevertheless represents a case in which Wesley's religious vision was consciously inspired by that of an ancient Christian work.

In the earliest decade of the revival, Wesley had to defend the Methodist movement against frequent charges of "enthusiasm," that is, of unjustified claims to religious inspiration. In his defense of the

Methodists' claims to divine "assurance" and inspiration, Wesley sometimes appealed to similar claims made by the early Christians. In his *Farther Appeal to Men of Reason and Religion* (1744), for example, Wesley had to respond to charges by Richard Smalbroke (1672–1749), an Oxford-educated bishop and scholar of early Christianity who had advised the clergy in his diocese to avoid the "enthusiastic" pretensions of the Methodists. Wesley's *Farther Appeal* responded by showing that early Christian writers held immediate divine inspiration to be an "ordinary" as well as an "extraordinary" gift of the Holy Spirit.[77] Similar issues regarding divine inspiration in the ancient church emerged in the period between 1745 and 1747 in Wesley's correspondence with an anonymous Anglican who signed his letters "John Smith." "Smith," whose identity must in all likelihood remain unknown, picked up on the argument of the *Farther Appeal* and questioned whether "perceptible inspiration" was as common in the early church as Wesley supposed. Wesley responded that "perceptible inspiration" was "the main doctrine of the Methodists," and pressed his argument that it was the teaching of the early church, backing up his claims with more citations of early Christian authors.[78]

It was at some point during the first decade of the revival—that remarkable and formative period between 1738 and 1748—that Wesley's attitudes toward ordination and episcopacy began to shift corresponding to a change in his understanding of the ancient church. When exactly is difficult to tell, but it is clear that at some point during the mid-1740s Wesley read both Stillingfleet's *Irenicum* and King's *Enquiry*, and on the basis of these works became convinced that an elder (or presbyter) in the church had an "inherent right" to ordain other elders, though this right should not be exercised except in cases of dire necessity. When in the 1780s Methodists in America needed ordained ministers, Wesley would turn to the new insights he had gained during this period.[79]

By 1748 Wesley's movement had developed most of its characteristic institutions. In that year—ten years after his Aldersgate Street experience—Wesley wrote an apology for the movement in the form of an open letter to the Reverend Vincent Perronet, Vicar of Shoreham in Kent. Wesley had made Perronet's acquaintance in 1744 and had come to rely on him as an advisor, one who returned the compliment by encouraging Methodist activities in his own parish. The letter, entitled "A Plain Account of the People Called Methodists," is dated 1748 and was published in January of 1749.[80] It reveals in several particular respects how Wesley understood the distinctive institutions of Methodism as emerging from his vision of the ancient church.

Wesley described in this work the "economy" or organization of Methodism. He explained in the beginning of the work that the Methodist institutions described in it were not planned beforehand, but developed in response to the needs of the movement. Nevertheless, Wesley maintained, the early Methodists "generally found, in looking back, something in Christian antiquity likewise, very nearly parallel" to the Methodist institutions.[81] In almost every section of the work Wesley pointed to specific parallels between Methodist and ancient Christian institutions: the Methodist societies and ancient catechetical classes; penitent bands and the segregation of penitents in the ancient church, and so on.[82] Thus, as Wesley's movement came to the end of its first decade, the motif of the revival of ancient Christian life, thought, and institutions remained prominent in Wesley's vision.

Christian Antiquity and the Methodist Enterprise

The year 1749 represents in many ways a new period for the Methodist movement. It was the year in which, with his own institutions firmly in place, Wesley began to reach out to other Evangelical leaders to secure greater cooperation, and (he hoped) organizational merger. It was also the year when two of his most celebrated "ecumenical" expressions appeared: his "Letter to a Roman Catholic" and the first volumes of his eclectic *Christian Library*.[83] Wesley's writings and other works in this and the following years also showed Wesley's continuing concerns with the ideal of early Christian life, as he tried to educate and defend his movement. The year began, in fact, with one of Wesley's longest original works—his "Letter to the Reverend Dr. Conyers Middleton"—a work which was wholly concerned with the question of "miraculous powers" in the first Christian centuries and which was written in the light of Methodist challenges to the newly emerging culture of the Enlightenment in England.[84]

Beginning in 1749, and continuing for several years after, John Wesley published a series of translations, editions, and abridgements designed especially for Methodist preachers. Many of these were ancient Christian works, or works concerned with Christian antiquity, and it is often possible to see their relevance to the Methodists' challenges to their culture. For instance, in January 1749 Wesley published a new revision of the edition of Claude Fleury's *Moeurs des Chrétiens* which he had originally prepared in Georgia. This revision is particularly interesting, because it shows a number of deletions—references to ancient penitential discipline and ordinations—which may indicate changing emphases in Wesley's views of ancient Christianity.[85] Wesley must have been at work on his edition of Fleury late in 1748 when he came upon Middleton's *Free Inquiry*. He was almost certainly also engaged in work on the first volume of his *Christian Library*, which began with a translation—partly his own work—of the early second century Apostolic Fathers. The period of the Apostolic Fathers was critical to Middleton's argument, and so it is likely that Wesley's immersion in this literature in late 1748 made him feel particularly well prepared to respond to Middleton.[86] Wesley indicated a high approbation of these works, as his introductory comments (taken over verbatim from the introduction of Archbishop William Wake) indicate, and held them up as models for Christian life and thought.[87]

The second work contained in the first volume of Wesley's *Christian Library* was an abridgement of a translation of the fifty "Spiritual Homilies" attributed to "St. Macarius the Egyptian." The author of the translation, entitled *Primitive Morality*, is unknown, but it is clear that Wesley worked from this version. The homilies are principally concerned with the Christian's pursuit of "perfection," and thus Wesley's edition of the work shows how he saw early Christian teachings as models for understanding sanctification.[88]

Much later in the *Christian Library*—in the twenty-ninth volume, published in 1752—Wesley included an abridgement of Anthony Horneck's *Happy Ascetick*, which contained "A Letter to a Person of Quality, concerning the Heavenly Lives of the Primitive Christians." This letter is itself a summary of a Latin letter dating from 1660, and describes in systematic fashion the virtues of the early Christians, holding them up as models for contemporary Christian life.[89] Like his edition of Fleury, then, Wesley's edition of this work reflects his views of the particular moral traits and institutions of the first Christian centuries that Wesley held up as models for his generation.

Finally, in the thirty-first volume of his *Christian Library* (this volume published in 1753) Wesley included an abridgement of Cave's classic work on *Primitive Christianity*. Cave's work was, in part, based on the 1660 Latin work upon which Horneck's "Letter to a Person of Quality" had been based, and thus adds to the stream of concern with revival of the moral life of the early church that seems to have been so prominent in Wesley's concerns in this period.[90]

Although it did not appear in the *Christian Library*, Wesley published in 1771 an edition of Johann Lorenz von Mosheim's *Ecclesiastical History*. Like the works in the *Christian Library*, the edition of Mosheim was intended for the instruction of the Methodists, especially for the Methodist lay preachers. Although Wesley's work in editing Mosheim was largely a work of deletion, there are a few added paragraphs (for instance, one on Pelagius) that reveal some particularities of Wesley's views of early Christianity.[91]

In addition to his edited works, Wesley's vision of Christian antiquity is also reflected in the "Address to the Clergy" which he wrote in the middle of the 1750s. His suggestions for reading in the "Address" are reminiscent of Samuel Wesley's advice to younger clergy. He listed particular early Christian writers by a scheme of centuries, and suggested that all Christian clergy should be familiar with their works.[92] The "Address" is particularly interesting since, not being addressed to the Methodist societies or preachers as so many of his works were, it reveals his concerns and hopes for the general welfare of the church—and among his concerns in this regard, his concern for education in the life and thought of Christian antiquity is prominent.

A Sketch of Wesley's Vision of Christian Antiquity

If Wesley's edition of Fleury gave a compressed portrait of the vision of the church in antiquity that Wesley held while in Georgia, it is possible to sketch with more detail his understanding of the ancient church, especially in the period between 1749 and the early 1770s, that is, in the middle years of the revival when so many of the editions noted above (including his second edited version of Fleury) were produced. What follows is a composite sketch of the content of John Wesley's vision of ancient Christianity as he consistently taught it during these three decades.

Consistent with the general church histories he had studied, Wesley understood the early history of Christianity within a framework of centuries or "ages." He used the terms "century" and "age" interchangeably: "With what colour," Wesley asked Conyers Middleton, "can you assert, that [the miraculous gifts] were less wanted for these ends, in the second and third, than in the Apostolic age?"[93] The structure of his conception of the earliest Christian centuries can be seen in the following paragraph from his sermon "On Laying the Foundation of the New Chapel, near the City-Road, London":

> This is the religion of the primitive Church, of the whole Church in the purest ages. It is clearly expressed, even in the small remains of Clemens Romanus, Ignatius, and Polycarp; it is seen more at large in the writings of Tertullian, Origen, Clemens Alexandrinus, and Cyprian; and, even in the fourth century, it was found in the works of Chrysostom, Basil, Ephrem Syrus, and Macarius.[94]

Century divisions are clearly marked out in this passage: Clement of Rome, Ignatius of Antioch, and Polycarp belong to the second century; Tertullian, Origen, Clement of Alexandria, and Cyprian belong to the third; and Chrysostom, Basil, Ephraem Syrus, and [pseudo-]Macarius to the fourth. As the passage suggests, and as the following account shows, Wesley perceived a break in the history of early Christianity in the early fourth century, coinciding with the reign of Constantine. The following account is thus organized to reflect Wesley's conceptions of ancient Christian history before and after Constantine.

Pre-Constantinian Christianity

"As the Christian religion is not an invention of men, but the work of God," begins Wesley's translation of Fleury's *Moeurs des Chrétiens*, "it received its full perfection in the beginning of it."[95] John Wesley consistently reflected the opinion that Christian faith and morals were purest at their source in Christ, and in the earliest, apostolic community, and declined as the years passed. He believed the earlier Christian writers to have had greater piety and holiness than later ones, and thought that for that reason God had given the earlier Christians more aid in avoiding delusions. Wesley omitted from his edition of Horneck a phrase asserting that the church's "Merits increased with its Years,"[96] probably because of his commitment to this general belief in the deterioration of the church.

Wesley ascribed a special excellence to the ages prior to Constantine. The passage from Wesley's sermon "On Laying the Foundation of the New Chapel . . . " given above suggests that Wesley ascribed an exceptional unity and purity to the pre-Constantinian church. He believed that miraculous gifts had continued in the church in this period, and he supposed that for all the saints known from the early centuries, far more remained unknown. He recommended the study of the early Christian writers, whom he held to be

> . . . the most authentic commentators on Scripture, as being both nearest the fountain, and eminently endued with that Spirit by whom all Scripture was given. It will be easily perceived, I speak chiefly of those who wrote before the Council of Nice. But who would not likewise desire to have some acquaintance with those that followed them?[97]

Wesley frequently recommended "the Ante-Nicene Fathers" or "the writings of the first three centuries," the esteem of which, he claimed, "never carried any man yet into dangerous errors, nor probably ever will."[98]

The First Century. The Roman Empire, states Wesley's version of Fleury, was "the most enlightened that ever it was, as well as the most corrupted" when Christianity came into it.[99] Into this enlightened and corrupted world, the Christian community grew from its base in Jerusalem, "the pattern and mother of all churches . . . taught and governed by the apostles themselves."[100] Wesley's vision of first-century Christianity is largely based on his study of the New Testament. From post-canonical sources, though, he knew the legend of the flight of the Jerusalem church to Pella after the destruction of Jerusalem. He believed, moreover, that the apostles had passed on the leadership of the church to their closest associates, among whom were St. Mark, St. Clement (of Rome), St. Timothy, St. Titus, St. Luke, and St. Polycarp. These, in turn, took disciples whom they instructed, and to whom they passed the leadership of the church. His edition of Mosheim recognizes that the "Apostles' Creed" was of later than apostolic origin, and suggests that the Ebionite heresy originated late in the first century.[101]

The Second Century. Although Wesley knew that some of the Apostolic Fathers' works dated from the first century, his mental framework of early Christian "ages" generally placed them within the second century. He suggested that clergy should read "over and over the golden remains of Clemens Romanus, of Ignatius and Polycarp." He suggested in the same address that clergy should give "one reading, at least," to Justin Martyr and third-century writers, thus indicating the higher esteem in which Wesley held the Apostolic Fathers.[102] He recognized that even the Apostolic Fathers were liable to "weakness," as exemplified in Clement's use of the legend of the Phoenix, but he insisted that such weaknesses did not mean that Clement or the other Apostolic Fathers were devoid of extraordinary spiritual gifts.

Although Wesley was aware of second-century corruptions in the biblical texts, he held that by the middle of the second century most of the books of the New Testament were read in the churches "as a divine rule of faith and manners."[103] His edition of Cave suggests that the second-century Christians had "fixed places of worship" in homes or cemeteries, although they could not yet undertake the construction of public church buildings.[104]

John Wesley saw the purity of the second-century church especially in its courage under persecutions and martyrdoms. His editions of various authors include vivid accounts of the persecutions—some delve into gruesome details. Wesley prepared for the *Christian Library* his own versions of the "Martyrdoms" of Ignatius and Polycarp. He asserted, against Conyers Middleton, that the same conditions which made miraculous gifts necessary in the first century, namely, persecutions of the church and the church's propagation of the gospel, continued in the second and third centuries, and so made miraculous gifts necessary in those ages as well.[105] He did, however, alter or omit passages from the martyrdom narratives which suggested that the early Christians were eager for martyrdom, did not attempt to escape martyrdom, or were given a special grace that enabled them to undergo torments without actually feeling them.[106]

The Third Century. Wesley regarded the third century as an age in which the primitive purity of the church still shone in many areas, but began to decline in others. He believed that Tertullian, Origen (*sic!*), Clement of Alexandria, and Cyprian expressed "the religion of the primitive church," and he suggested that clergy should read their works at least once.[107] In actual usage, Wesley referred to these authors more than he referred to any others, with the exception of Augustine (and his references to Augustine were often critical).[108] Nevertheless, Wesley held "that before the end of the third century the Church was greatly degenerated from its first purity," and cited Cyprian as giving evidence of the third-century church's corruptions.[109] Where other writers had seen the early church's councils as standards of Christian unity and orthodoxy, Wesley deplored the councils of the third century and later (this in spite of his affirmation of the language of Nicea, Constantinople, and Chalcedon; see below under "A Pattern for Christian Teachings" in chapter 5). His comment on Baxter's *History of the Councils* antedates Voltaire's mockery of the ancient councils:

> What a company of execrable wretches they have been (one cannot give them a milder title,) who have almost in every age, since St. Cyprian, taken upon them to govern the Church! How has one Council been perpetually cursing another; and delivering all over to Satan, whether predecessors or contemporaries, who did not implicitly receive their determinations, though generally trifling, sometimes false, and frequently unintelligible or self-contradictory. Surely Mahometanism was let loose to reform the Christians![110]

But in the next century, as Wesley saw it, the evils present here and there were to grow into a flood that would ravage ancient Christianity to its foundations.

Constantinian and Post-Constantinian Christianity

The Constantinian Crisis and Its Effects. Wesley asserted on numerous occasions throughout his life his belief that, with Constantine's supposed conversion to Christianity, the church lost a great deal of its original purity, that the corruptions which had been creeping in drop by drop during the second and third centuries poured in upon the church with a full tide from the beginning of the fourth century, when Constantine called himself a Christian.[111] In opposition to Bishop Thomas Newton of Bristol, whose *Dissertations on the Prophecies* had identified Constantine's conversion with the advent of the new Jerusalem foretold in the Revelation, Wesley asserted that "Constantine's calling himself a Christian" was "productive of more evil to the Church than ten persecutions put together."[112]

Wesley believed, in particular, that Constantine's donations of wealth to the church, and his according honor to Christians (especially to the clergy) led to the church's moral decline. The church became intermixed with "paganism," and thus Christians became "lovers of the world, lovers of themselves, lovers of pleasure more than lovers of God."[113] His edition of Mosheim notes that from the time of Constantine Christians began to utilize philosophy and the liberal arts more than they had done in the past, and that Constantine arrogated to himself the authority to rule the church through ecumenical councils.[114]

As Wesley saw it, Constantine's taking up the Christian cause had debilitating effects on the church's life. The clergy began to seek wealth and power. Ministerial orders, formerly divided according to a number of functions, were consolidated under the office of bishop. Church buildings were erected, images were placed in them, and people began to pay homage to the images. Church rituals multiplied beyond their ancient simplicity. The miraculous gifts ceased to be commonly exercised, and only the "dead form" of Christianity remained in most areas.[115]

True Christianity after Constantine. Nevertheless, Wesley held that some pockets of true Christianity remained after the age of Constantine. He insisted, for instance, that clergy should have "some acquaintance" with such post-Nicene writers as Chrysostom, Basil, Jerome, Augustine, "and, above all, the man of a broken heart, Ephraem Syrus."[116] In a similar list, Wesley omitted Jerome and Augustine and included Macarius, and in a third list he included only Ephraem Syrus and Macarius.[117] What is to be especially noted in these lists is the preponderance of Eastern Christian writers. Although Augustine and Jerome appear on one list, and although Wesley actually cited Augustine more than any other patristic writer, Wesley's comments on Augustine could be extremely negative.[118] Within the Eastern writers in these lists, he sometimes attached special importance to the ascetics, Ephraem Syrus and Macarius. Although he never made it explicit, Wesley seems to have understood true Christianity after the age of Constantine to lie principally in isolated pockets of Eastern Christendom, and among the ascetics in particular.

The overall impression that emerges from this sketch of Wesley's understanding of ancient Christian history is a clear sense of the decline in the purity of the ancient church throughout the first four centuries, with a particularly precipitous decline in the age of Constantine, but with some pockets of pure faith remaining even in the fourth century and beyond. With a degree of caution almost always present, however, Wesley could point to models of corporate and individual life within these centuries as models to be emulated by the Christians of the eighteenth century; models which sometimes affirmed, but which more often challenged, inherited cultural patterns in Wesley's own age.

The Maturing of Wesley's Estimation of Christian Antiquity

In the 1770s, the Methodist movement again entered a new phase: the Methodists in England and America, despite Wesley's protestations to the contrary, were becoming very much *like* a church if they had not already become a *de facto* church. A significant indication of this new era for the Methodists is the Chapel on City Road in London, for which the cornerstone was laid in 1777. This chapel, unlike earlier Methodist "preaching houses," was designed for sacramental worship as well as preaching: behind its pulpit was an apse encircling an altar on which the eucharist was to be celebrated. On the occasion of his laying the cornerstone of this chapel, Wesley preached a sermon in which he professed his belief that the Methodist movement represented "the old religion, the religion of the Bible, the religion of the primitive church, [and] the religion of the Church of England."[119] In explaining Methodism's following "the primitive church," Wesley laid out his understanding of the ancient writers in whose works he saw the pure religion of Christian antiquity: Clement of Rome, Ignatius, and Polycarp in the second century; Tertullian, Origen (yes!), Clement of Alexandria, and Cyprian in the third century; Chrysostom, Basil, Ephraem Syrus, and "Macarius the Egyptian" in the fourth century.[120]

The issue of Methodism and its being a "church" was raised especially during and just after the American Revolution, when many Anglican clergy had left North America. When in 1784 John Wesley decided to ordain elders, consecrate (or "ordain," as he said in his diary) a "superintendent," and devise a Prayer Book for the American Methodists, he again turned to ancient Christian precedents. The American Methodists, he wrote in a letter to accompany Thomas Coke, "are now at full liberty simply to follow the Scriptures and the Primitive Church."[121] In justifying his consecration of Coke, Wesley

51

indicated that it was his reading of King's *Enquiry* (though, in fact, it may have been Stillingfleet's *Irenicum*) which had led him to the conclusion that elders have an inherent right to ordain. Coke and Francis Asbury themselves would point to the precedent of the ancient church of Alexandria, which elected its bishops from among the presbytery, in justification of their assuming episcopal offices.[122]

There is some evidence that as Wesley reached his maturer years he began to espouse a more realistic estimate of Christianity in its first centuries. His sermon on "The Mystery of Iniquity" (1783) has six paragraphs devoted to a description of the growth of corruption in the early centuries, focusing on the deterioration of the church in the age of Constantine, although the sermon allows that there were revivals of true religion in the early centuries.[123] Similarly, his sermon "Of Former Times" (1787) aimed at showing that "the former days" were not necessarily better than the present. In doing so, he again described the growth of corruptions in the early church, especially associated with the period of Constantine.[124]

Two years before his death, however, Wesley again called on an ancient Christian precedent in order to defend Methodist practice. His sermon on "Prophets and Priests" (or, "The Ministerial Office," 1789) argued in defence of the Methodist lay preachers that laypersons could hold a "prophetic," but not a "priestly," office. He called upon biblical evidence and evidence from the earliest Christian centuries to demonstrate the existence of a prophetic office which, he held, was different from the priestly office. Characteristically, he maintained that it was during the age of Constantine that the prophetic office ceased to be exercised in the church.[125] In Wesley's maturer years, then, he developed a somewhat more pessimistic (or realistic) view of the ancient church, coupled with a somewhat more optimistic view of historical progress. Nevertheless, the difference is in emphasis, since his principal conviction of the fall of the church in the age of Constantine remained firmly fixed, and he did not cease to look upon the early centuries as an exemplary period in the life of the Christian community.

Throughout John Wesley's career a concern with "Christian antiquity" in tension with the culture of Wesley's age developed: from his passionate concern in his Oxford and Georgia days for the reinstitution of ancient liturgical practices, to his concern during the revival for the renewal of ancient Christian morality and spirituality, through his later concerns for church structure and institutions patterned after those of the ancient church. In almost every case, however his vision of Christian antiquity may have changed, Wesley characteristically *utilized* his vision of Christian antiquity in what I have identified as a "programmatic" manner. The next two chapters will lay out this programmatic thrust in a more detailed and analytical fashion.

Chapter 4

"THE MANNERS OF THE ANCIENT CHRISTIANS": CHRISTIAN ANTIQUITY AS A VISION FOR INDIVIDUAL LIFE

The previous chapter has suggested that although Wesley's vision of Christian antiquity shifted throughout his career, his vision was consistently utilized in what we have called a "programmatic" configuration. This chapter will examine this claim in closer detail by focusing on the ways in which Wesley used Christian antiquity as a vision for individual life, with the next chapter focusing on Christian antiquity as a vision for the corporate life of the Christian community.[1]

Wesley believed that one of the foremost duties of the Christian community was to "describe" and "promise" an ideal of individual Christian life.[2] Consistent with this view of the church's task, Wesley set about describing and illustrating this ideal, and in this work his vision of ancient Christian life came to the fore. A large number of his sermons describe this vision for individual life, his letters clarify its meaning for various persons, and his *Journal* recounts cases of individuals who sought it. Wesley developed a specialized vocabulary for describing this ideal, the stages on one's way to it, and the problems one might face on the way to it: "Christian perfection," "entire sanctification," "assurance of pardon," "the wilderness state," "heaviness through manifold temptations," are among the terms of this vocabulary.[3]

Wesley stated explicitly his conviction that the lives of the saints throughout the church's history should provide patterns to be imitated by latter-day Christians. In 1771, he wrote to a member of one of the Methodist societies,

> Mr. Norris observes that no part of history is so profitable as that which relates to the great changes in states and kingdoms; and it is certain no part of Christian history is so profitable as that which re-

lates to great changes wrought in our souls: these, therefore, should be carefully noticed and treasured up for the encouragement of our brethren.[4]

The "Mr. Norris" referred to in this letter is John Norris of Bemerton, who transmitted to Wesley the Cambridge Platonists' concern with religious experience as a valid source of human knowledge. Wesley again indicated his concern for finding patterns for individual Christian life in Christian history when he criticized Mosheim's treatment of the "Internal State of the Church." He argued that this expression ought to refer not to rites and doctrines, but to the presence or absence of the Holy Spirit in "individual Christians, and the Christian Church in general," and in fact Wesley went so far as to doubt whether Mosheim was familiar with true, inward Christianity.[5] He faulted Mosheim's account of Christian history because it failed to recount the inward or spiritual depth of the lives of Christians.

Wesley received much of the material about Christian antiquity that he used as patterns for individual Christian life in works that other authors had prepared for this same purpose. His edition of Fleury's *Manners of the Ancient Christians* asserts in one place,

> After the apostles had received the Holy Ghost they were living images of Jesus Christ. And by them all the following servants of Christ were to form their hearts and lives.[6]

And again it states,

> It is among the first Christians, therefore, that we must look for a pattern of the most perfect life, and by consequence of the most happy, that can be upon earth.[7]

The use of Christian antiquity as a pattern for individual life asserted in these passages is consistent with Wesley's beliefs about the exceptional virtues of the early Christians, and continues a long tradition of Christian hagiography which had pointed to the saints of the church as illustrative of a Christian vision for individual life.

Like Fleury's book, Cave's *Primitive Christianity* was also designed by its author to offer the model of the ancient Christians' lives in place of the corrupt lives Cave perceived in his own society:

> I had not been long an Observer of the Manners of Men, but I found them generally so Debauched and Vitious, so Corrupt and Contrary to the Rules of this Holy Religion, that if a modest and honest Heathen was to estimate Christianity by the Lives of its Professors, he would certainly Proscribe it as the vilest Religion in the World.[8]

Cave began to inquire into the lives of the ancient Christians, he explained, and presented their model to his readers in *Primitive Christianity*.[9] Similarly, Horneck's "Letter to a Person of Quality, concerning the Heavenly Lives of the Primitive Christians," as its title suggests, amounts to an encomium upon the virtues of the ancient Christians, and urges its readers to imitate them.[10]

The most explicit assertion of Wesley's esteem for Christian antiquity as a vision of the individual Christian life, comes in one of his original works, the conclusion of his "Letter to Conyers Middleton." After admitting that the ancient Christians exhibited some weaknesses, Wesley wrote,

> And yet, I exceedingly reverence [the ancient Christians], as well as their writings, and esteem them very highly in love. I reverence them, because they were Christians, such Christians as are above described. And I reverence their writings, because they describe true, genuine Christianity, and direct us to the strongest evidence of the Christian doctrine. . . .
>
> I reverence these ancient Christians (with all their failings) the more, because I see so few Christians now; because I read so little in the writings of later times, and hear so little, of genuine Christianity; and because most of the modern Christians, (so called,) not content with being wholly ignorant of it, are deeply prejudiced against it, calling it enthusiasm, and I know not what.[11]

This passage merits quotation at length because it reveals at least part of the motivation behind Wesley's lengthy response to Conyers Middleton. Middleton's attack on the ancient Christians' claims to miraculous powers impugned the *character* of the ancient Christians. Wesley defended their character throughout his response to Middleton, and, in the conclusion quoted here, held them up as models to be emulated by eighteenth-century Christians.

Others of Wesley's works reveal less directly his general use of Christian antiquity as a pattern for individual Christian life. Wesley's "Character of a Methodist," inspired by Clement of Alexandria's description of the Christian ideal, carries the inscription "Not as though I had already attained,"[12] thus indicating that the treatise sets out more an ideal than an actual description of a Christian. Similarly, Wesley wrote in closing the preface to the work,

> And perhaps some of you who hate what I am called, may love what I am by the grace of God; or rather, what 'I follow after, if that I may apprehend that for which also I am apprehended of Christ Jesus.'[13]

Like the inscription, this passage suggests that Wesley used the material in "The Character of a Methodist," inspired as it was by an ancient portrayal of the Christian ideal, as presenting a vision for the lives of modern Christians.

Both in his original works, therefore, and in the works he edited, Wesley consistently and explicitly stated his intention to utilize the resources of antiquity as a vision after which modern Christians might model their lives. He also expressed this intention with respect to more specific aspects of the Christian life, namely, Christian religious experience, the order of the Christian life, and Christian virtue.

The Centrality of Religious Experience

John Wesley was part of a widely dispersed movement in Western European culture in the seventeenth and eighteenth centuries that stressed the centrality of personal religious experience. In this respect, it is critical to note in beginning an examination of his views of ancient Christianity as providing a vision of the individual Christian life that he consistently called upon Christian antiquity as a pattern for the sort of religious experience which he believed to be normative for individual Christian life. This was particularly critical in the light of the eighteenth-century British cultural millieu, which valued experiential (or, "experimental") epistemologies. Wesley held, in particular, that there is a general religious experience, a "spiritual sensation" (to use his terms) which persons are aware of in varying degrees. Wesley could term this sort of religious experience "faith," in a general sense (but not in the specific sense of "the proper Christian faith" of "justifying faith," from which he distinguished this more general sense of the term). His *Explanatory Notes upon the New Testament*, for example, defines "faith" in this general sense, following Hebrews 11:1,

> Now faith (supposing the Scripture to be of God) is *elenchos ton ou blepomenon*—the demonstrative evidence of things unseen, the supernatural evidence of things invisible, not perceivable by eyes of flesh, or by any of our natural senses or faculties. Faith is that divine evidence whereby the spiritual man discerneth God and the things of God. It is with regard to the spiritual world what sense is with regard to the natural. It is the spiritual sensation of every soul that is born of God.[14]

Elsewhere he maintained that this "spiritual sense" characterizes not only the regenerate, but, to some degree, every human. It might involve "conviction of sin" as well as "assurance of pardon" and the awareness of other spiritual states.[15] In his correspondence with "John Smith," he termed it "perceptible inspiration," and claimed that it was "the main doctrine of the Methodists."[16]

Given this general stress on the immediate experience of God, it is important to note that Wesley and at least one of his interlocutors recognized a conceptual distinction between inward, divine inspiration, and the power to perform externally attested, miraculous acts. "John Smith" wrote to Wesley:

> There are three ways in which the Holy Spirit may be said to bear witness: first, by external, miraculous, sensible attestations (as by an audible voice from heaven, by visible signs, wonders, etc.); or secondly by internal, plainly perceptible whispers ('Go not into Macedonia', 'Go with these men', 'Join thyself unto this Christ', etc.); or third [and] lastly, by his standing testimony in the Holy Scriptures.[17]

Although Wesley disagreed with "Smith" over the ages in which the first two forms of witness ceased, and wished to clarify the second form of witness, he accepted the conceptual distinctions laid down by "Smith."[18] His principal point of contention with "Smith" (and with Bishop Smalbroke in the *Farther Appeal*) was over the second form of witness, that is, internal, divine inspiration, whereas the principal point of contention with Middleton was over the first form of witness, that is, publicly attested divine acts.

Wesley's *Farther Appeal* attempts to prove that immediate, divine inspiration was considered by the early Christians among the "ordinary" operations of the Holy Spirit available to Christians of every generation. Wesley undertook this argument in response to Bishop Richard Smalbroke, a noted scholar of ancient Christianity who had attempted to prove that immediate divine inspiration was considered by Augustine, Jerome, Origen, and Chrysostom as belonging among the "extraordinary" gifts of the Holy Spirit reserved only for the apostolic age. Wesley responded to Smalbroke by producing *loci* from each of these four early Christian writers which illustrate their belief that the immediate divine inspiration (referred to by several scriptural passages) continued to be experienced by the Christians of their own ages.[19] Wesley cited, for example, a long passage from John Chrysostom asserting that the witness of the Spirit of which Paul speaks in Romans 8:15–16 was the common possession of Christians.[20] He conceded that some of the scriptural passages referring to divine inspiration were understood by ancient Christian writers as relating primarily to the apostolic age; but even in these cases, Wesley maintained, the writers held that in another sense the passages referred to their own age. His conclusion to this section of the *Farther Appeal* summarizes his views:

> Therefore, upon the whole, the sense of the primitive church, so far as it can be gathered from the authors above cited, is that 'although some of the Scriptures primarily refer to those extraordinary gifts of the Spirit which were given to the apostles and a few other persons in the apostolical age; yet they refer also, in a secondary sense, to those ordinary operations of the Holy Spirit which all the children of God do and will experience, even to the end of the world.'[21]

The *Farther Appeal* indicates that Wesley held Christians through the fifth century to have experienced such inspirations.

Wesley's specific understanding of this immediate divine inspiration becomes even clearer in his correspondence with "John Smith." "Smith's" question was whether the ordinary operations of the Holy Spirit were "perceptible" to Christians:

> The dispute [in the *Farther Appeal*] was about the ordinary and extraordinary operations of the Holy Ghost. But of the perceptibility of the ordinary operations, as directly felt to be worked by him, there is not one word said, neither there, nor that I know of in one place in the Bible.[22]

"Smith" actually conceded that "internal, plainly perceptible whispers," or "internal prophetic inspiration," remained through the fifth century, although he held that it was not experienced by Christians of the middle ages, such as Bernard of Clairvaux.[23] Wesley responded that Christians of all generations should expect the same divine inspiration known to the ancient Christians.[24] His conception of this divine inspiration is revealed in a passage where Wesley cited "Smith's" definition of it, and comment parenthetically thereon:

> '... by internal, plainly perceptible whispers' (I must add, not in words, at least not always, but by some kind of impressions equivalent thereto). . . .[25]

Wesley's comment in this instance suggests that he understood the divine inspiration of the ancient (and modern) Christians as being a form of knowledge gained by impressions upon some organ other than the bodily senses. This conforms to his conception of faith, in a general sense, as a form of spiritual perception.[26]

Wesley's interest in ancient Christian religious experience was motivated by Methodist claims to similar experiences. The Methodists' teaching of, and testimonies to, this sort of religious experience provoked considerable response from Anglican leaders. Wesley summarized their objections in introducing a section of his *Farther Appeal, Part I,*

> Accordingly, whenever we speak of the Spirit of God, of his operations in the souls of men, of his revealing unto us the things of God, or inspiring us with good desires or tempers, whenever we mention the feeling his mighty power working in us according to his good pleasure, the general answer we have to expect is: 'This is all rank enthusiasm. So it was with the apostles and first Christians. But only enthusiasts pretend to this now.'[27]

The issue of Christian religious experience was generally controverted in Wesley's age under the heading of "enthusiasm," and one of the central issues was whether perceptible (religious) experience was limited to "the apostles and first Christians," or available to persons of all time.

This was the issue between Wesley and Bishop Smalbroke. Wesley understood the controversy in the following terms:

> That I confound the extraordinary with the ordinary operations of the Spirit, and therefore am an enthusiast, is also strongly urged in a *Charge* delivered to his clergy and lately published by the Lord Bishop of Coventry and Lichfield.[28]

Smalbroke took immediate, divine inspiration to be among the "extraordinary" operations of the Holy Spirit reserved for the apostolic age. Wesley undertook to show, in response to Smalbroke, that Christian writers through the fifth century considered immediate inspiration to be commonly experienced by Christians.[29] In this manner, Wesley defended by appeal to ancient Christian precedents the view of religious experience that he and the Methodists advocated.

Similarly, it was the issue of "enthusiasm" that lay behind Wesley's polemical correspondence with "John Smith." The controversy took a differently nuanced form in this case, since "Smith's" question was whether the ordinary operations of the Holy Spirit were to be considered "perceptible," and since Smith conceded that Christians through the age of Constantine did indeed perceive the Spirit's operations. Nevertheless, "Smith" maintained that the operations of the Holy Spirit were no longer perceptible by Christians after the age of Chrysostom.[30] Wesley argued in reply that, if there is good reason to believe that internal, "prophetic assurance" continued in the days of Origen and Chrysostom, then there is good reason to believe that it continued in the days of Bernard, and that it continues in modern times.[31] Again, Wesley justified his view of religious experience by appeal to patristic precedent.

The controversy over "enthusiasm" continued, and Wesley continued to defend Methodist views by appeal to ancient Christian precedents. Bishop George Lavington's *Enthusiasm of Methodists and Papists Compar'd* (1749) attempted

> to draw a comparison between the wild and pernicious enthusiasms of some of the most eminent saints of the popish communion, and those of the Methodists in our own country.[32]

Wesley argued that the Bishop's censures upon the Methodists could be applied with equal force against the "enthusiasm" of the martyrs of the ancient church.[33]

Wesley's appeal to ancient Christian accounts of religious experience in order to demonstrate the validity of, and provide positive models for, modern religious experience was consistent throughout his career in the Evangelical Revival. It shows how he regarded the developing spiritual epistemologies of his age as a revival of the "vision" of the ancient Christians which contrasted with the conventional "dullness" or "darkness" of contemporary, nominal Christians. His struggles with "Smith," Smalbroke, and Lavington over the issue of "enthusiasm" show that this vision clearly contrasted with the vision of religious life that was being handed down by more conventional Anglican teachers.

A Vision of the Christian Life

Given this understanding of religious experience, Wesley was vitally concerned with the process by which persons come to Christian faith and live out that faith. He held up the ethos of ancient Christianity as a pattern for the order in which he believed the Christian life was normally structured. Although his opinions on particular moments in the Christian life changed with his own experience and reflection, his thought can be consistently understood in terms of an *ordo* or *via salutis*, a "way of salvation." For Wesley, the "way of salvation" reached from the first "stirrings of conscience," through the "relative change" described as justification, through the "real change" described as sanctification, to its goal, "entire sanctification" or "Christian perfection."[34] Wesley's deletion of material extraneous to the *via salutis* from the Macarian homilies indicates the importance with which he viewed (and used) the idea of the *via salutis*.[35] He found in ancient Christian writings, and in works describing the faith of the ancient Christians, patterns for some of the specific stages of the *via salutis*, although there are not specific references to Christian antiquity for all the stages which he conceived of the *via salutis* as involving.

The Human Condition. Of all the material Wesley did include on the *via salutis*, however, very little deals with the state of persons apart from the influence of divine grace. He included a passage from Cave describing the natural human soul as "Heaven-born" and yet "clogged and overborne with the earthly and sensual Propensions of the lower Appetites."[36] This inclusion is exceptional, however, given Wesley's general tendency to avoid passages enunciating obviously Hellenistic conceptions. Wesley omitted from his edition of Macarius several passages detailing the state of Adam before his transgression, the fallen condition of humankind, and the origin of infirmities and illness.[37] In these cases, however, it is not clear whether Wesley omitted these passages because he disagreed with them, or because he thought them trifling.

Divine Initiative and Human Response. The *Spiritual Homilies* attributed to Macarius of Egypt must have presented a challenge to Wesley. Although they state in some places that it is God's grace that enables the Christian to perform God's commandments, in other places they speak of human beings as having the ability of themselves to turn to God. Wesley generally included passages of the first sort in his own version of the *Spiritual Homilies*. An example would be his inclusion of a passage asserting that the Spirit indwelling the Christian performs the commandments of the Lord.[38] He consistently omitted passages of the second sort, such as a passage describing the human's guarding the soul, which results in the advent of divine grace, or a passage suggesting that humans ought to give themselves up to God in the hope that God would impart his grace to them. Wesley omitted no less than twenty-nine passages from the Macarian *Homilies* containing this sort of material,[39] and thus avoided giving the impression that Macarius believed in human initiative prior to, or apart from, divine grace. A similar pattern can be discerned in Wesley's editions of other works. For example, he omitted from I Clement a passage asserting that Christians are "justified by [their] Actions, not [their] Words."[40]

On the other hand, Wesley was convinced that early Christian writers insisted upon a free human response to God's grace. In his "Dialogue between a Predestinarian and his Friend," Wesley had the "Predestinarian" assert the authority of Augustine for the doctrine of predestination. The "Friend" (that is, Wesley) then replies:

> Augustine speaks sometimes for [the doctrine of predestination], sometimes against it. But all antiquity for the first four centuries is against you. . . .[41]

On another occasion, Wesley cited Augustine's expression, "He who created us without ourselves, will not save us without ourselves" against the doctrine of predestination.[42] The manner in which this statement is cast suggests that Wesley understood the issue between Augustine (or, Augustine some of the time) and "all antiquity for the first four centuries" to be that of the possibility of a free human response to divine grace, which he evidently held Augustine to deny insofar as Augustine taught predestination.[43]

Wesley's outlook on the issue of divine initiative and human response in salvation may be clarified somewhat by considering his estimate of two Christian heresies with which Augustine had dealt, namely, Manicheanism and Pelagianism. Wesley unambiguously rejected what he perceived as the determinism of the Manichean outlook. As early as 1729, in a letter to his father, Wesley referred to the "monstrous scheme" by which the Manicheans had attempted to explain the origin of evil, and regarded Augustine as having sufficiently refuted the Manichean outlook.[44] In his later "Thoughts on Necessity," Wesley held up Manicheanism as one of the earliest systems of determinism, and pointed to it as one of a number of contradictory accounts given by determinists of what the determining principle of the universe is.[45]

Wesley's attitude toward Pelagianism was considerably more ambiguous. He could recognize "Pelagianism" as being as dangerous an extreme as Calvinism,[46] but he was not sure that the historical Pelagius (so to speak) could be handily condemned as a heretic, if for no other reason than that none of Pelagius's own writings had survived. Moreover, Wesley argued, Augustine was angry at Pelagius, and for that reason Augustine's account of Pelagius could not be trusted. Wesley added the following note to Mosheim's conventional description of Pelagius:

> It is scarce possible at this distance of time to know, what Pelagius really held. All his writings are destroyed: and we have no account of them but from Augustin [sic], his furious, implacable enemy. I doubt whether he was any more an Heretic than Castellio, or Arminius.[47]

Elsewhere Wesley stated his guess that Pelagius was "both a wise and holy man,"[48] whereas of Augustine he wrote: "A wonderful saint! As full of pride, passion, bitterness, censoriousness, and as foul-mouthed to all that contradicted him, as George Fox himself."[49] Pelagius, Wesley wrote to John Fletcher, "very probably held no other heresy than you and I do now."[50] He therefore doubted, if I may put it in this manner, whether Pelagius himself would have subscribed to "Pelagianism," meaning by the latter the view foisted on Pelagius by Augustine and identified as "Pelagian" in the subsequent Christian tradition, according to which human beings have a natural ability to keep God's commandments. Wesley may have felt that Pelagius was a kindred spirit, accused (as Wesley was accused) of denying the priority of grace in his stress on the necessity of following God's law.[51]

Faith and Assurance. Wesley was convinced that the early Christians taught salvation by faith alone, but on at least two occasions he had to alter the texts of the Apostolic Fathers to ward off appearances to the contrary. He omitted from the Epistle of Polycarp an assertion "that by your good Works, . . . ye your selves may receive praise. . . ."[52] The second instance is rather bold: where Wake had rendered a passage from I Clement "By Hospitality and Godliness [*dia philoxenian kai eusebian*] was Lot saved out of Sodom," Wesley's version reads, "By faith was Lot saved out of Sodom."[53] These alterations do not have to be interpreted as meaning that Wesley thought that the Apostolic Fathers taught that human beings could achieve merit by good works; they indicate rather what he perceived as unfortunate expressions in their writings, which he felt obliged to amend.

Wesley also utilized the resources of the ancient church in his attempt to demonstrate that Christian faith (now using "faith" in a more restricted sense, where it is understood to have Christ as its object) is normally accompanied by an "assurance of pardon." Although Wesley's opinion varied as to whether this "assurance" was the necessary concomitant of Christian faith, he nevertheless maintained consistently that assurance was the usual concomitant of true Christian faith.[54] Readers of Wesley's edition of the Macarian *Homilies* would have found references to "the Full Assurance of Faith" and to the Christian's assurance of eternal life.[55] In two letters dating from the 1750s to Richard Tompson, Wesley asserted that Clement of Rome, Ignatius of Antioch, Polycarp, and Origen all taught the doctrine of the assurance of pardon, although he could not recall any who had dealt with the subject "professedly," nor did he feel that he had "leisure to wade through that sea" of ancient Christian literature in order to locate specific passages upholding the doctrine.[56]

Sin in, and Repentance of, Believers. The mature Wesley taught that sin remained in believers after regeneration, and that believers had therefore continually to repent of their sins. He vindicated this teaching by appeal to ancient Christian writings. The poem "On Clemens Alexandrinus's Description of a Perfect Christian" describes the struggle against sin in which the believer is engaged:

> Learn thou the whole of Mortal State
> In stillness to sustain:
> Nor sooth with false Delights of Earth
> Whom God has doom'd to Pain. . . .[57]

His edition of the Macarian *Homilies* in the first volume of *A Christian Library* presented to his readers the struggle between a Christian and indwelling sin.[58] This edition includes numerous passages affirming the Christian's battle with sin, and stating that the Christian can fall from grace and thus ought to "lament, and grieve, and mourn" over their sins.[59] In the early 1760s Wesley was forced by "a mistake which some were labouring to propagate,—that there is no sin in any that are justified,"[60] to defend his teachings "On Sin in Believers." In 1763 he composed a sermon by that title, the second paragraph of which asserts that "the whole body of ancient Christians, who have left us anything in writing, declare with one voice" their belief in sin remaining in believers.[61]

Holiness and Perfection. Wesley also appealed to the early Christians as teaching the necessity of holiness, and as holding up the goal of Christian perfection. His edition of I Clement has the expression "holiness of heart" (*hosiotes kardias*) that became part of Wesley's vocabulary for describing the goal of the believer's relationship to God.[62] Where Wake rendered a passage from Ignatius's Epistle to the Ephesians as "But all other things are the followers of Piety" (*ta de* *allapanta akolouthenta tes eusebias*), Wesley translated it, "All other things pertaining to perfect holiness follow."[63] Here, distinctively Wesleyan vocabulary for the higher Christian life is more or less written back into an ancient Christian text. His edition of the "Martyrdom of St. Ignatius" includes a sentence asserting that in his early life Ignatius knew "that he had not attain'd to the pitch of a perfect disciple."[64] The poem "On Clemens Alexandrinus's Description of a Perfect Christian" also holds up the goal of Christian perfection. It begins with the stanza:

> Here from afar the finish'd Height
> Of Holiness is seen:
> But O what heavy tracts of Toil,
> What Deserts lie between.[65]

Wesley's edition of Horneck's "Letter to a Person of Quality," moreover, states that the early Christians considered it the duty of their pastors to lead them to perfection.[66]

Wesley was aware of the Gnostics' teachings on perfection, and was sensitive to the accusation that his doctrine was like theirs. He tried to contrast their notions with his own in this manner:

> The doctrine of the Gnostics was not that a child of God does not commit sin, i.e., act the things forbidden in Scripture, but that they are not sin in him, that he is a child of God still; so they contended not for sinless but sinful perfection: just as different from what I contend for as heaven is from hell.[67]

It may be noted, however, that on other occasions Wesley himself disavowed the notion of "sinless perfection."[68] Wesley maintained that the earliest Christians strived for a perfection integrally related to the moral holiness they inculcated.

It is likely that the reason why Wesley was attracted to the *Spiritual Homilies* of Macarius was because of the stress that the Homilies laid on holiness and perfection. Indeed, these *Homilies*, as other Eastern Christian literature, regarded the goal of humankind as "deification" (*theiosis* or *apotheiosis*); but Wesley eliminated this controversial term from his edition of the *Homilies*.[69] The *Spiritual Homilies* assert that the Christian ought to do good "by violence" until he can do it freely; they also describe "Degrees of Perfection."[70] The *Homilies* speak of a "Sanctification of the Spirit" which can be termed "an Entire Redemption from Sin,"[71] or "the Baptism of Fire and of the Holy Ghost."[72] Similarly, those who attain to spiritual perfection are described as "baptized into the Holy Spirit."[73] The Christian's quest for holiness and perfection is a persistent theme in the Macarian *Homilies* which shines through Wesley's edition of them.[74] Wesley saw "Macarius," then, as a fourth-century advocate of the quest for holiness Wesley believed to have characterized the church as a whole in its purer ages.

Moreover, the particular English translation of the Macarian *Homilies* which Wesley used (*Primitive Morality*) understood the import of the work to be its contribution to Christian sanctification and "morality." The prefatory material which Wesley took over from *Primitive Morality* makes clear what Wesley and the translator of the work took to be its essential message,

> What [Macarius] continually labours to cultivate in himself and others is, The real life of God in the heart and soul, that kingdom of God, which consists in righteousness and peace, and joy in the Holy Ghost. He is ever quickening and stirring up his audience, endeavouring to kindle in them a sturdy zeal, an earnest desire, and inflam'd ambition, to recover that divine image we were made in; to be made conformable to Christ our head; to be daily sensible more and more of our living union with Him as such; and discovering it, as occasion requires, in all the genuine fruits of an holy life and conversation, in such a victorious faith as overcomes the world, and working by love, is ever fulfilling the whole law of God. He seems indeed never to be easy, but either in the height, or breadth, or length of divine love, or at least in the depths of humility.[75]

In the case of the Macarian *Homilies*, therefore, Wesley received an ancient Christian text already prepared to present the ideal of holiness to eighteenth-century English Christians.

A Vision of Christian Virtue

John Wesley believed that the Christians of the first two to four centuries lived exemplary, virtuous lives, even though later in his life he seems to have recognized that certain corruptions had been a part of the church's experience from its very earliest years. The sources that informed his understanding of the virtues of the early Christians include chapters from the *Stromateis* of Clement of Alexandria describing the "perfect Gnostic," which inspired Wesley's tract on the "Character of a Methodist." The works of Fleury, Cave and Horneck, which Wesley edited in the late 1740s and early 1750s, all extolled the virtuous lives of the ancient Christians. Mosheim's history, by contrast, presented a more cautious portrayal of the virtues of the early Christians, and it either influenced Wesley's conceptions, or at least confirmed a notable shift in Wesley's emphasis, when in the 1770s and 1780s Wesley began to realize more of the corruptions of early Christianity.

Virtues of the Ancient Christians

Wesley's writings and editions through the 1750s not only reflect the high estimate of the virtues of the ancient Christians that his sources gave, but even go beyond them in some respects. His editions of Cave, Fleury, and Horneck retain descriptions of early Christian virtues, but omit passages suggesting that some Christians had committed immoral acts. For instance, Wesley omitted passages from Cave's *Primitive Christianity* which detail charges of incest and adultery against certain ancient Christians, and which give the excuses made by some ancient Christians for wearing fine clothing. He even omitted passages from Cave describing the pagans' accusations against the early Christians.[76] In Wesley's account, then, the virtues of the early Christians were magnified even beyond their portrayal in the accounts of his sources.

"Heavenly" Virtues. In the first place among the virtues Wesley ascribed to the ancient Christians is their love for God and their unity within the church. The early Christians loved God and despised the things of this world. To use Cave's term, they were "heavenly-minded," and had a continual sense of the presence of God.[77] As a consequence, they were always ready to profess their faith in Christ, and exhibited exemplary patience in enduring the torments to which their persecutors put them. The martyrdoms of the early Christians vouched for the credibility of their message.[78] The early Christians found their true home, not in the world, but in the Christian community, where they lived in unity and regarded each other as equals.[79]

Personal Virtues. In the second place were those virtues that describe the way in which the early Christians conducted their personal affairs. Wesley believed that the early Christians were happy in spite of their poverty.[80] They were chaste in all their relations with others, were continent in marriage, and regarded second marriages as "little better than adultery."[81] He consistently omitted from his edition of the Macarian homilies the erotic imagery, especially the imagery of the lover and the beloved, that punctuates the work,[82] probably because of his desire to avoid characterizing the ancient Christians as overly concerned with sexual matters. The early Christians practiced temperance and abstinence (from meat and drink) in their regular meals and sobriety in their dress.[83] These virtues followed from their humility and meekness, a further instance of which was the "true primitive simplicity" of the language in which they expressed themselves.[84]

Social Virtues. Finally, there were those virtues grounded in the ancient Christians' relationships with the world outside of their own community. Wesley believed that the ancient Christians loved their neighbors, and that this love expressed itself in acts of charity: providing for the poor, visiting the sick, caring for those in captivity, looking after the welfare of children. The early Christians expressed this love to their fellow Christians and to non-Christians as well.[85] Wesley's edition of Cave stresses the early Christians' justice and honesty in their dealings with other persons. It claims, further, that the ancient Christians were subject and obedient to civil government, although Wesley consistently omitted the term "subjection" in his edition of Cave.[86]

Ancient Images of Virtue and the Methodist Movement

Despite his acknowledgment of corruptions in the ancient church, Wesley called upon Christian antiquity as a pattern for Christian virtue. This particular use of Christian antiquity is illustrated in two of Wesley's original works from the early 1740s. His 1742 tract on "The Character of a Methodist" depicts the ideal Christian by the dull but characteristically eighteenth-century practice of listing specific virtues, many of which are the same virtues listed by Clement of Alexandria in describing the Christian ideal: hope of immortality, constancy in prayer, love of neighbor, obedience to God's commandments, and freedom from worldly desires. Although Wesley's tract does not refer to some of the virtues stressed by Clement (passionlessness and contemplation of the divine, for example), Wesley acknowledged that a passage from Clement's *Stromateis* had inspired "The Character of a Methodist." Similarly, the poem entitled "Primitive Christianity" which concludes Wesley's *Earnest Appeal* (1743) holds up the model virtues of the ancient Christians, and describes in particular their simplicity, constancy in prayer, fellowship, unity, and love for each other.[87]

This use of Christian antiquity as a vision of Christian virtue may be seen even more clearly in works Wesley produced in 1749 and in the early 1750s. His "Letter to Conyers Middleton" (1749) concludes with a description of "a Christian indeed" as one who abases himself before God, depends on God, confides in God, loves God and neighbor, seeks after the truth, is free from pride, accepts censure, and is happy in God. Wesley asserted in this work that ancient Christian writers from the second through the fourth centuries displayed this ideal, and these virtues.[88] Similarly, his "Letter to a Roman Catholic," composed during a visit to Ireland in the summer of 1749, includes a description of the moral and spiritual virtues of the Christian believer. Following this description, Wesley wrote: "This, and this alone, is the old religion. This is true, primitive Christianity."[89] Similarly, his edition of Horneck's "Letter to a Person of Quality, concerning the Lives of the Primitive Christians" concludes with the following paragraph,

> I am persuaded that you have chosen the better Part, and as I do not question your Belief of these Passages, so that these Saints may be your Pattern, and their Actions the great Rule of your Life, and the Spirit of God your Guide in these Ways of Holiness, is the hearty Wish and Prayer of,
>
> Sir,
Your affectionate Friend
and Servant,
Anthony Horneck.[90]

This passage indicates the intent of the work as a whole, which, in this case, was to hold up "the Lives of the Primitive Christians" as models for the lives of virtue to which Wesley and Horneck (and Fronteau) believed their own contemporaries had been called.

Omissions from works Wesley edited also suggest his use of Christian antiquity as a vision of Christian virtue, especially where Wesley omitted passages that might lead readers to question the moral purity of the early Christians. He omitted, for example, Clement of Rome's suggestion that the spies of Israel lodged with "Rahab the Harlot" in Jericho, and also omitted a passage from the Ignatian epistles asserting that Christians should not heed those who teach the necessity of following the "Jewish Law."[91] Although the "Law" referred to in this case probably meant the ritual observances of Judaism, Wesley may have feared that readers would take the passage as indicating that Christians were not obliged to observe the moral commandments inculcated by scripture.[92] In a similar manner, he omitted erotic imagery from his edition of the *Spiritual Homilies*, and omitted numerous references to (and suggestions of) the misdeeds of the early Christians in Cave's *Primitive Christianity*.[93] These omissions have the effect of distorting the presentation of ancient Christianity that Wesley made to his readers, and indicate most clearly his concern that the readers should find in ancient Christianity models of moral purity.

Wesley's emphasis on the virtues of the early Christians appears to have changed sometime in the 1760s or 1770s. At least, in introducing his version of Mosheim's church history in 1781, Wesley warned his readers not to expect "an History of Saints, of men that walked worthy of their high calling" in Mosheim or any other church history, since "the mystery of iniquity" began to work in the church from quite an early age.[94] The third chapter has noted how some of Wesley's later sermons stressed the corruptions which entered the church in the early centuries and overwhelmed the church in the fourth century.

Nevertheless, Wesley had acknowledged the presence of some corruptions in the early church since at least the time of his "Letter to Conyers Middleton" (1749), and maintained that the presence of these corruptions did not detract from the general purity of the church in the pre-Constantinian period.

In the "way of salvation," Wesley and other Evangelical leaders had offered a kind of blueprint for life. A blueprint for life, however, is precisely what culture gives, in passing on from one generation to another patterns for belief and behavior, so that the Evangelicals' work in expounding the "way of salvation" was a clear attempt at the enterprise of culture change. The Evangelical pattern stressed religious experience as central to the religious life as a whole, developed a specific pattern of life focusing on repentance, faith, and holiness, and pointed to a specific set of virtues as characterizing the true Christian. This chapter has delineated something of Wesley's particular vision of this blueprint for life, and has found that at critical points his vision for Christian individual life was informed and inspired by his vision of the lives of the ancient Christians.

Chapter 5

"The Whole Church in the Purest Ages": Christian Antiquity as a Vision for Corporate Life

Eighteenth-century Evangelicals like Whitefield and Wesley offered not only a vision of the "way of salvation" as a blueprint for Christian life, but also a vision of Christian community that could serve as a blueprint for the religious groups that they had formed. At first, the Evangelical groups existed within the Church of England as religious "societies" or associations, but by the end of the century many had become independent churches. Their needs for institutional structures, then, developed as their various movements developed, but in each case they needed a commonly-held vision of Christian community.

In this process of developing the Methodist community, John Wesley utilized ancient Christian teachings, customs and institutions as a vision of corporate Christian life. His intention to use ancient Christian beliefs and practices as normative patterns for the corporate life of the Methodist movement appears in his "Plain Account of the People Called Methodists," although the wording of this statement is problematic:

> But I must premise, that as [the early Methodists] had not the least expectation, at first, of anything like what has since followed, so they had no previous design or plan at all; but everything arose just as the occasion offered. They saw or felt some impending or pressing evil, or some good end necessary to be pursued. And many times they fell unawares on the very thing which secured the good, or removed the evil. At other times, they consulted the most probable means, following only common sense and Scripture: Though they generally found, in looking back, something in Christian antiquity likewise, very nearly parallel thereto.[1]

This suggests that Wesley's conceptions of Christian antiquity only confirmed Methodist institutions that had already developed, but not that they provided explicit models for the *development* of those institutions. But considering the particular institutions to which Wesley refers here, one must doubt whether the statement is uniformly accurate. It is true that in some cases he may not have recognized the parallels between ancient and Methodist institutions until he looked back and reflected upon them. For instance, he may not have recognized the parallel he drew between the ancient catechumenate and the Methodist societies until after the societies were functioning.[2] But in other cases, he could scarcely have failed to recognize the parallels beforehand, and one suspects in these cases that his conceptions of Christian antiquity did indeed provide the patterns upon which the Methodist institutions were based. For example, he had known of ancient penitential practices and of the ancient order of deaconesses long before he segregated "penitent bands" from the rest of the Methodist societies or instituted the office of deaconess among the Methodists.[3]

In fact, one can demonstrate how, in numerous specific cases (including many in the "Plain Account of the People Called Methodists"), Wesley's conceptions of Christian antiquity served as normative patterns upon which Methodist teachings and practices were based. This chapter examines specific instances of this utilization of Christian antiquity as a vision for the corporate life of the Christian community.

A Vision of Pure Christian Teaching

The Apostolicity of Ancient Christian Teachings

John Wesley explicitly held up the writings of the ancient church as a pattern, subordinate only to scripture, for Christian teaching. "The esteeming the writings of the first three centuries, not equal with, but next to, the Scriptures," Wesley wrote to Middleton, "never carried any man yet into dangerous errors, nor probably ever will."[4] Similarly, he wrote to Joseph Benson, "I regard no authority but those of the Ante-Nicene Fathers; nor any of them in opposition to Scripture."[5] This use of the ante-Nicene writers as a subordinate pattern of Christian teaching was Wesley's consistent use after 1737, when he recognized his error in having regarded antiquity as a "coordinate" rule with scripture.[6]

The special regard Wesley had for the Apostolic Fathers as presenting normative patterns of Christian teaching can be seen in the prefatory materials which he gleaned from Wake and prefixed to his own version of the Apostolic Fathers in *A Christian Library*:

> The authors of the following collection, were contemporaries of the holy Apostles. . . . We cannot therefore doubt, but what they deliver to us is the pure Doctrine of the Gospel; what Christ and his Apostles taught, and what these holy men had themselves received from their own mouths.[7]

And again, he stated,

> . . . we cannot with any reason doubt of what they deliver to us as the gospel of Christ; but ought to receive it, tho' not with equal veneration, yet with only little less regard, than we do the sacred writings of those who were their masters and instructors.[8]

The latter passage places the Apostolic Fathers in a position of authority nearest to scripture, but also expresses Wesley's insistence on the subordination of Christian antiquity to scripture.

Wesley linked the ancient church's teachings with the teachings of Scripture, and with the use of reason as doctrinal authorities. "We prove the doctrines we preach," he wrote in the *Farther Appeal*, "by Scripture and reason; and, if need be, by antiquity."[9] Similarly, in introducing the 1771 edition of his *Works*, Wesley wrote,

> . . . in this edition I present to serious and candid men my last and maturest thoughts, agreeable, I hope, to Scripture, reason, and Christian antiquity.[10]

Wesley also used the term "authority" in reference to Christian antiquity in his *Farther Appeal*.[11] He thus regarded the writings of Christian antiquity as having authority for subsequent Christian teachings; not, indeed, the authority which he ascribed to scripture alone, but a "subordinate" authority which he found nonetheless helpful. It is critical to note that although his use of early Christian writings in this way *generally* corresponds to the uses of ancient texts by conservative Anglicans, he nevertheless stressed a different set of *particular* texts, giving preference to earlier texts (such as the Apostolic Fathers) over later texts (such as Augustine and the Councils) stressed by the Caroline theologians.

Given this approval of the authority of the ancient Christian writings, Wesley could find them particularly useful in the interpretation of the New Testament. He thought that most of the New Testament books were read from the second-century "as a divine rule of faith and manners."[12] He believed that the earliest Christian writers stood closest to the apostles, and were especially endowed with the Holy Spirit, so that they were "the most authentic commentators on Scripture."[13]

His edition of Fleury puts the case for the use of ancient Christian sources for interpretation in this manner:

> In the writings therefore of [the earliest disciples of the Apostles], not of modern reasoners and disputers, are we to search for that sense of scriptures hard to be understood, which they received from the apostles, and the apostles from Christ.[14]

Wesley did acknowledge that there were corruptions in second-century biblical manuscripts, and he held that Irenaeus had shown "weakness" in relying upon oral traditions, as opposed to the written scriptures. He maintained, moreover, that some later authors went to extremes in their allegorical expositions of scripture, but he held that they did this because they were "afraid of too literal a way of expounding the scriptures."[15] Wesley's "Address to the Clergy" recommends the study of the early Christian writers, whom Wesley called "the most authentic commentators on Scripture,"[16] and amongst whom he especially valued the second-century writers. He often validated his own interpretations of biblical passages by citing patristic interpretations of them.[17]

Heresy, Ancient and Methodist

As the leader of a controversial religious movement, Wesley frequently faced the charge that he was (or his followers were) teaching heretical doctrine. He responded by defending the Methodists against the charges, and by going on the offensive to identify heretical teachings among his opponents. Given his high approval of ancient Christian teachings, it was natural that he should turn to ancient Christian sources as a kind of arbiter for the accusations of heresy that flew in so many directions in his age.

Wesley believed that the ancient Christians, especially those of the first three centuries, faithfully followed the apostles' teachings, and strove to avoid heresy, which his edition of Horneck defines as "Doctrine . . . unknown to the Apostles."[18] He suspected that although heresies were more frequently mentioned in the earlier centuries than in later ages, nevertheless there may have been *more* heresies in later ages, against which the church did not protest as frequently as it had done against the earlier ones. He was aware of heretical literature in the early centuries, and maintained that, although some heretical books were forged in the name of apostles and other early Christians, others were "compiled by weak, well-meaning men, from what had been orally delivered down from the Apostles."[19]

John Wesley held up the teachings of the ancient Christians in his protests against the revivals of ancient heresies in his age. At least ten passages in Wesley's *Sermons, Journal,* letters, and doctrinal writings warn the Methodists against Arianism, which Wesley understood to be not only an ancient heresy, but also a modern one.[20] He once reflected upon Swedenborg's "Account of Heaven and Hell," and warned against its Sabellianism and Anthropomorphitism.[21] In his original works, he cited Augustine (*sic*!) and Chrysostom against predestinarianism, which he also regarded as a false teaching.[22]

Wesley's opponents accused the Methodists of reviving ancient heresies, and this put him on the defensive. He sometimes responded by clarifying and defending Methodist teachings, as in his treatise on Arminianism, in which he clearly distinguished Arminianism from Arianism,[23] but sometimes he merely pointed out the absurdity of his opponents' claims. Attempts to tag the Methodists with ancient heretical labels reached their pitch in John Downes's assertion that

> All ancient heresies have in a manner concentrated in the Methodists; particularly those of the Simonians, Gnostics, Antinomians, Valentinians, Donatists, and Montanists.[24]

Wesley responded,

> While your hand was in, you might as well have added Carpocratians, Eutychians, Nestorians, Sabellians. If you say, 'I never heard of them,' no matter for that; you may find them, as well as the rest, in Bishop Pearson's index.[25]

This was a way of saying that the heresies of which Downes had accused the Methodists were themselves so contradictory that Downes's arguments could not be seriously received.

Wesley's attitudes towards the ancient heresies provide an interesting test of his use of Christian antiquity in relation to his culture. Whereas he assented to the fourth-century condemnations of Arianism and Sabellianism, and could give scriptural and ancient Christian evidence against both, he was at least uncertain about the heresies of the fifth century (Pelagianism, Nestorianism, and Eutychianism, in particular). In at least three cases, moreover (Montanism, Donatism, and Novatianism), he saw the ancient "heresies" as representing "scriptural Christianity" in their ages.[26] In these instances, it is clear, he did not assent to the church's condemnations, and in fact he saw the so-called heretical groups as more faithfully representing the apostolic faith. This shows, above all, the seriousness with which his view of ancient authority had changed as indicated in his writings in 1737: no longer was the *consensus* of ancient teachings in itself a normative authority for Wesley, but instead, the ancient church's teachings held authority so far as they "well agreed with the practice and writings of the apostles" and thus reflected the purity of the New Testament church.[27] Thus, his uses of Christian antiquity in clarifying accusations of heresy conformed to the conservative Anglican patterns in some respects, but very clearly diverged in others.

Ancient Creeds and Councils

As the second chapter has shown, Wesley assumed from late 1737 a critical attitude toward ancient Christian councils themselves, asserting on one occasion that the determinations of the ancient councils were "generally trifling, sometimes false, and frequently unintelligible or self-contradictory."[28] It is more difficult to assess his estimate of the creeds and other statements produced by the ancient councils, since many of them were used by Anglicans, and Wesley affirmed at least some of them. The evidence for Wesley's views of ancient creeds and conciliar statements is relatively scant. His edition of Mosheim includes the assertion that the Apostle's Creed was not of apostolic origin, but developed in postapostolic times to banish heresies. He indicated elsewhere his general subscription to the Nicene Creed (including the *filioque* clause), the Chalcedonian doctrine of two natures in Christ, and the Trinitarian theology of the "Athanasian" Creed. One would expect this of an Anglican, whose eighth Article of Religion asserted that the Apostles', Nicene, and Athanasian Creeds "ought thoroughly to be received and believed; for they may be proved by most certain warrants of Holy Scripture."[29] Wesley's own version of the Anglican Articles included the first, second, and fourth articles, which reflect Nicene, Constantinopolitan, and Chalcedonian language; but the eighth Article, which explicitly affirmed the "Three Creeds," was one of the Articles omitted in his *Sunday Service of the Methodists in North America*.[30] One gains the impression that, although Wesley found the ancient creeds generally faithful to the apostolic teaching, he did not find their precise formulations particularly helpful.

Given this relatively ambivalent attitude toward the ancient councils, it is interesting to note that when defending the Methodists Wesley asserted that his followers did accept ancient, and even post-Nicene doctrinal formulations. "The fundamental doctrine of the people called Methodists," he wrote on two occasions to the editor of *Lloyd's Evening Post*, "is, Whosoever will be saved, before all things it is necessary that he hold the true [*sic*] faith."[31] Answering the charge that he had altered the text of the Athanasian Creed in this instance (from "catholic" to "true"), Wesley wrote, "Sir, shall I tell you a secret?—It was for the readers of your class that I changed the hard word Catholic into an easier."[32] His *Explanatory Notes on the New Testament* attempts to show that the Holy Spirit "proceeds from the Son, as well as the Father" on the basis of John 15:26, and thus indicates his subscription to the Western *filioque* clause of the Nicene Creed.[33]

Ancient Trinitarian Theology and Christology

Wesley regarded the ancient church's doctrine of the Trinity as consistent with the Apostolic faith, although he questioned later and more "philosophical" expressions of it. He accepted the authenticity of the "Johannine Comma" (I John 5:7; following Bengel) on the basis of the attestation of the verse in the first three centuries, in spite of what he believed were the Arians' attempts to expunge it. Beyond his general acceptance of the doctrine, however, he regarded all philosophical "explications" of the Trinity as failures. Even the teaching of the Athanasian Creed, which he held to be the "best" explication he had encountered, could not be insisted upon as necessary doctrine, as he explained in his sermon "On the Trinity":

> It was in an evil hour that these explainers began their fruitless work. I insist upon no explication at all; no, not even the best I ever saw; I mean, that which is given us in the creed commonly ascribed to Athanasius. I am far from saying, he who does not assent to this "shall without doubt perish everlastingly." For the sake of that and another clause, I, for some time, scrupled subscribing to that creed; till I considered, (1.) That these sentences only relate to *wilful*, not involuntary, unbelievers; to those who, having all the means of knowing the truth, nevertheless obstinately reject it: (2.) That they relate only to the substance of the doctrine there delivered; not the philosophical illustrations of it.[34]

In spite of the fact that he himself used a range of philosophical terms that had come into the Christian tradition from ancient, extra-biblical sources (terms such as "substance," "nature," and so forth), Wesley seems to have viewed the use of (Hellenistic) philosophical conceptions as a sign of the church's decline from its original simplicity. He carefully screened out references in the Macarian literature to obviously Platonic teachings (the ruling powers of the soul, the five senses of the soul, and so forth).[35] Such omissions reflect his resistance to unhelpful elaborations on the church's primitive, and simple, teachings.

As mentioned briefly above, Wesley knew Arianism not only as an ancient heresy, but also as a contemporary option in Christian thought, since William Whiston and others had attempted to revive Arian teachings. Wesley had studied the fourth-century controversies over Arianism, and realized that Arianism had prevailed so widely that *Athanasius contra mundum* ("Athanasius against the world") became a byword, and the fourth century was later styled the *saeculum arianum* ("Arian century" or "age").[36] He frequently condemned Arianism hand-in-hand with Socianism, but he did distinguish between the two: "For, whereas [Socinians] deny Christ to be any God at all, [Arians] do not, they only deny him to be the great God."[37] But, as Wesley saw it, the distinction was finally meaningless:

> An Arian is one who denies the Godhead of Christ; we scarce need say, the supreme, eternal Godhead; because there can be no God but the supreme, eternal God, unless we make two Gods, a great God, and a little one.[38]

Wesley condemned, in strong terms, contemporary attempts to reintroduce Arian teachings.[39] On the other hand, Wesley also condemned what he understood as Swedenborg's Sabellianism in even harsher terms, condemning it along with Arianism and Socinianism.[40] In this instance, Wesley's use of ancient Christian sources conforms to conservative Anglican uses, in which trinitarian orthodoxy was a principal concern.

Wesley knew of ancient Christological teachings also, but wrote on them on relatively few occasions. In commenting on a contemporary work entitled *The Glory of Christ as God-Man Unveiled*, Wesley wrote:

> I will not, dare not move those subtle, metaphysical controversies. Arianism is not in question; it is Eutychianism—or Nestorianism. But what are they? What neither I nor any one else understands. But they are what tore the Eastern and Western Churches asunder.[41]

The last sentence is genuinely puzzling: Wesley may have been thinking of the title of the Nestorian communion as "the Church of the East." If he was confused, he may have been thinking of the conflict between Constantinople and Alexandria in the fifth century (hardly East and West), or perhaps the medieval controversies over the *filioque* clause. The passage as a whole suggests that Wesley regarded later ancient developments in christology in much the same manner as he regarded the ancient church's elaboration of Trinitarian teaching, namely, as unhelpful additions of philosophical conceptions to the simply-expressed teachings of the apostolic, and the early post-apostolic, church. In these cases, Wesley may be seen as diverging somewhat from the more conservative Anglican patterns according to which subscription to ancient creeds and conciliar canons was stressed.

There is, moreover, one aspect of the earlier Christological tradition with which Wesley seems to have had some difficulty. He omitted, with remarkable consistency, passages from the Ignatian epistles which vividly assert Jesus' real humanity, especially passages stating that Jesus was born "of the Race of David according to the Flesh."[42]

There can be no question that Wesley accepted the authenticity of these passages. He must have feared that their inclusion would lead believers toward heterodox opinions—perhaps towards Arianism or Socinianism. The omission of these passages is consistent with a general pattern in Wesley's christology, according to which he emphasized the divine nature of Christ (although, of course, he did acknowledge Christ's human nature).[43]

In summary, then, Wesley held up the teachings of the ancient Christians, so far as they represented the purity of the apostolic faith, as standards to be affirmed and followed by the Methodists. The quotation from the edition of Fleury (above) indicates his belief that there was an oral tradition from the apostles maintained in the early church which gave its interpretations of scriptural teachings a special authority. This may be confirmed to some extent by the distinction between a public *kerygma* and secret *dogmata* drawn in Wesley's edition of Cave.[44] In this respect Wesley could maintain that the ancient church's teachings offered a significant complement to the authority of scriptural teachings. He reflected both the conservative Anglican tradition of using ancient writings in defence of the church's received doctrinal traditions, and some significant departures in that he was willing to see a few "heretical" groups (like the Montanists and Donatists) as representing the true faith.

A Vision of Christian Evangelization

The Gospel for Modern Pagans

Wesley's ministry of teaching was part of his more general ministry of evangelization, and in this too he turned to the patterns of ancient Christian communities as guidelines for the Methodist movement. In contrast to Anglican leaders who understood themselves as administering the Christian religion in an essentially Christian culture, Wesley understood himself as proclaiming the gospel to a largely pagan culture, as the ancient Christians had done. As he thought of the ancient Roman world in which Christianity arose as "the most enlightened that ever it was, as well as the most corrupted,"[45] so he thought of his own world as enlightened and corrupted. In the words of one modern interpreter, Wesley's was the age of "the rise of modern paganism,"[46] and Wesley was well aware of the new "pagan" or "heathen" environment in which the church's mission had to be carried on.

Wesley's *Earnest Appeal to Men of Reason and Religion*, for instance, asserts that, although many persons in England called themselves

81

Christians, they were in fact as pagan as the American natives whom Wesley had known in Georgia.[47] His treatise on "The Doctrine of Original Sin" considers modern heathenism, "Mahometanism," and Christianity, and concludes that modern Christians (so-called) are little better, if at all, than heathens or "Mahometans."[48] Similarly, his sermon on "The General Spread of the Gospel" concludes that modern Christians (again, so-called) are little better than Muslims and heathens, then describes the origin of Methodism as a means used by God for reforming the nominally Christian people of England.[49] Here the Methodists' conflict with contemporary culture becomes explicit.

Wesley thought of the early Christians as constantly engaged in the work of proclaiming the gospel in this pagan environment, and of drawing converts into their societies.[50] It is significant that although his 1736 manuscript translation of Fleury's *Moeurs des Chrétiens* represented the ancient Christians as refusing to speak of the gospel to any but the most attentive listeners, Wesley omitted these passages in his 1749 published edition of the work, after the evangelistic work of the Revival was underway.[51]

Extraordinary Ministry

Wesley distinguished between "ordinary" and "extraordinary" ministries in the ancient church (the distinct ministries of administering previously-established congregations and preaching the gospel in order to bring in new converts) and believed that the Methodists had an "extraordinary" ministry of proclaiming the gospel, in contrast to the "ordinary" ministry of the Anglican clergy. This peculiar calling, Wesley argued, justified the Methodists' itinerant preaching, and their utilization of lay preachers. He stressed that Methodist lay preachers did not claim the "ordinary" ministry of the administration of the sacraments.[52] Consistent with this defense of lay ministry, he omitted passages from Fleury representing the ancient Christians as refusing to speak of the gospel to any but the most attentive and least quarrelsome listeners, perhaps because he wanted to avoid giving the impression that the early Christians did not engage in the sort of widespread preaching that by 1749 had come to characterize the Methodist movement.[53] Fleury's vision of the ancient church is thus distorted or skewed in such a way that it bolsters Wesley's new evangelistic vision.

Persecution

Wesley liked to draw a parallel between the persecution that the ancient Christians faced in their evangelistic task, and the "persecution" of the Methodists. He suggested this in a letter to William Dodd when he wrote,

> What the Donatists were I do not know. But I suspect they were the real Christians of that age, and were therefore served by St. Augustine and his warm adherents as the Methodists are now by their zealous adversaries.[54]

His *Journal* abounds in stories of the persecution of the Methodists as they carried on their evangelistic task, and (as the previous chapter shows) Wesley's editions of the Apostolic Fathers, Cave, Fleury, Horneck, and Mosheim all depict the patience of the ancient Christians during the persecutions.[55] Where the parallels were not explicitly drawn (as they were in the letter to Dodd), readers were left to draw their own conclusions.

Attestation by Miraculous Signs

Wesley extended this parallelism by claiming for the Methodists the attestation by miraculous signs that had accompanied the ancient Christians' evangelization, according to many ancient writers. He believed that the ancient church had a "standing power" to perform miracles, which accompanied, and attested the truth of, their proclamation of the gospel. His long public letter to Conyers Middleton focuses on the persistence of the miraculous powers in the ancient church, and shows that his concern was also for their revival in the Methodist movement.[56]

Wesley knew of a number of specific miraculous "powers" claimed by the ancient Christians. Some idea of the variety of these miraculous gifts appears in the following passage, in which he listed the *charismata* of the apostolic age:

> Hence we may observe, that the chief *charismata, spiritual gifts,* conferred on the apostolical church, were 1. Casting out devils: 2. Speaking with new tongues: 3. Escaping dangers, in which otherwise they must have perished: 4. Healing the sick: 5. Prophecy, foretelling things to come: 6. Visions: 7. Divine dreams: And, 8. Discerning of Spirits.[57]

It may be noted that Wesley understood "Speaking with new tongues" to denote the miraculous gift of understanding human languages in order to assist in the propagation of the faith.[58] Wesley also included references to healings, revelations and prophecies in his edition of the Macarian *Homilies.*[59]

As noted above in the discussion of ancient heresies, Wesley came to have a high appreciation for Montanism. He regarded Montanism as a second-century resurgence of the miraculous powers described in the New Testament. Even in the "Letter to Conyers Middleton," where one might expect him to be more circumspect, he expressed his belief that the miraculous powers claimed by the Montanists (especially visions and prophecies) were none other than those claimed in the New Testament.[60] A very clear approval of Montanism came a year after the "Letter to Conyers Middleton," in 1750:

> By reflecting on an odd book which I had read in this journey, *The General Delusion of Christians with Regard to Prophecy*, I was convinced of what I had long suspected: (1) That the Montanists, in the second and third centuries, were real, scriptural Christians; and (2) That the grand reason why the miraculous gifts were so soon withdrawn, was not only that faith and holiness were wellnigh lost, but that dry, formal, orthodox men began even then to ridicule whatever gifts they had not themselves, and to decry them all as either madness or imposture.[61]

Except for a letter of 1761, which might be construed as meaning that Wesley placed some distance between himself and the practices of the Montanists, his comments on Montanism after 1750, including a note appended to his edition of Mosheim and a separate tract on "The Real Character of Montanus," regard the movement as a revival of the moral virtues and the miraculous gifts that characterized Christianity in the apostolic age.[62]

Despite his view of Montanism as an isolated resurgence of the miraculous powers, however, he believed that these powers subsisted in the church at large in the second and third centuries. Just as Christ "shewed that he came from God by his miracles," and as the miraculous gifts of the apostolic age were needed in order to convince the heathen of the truth of Christianity, so he believed that the miraculous powers continued to be used in the second and third centuries in the church's evangelistic task.[63] He suggested that, for all the saints who are known from the first three centuries, there were far more who remain unkown. These, Wesley speculated, may have held miraculous powers for which there is but little evidence in the writings which have come down to us from those centuries.[64] Wesley's edition of Mosheim is somewhat more guarded, but notes that the miraculous powers were known to have continued in the church at least in the second century.[65]

Wesley consistently associated the decline of the miraculous powers in the early church (as well as the decline of morals) with the age of

Constantine. The "Letter to Conyers Middleton" states frequently his belief that it was because of the waning of faith and morals among the ancient Christians that the miraculous powers declined:

> You will naturally ask, "Why do you stop there? What reason can you give for this? If you allow miracles before the empire became Christian, why not afterwards too?" I answer, Because "after the empire became Christian," (they are your words,) "a general corruption both of faith and morals infected the Christian Church; which, by that revolution, as St. Jerome says, 'lost as much of her virtue, as it had gained of wealth and power.'" (Page 123).[66]

Wesley argued throughout the "Letter to Conyer Middleton" that "the generality of the Protestant Doctors" held that the miraculous powers ceased with the age of Constantine, and defended this position.[67] Consistent with this conviction, he omitted from his edition of Cave an assertion that the miraculous powers continued "some considerable time after Constantine."[68] A 1787 sermon on "The More Excellent Way" reiterates his view that after Constantine had heaped riches upon the church, especially upon the clergy, the church became mostly heathen, and the miraculous powers all but ceased.[69]

Wesley made the parallels between the ancient and Methodist miracles quite explicit. His *Journal* is filled with reports of answers to prayer and "providences" such as the following,

> I met with a fresh proof that "whatsoever ye ask, believing, ye shall receive." A middle-aged woman desired me to return thanks for her to God, who, as many witnesses then present testified, was a day or two before really distracted, and as such tied down in her bed. But upon prayer made for her, she was instantly relieved and restored to a sound mind.[70]

Similarly, the *Journal* recounts miraculous conversions, healings, and deliverances from diabolical powers, which Wesley attributed to the interposition of God in the natural order.[71] He explained,

> I acknowledge that I have seen with my eyes, and heard with my ears, several things, which, to the best of my judgment, cannot be accounted for by the ordinary course of natural causes, and which, I therefore believe, ought to be "ascribed to the extraordinary interposition of God." If any man choose to style these miracles, I reclaim not.[72]

Such claims made by the Methodists were the reason why Wesley devoted so much energy to refuting Middleton's thesis that the miraculous powers were needed only in the apostolic age. Even though Wesley acknowledged that the miraculous powers had waned in the fourth century, he could write: "Sir, we do not pretend the revival of [the miraculous powers], seeing we shall believe they never were intermitted, till you can prove the contrary."[73]

In spite of his frequent references to miraculous events, however, he tempered his appeals to them in two respects. First, in response to the demands of "John Smith" and others that he should produce publicly witnessed miracles in order to substantiate his claims to inward, divine inspiration, Wesley responded that the Methodists did not need miracles as "proofs," since they proved their claims by Scripture, reason, and Christian antiquity.[74] Second, he denied that he himself had any miraculous power, but claimed only to have witnessed miraculous events that he believed had occurred as answers to prayers.[75]

A Vision of Christian Fellowship

Christian Societies

The Methodists' work of evangelization led to the incorporation of women and men into distinctively Methodist structures for Christian fellowship. Here again, in almost every case, Wesley called on ancient Christianity for precedents or confirmations for Methodist institutions. He conceived of the early Christian communities as "societies," sharing at least some of their possessions in common, and committed to the common task of evangelization. He understood the term "societies" (or "conventicles") as rendering the Greek term *hetairiai*, which appears transliterated as *hetaeriae* in Pliny's letter to Trajan concerning the punishment of Christians. This letter represents the *hetaeriae*, which could denote a variety of "trade guilds and social or political clubs," as forbidden by decree of Trajan.[76] The term would have presented, to Wesley's age, a much more intense image of Christian fellowship than the term "churches," which might have suggested parishes whose memberships were determined more by ancestral association than by voluntary commitment. Indeed, the Methodist societies did not require a profession of Christian faith for membership, but only "a desire 'to flee from the wrath to come, and be saved from their sins.'"[77] Since the Methodist societies were organized for persons seeking Christian faith, Wesley could see a parallel between them and the catechetical institutions of the ancient church, a parallel which would not have been as apparent in the Anglican (and more broadly Western Christian) practice of catechizing children at the point of confirmation.

John Wesley believed that the Methodists' use of class tickets to identify members of the societies paralleled the ancient church's use of commendatory letters. The "Plain Account of the People Called Methodists" states,

Those who bore these tickets (these *symbola* or *tesserae*, as the ancients termed them, being of just the same force with the *epistolai systatikai*, commendatory letters, mentioned by the Apostle,) wherever they came, were acknowledged by their brethren, and received with all cheerfulness.[78]

Wesley had been familiar with the ancient commendatory epistles since his Oxford reading in Cave's *Primitive Christianity*, and he would have encountered references to this institution in his Georgia reading in Fleury's *Moeurs des Chrétiens*. It is possible, then, that Wesley's knowledge of the ancient custom, as well as the practical needs of the Methodist societies, led him to develop the practice of issuing class tickets.

Segregation of Penitents

Wesley held that the Methodists' segregation of penitents from other persons in the societies paralleled the penitential discipline of the ancient church. His edition of Cave's *Primitive Christianity* closes with a quotation from the Prayer Book commination which noted the ancient penitential discipline, and urged that this discipline "might be restored again."[79] Similarly, Nathaniel Marshall's *Penitential Discipline of the Primitive Church*, with which he had been familiar since his Georgia days, suggested a program for restoring the ancient discipline in the Church of England.[80] Wesley understood the Methodist "penitent bands" as a restoration of the ancient discipline:

In prescribing hair-shirts and bodily austerities, we durst not follow even the ancient church; although we had unawares, both in dividing *hoi pistoi*, the believers, from the rest of the society, and in separating the penitents from them, and appointing a peculiar service for them.[81]

Given Wesley's familiarity with Cave, Marshall, and other writers who had described the ancient discipline (and given the fact that he used the term "penitents") it is difficult to believe that he was wholly unaware of the ancient pattern when he established the Methodist penitent bands (as the introduction to the "Plain Account of the People Called Methodists" had suggested).

Community of Possessions

Wesley's edition of Fleury represents Christ and the Apostles as living "in common, as one family."[82] Whether he thought the idea originated with Christ, or with the Jerusalem church (Acts 2:44–45), Wesley believed that a community of possessions characterized the

87

Christian societies in their earliest centuries. His edition of Cave states that Constantine returned the possessions of the churches because he recognized that the Christians were

> known to have had other Possessions [besides their church buildings] which were not the Propriety of any single Person, but belong to the whole Body and Community.[83]

His edition of Horneck represents the earliest Christians as sharing their possessions with each other, and depicts later Christians as giving at least the first fruits of their lands for the church's ministries to the sick, the poor, captives, and others in need. Similarly, Wesley thought of ancient "ecclesiastical revenues," even in later centuries, as "sacred to God and to the poor."[84] He thus imagined the possessions held in common by the ancient Christians as declining through the early centuries.

John Wesley held up this distinctive ancient precedent as a pattern for the Methodists' common ownership of property. His intentions are revealed in a passage from John Bennett's copy of the Minutes of the Annual Conference of 1744. The question was posed, "What are the Rules of the Select Societies?" Wesley responded, according to Bennett's notes, that they are the same as the rules for the bands, with the addition of three rules, the third of which was, "Every member, till we can have all things common, will bring once a week, *bona fide*, all he can spare towards a common stock."[85] Just as Wesley conceived of the possessions held in common by the ancient Christians as dwindling through the years, so, this passage suggests, Wesley intended to build a "common stock" until at least the members of the select societies could "have all things common."

Common Works of Charity

Wesley believed that the corporate charitable enterprises sponsored by the Methodists paralleled the charitable enterprises of the ancient Christian church. In particular, he saw the Methodist "Visitors of the Sick" as corresponding to the ancient deacons and deaconesses, and the "widows" who administered the Methodist Poor House as corresponding to the "widows" of the ancient church.[86]

The institutions of the Methodist fellowship described here represent the most distinctive formal structures of the movement in its earliest decades. Considered innovative and threatening by many of his peers, the evangelist labored to justify their development. In doing so he linked them to the structures of the ancient church and in this way they were understood as embodying the religious ideal or vision of

Christian community which he believed to have been realized in the earliest centuries.

A Vision of Christian Polity

So long as the Methodists remained within the Anglican communion, Wesley did not have to deal directly with questions of church polity. He believed, evidently to the end of his life, that the Church of England was "the best constituted National Church in the world," and he forbade his followers in England from separating from the Established Church.[87] When in 1784, however, he felt it necessary to constitute the American Methodists as a church distinct from the Anglican communion, he had to deal directly with the question of church polity. The crucial issue that faced him was the issue that had faced the framers and defenders of Anglican polity from the time of the Reformation, through the age of Richard Hooker, up until Wesley's own day. The issue was that of episcopacy. And just as Anglicans such as Hooker and Ussher had scoured the resources of Christian antiquity in their attempts to define an episcopal polity, so Wesley turned to Christian antiquity to find a pattern for his own church polity.

Orders of Ministry

In the first place, Wesley was aware of a variety of ministerial and religious orders in the ancient church. He distinguished the "extraordinary" ministry of those who preached and propagated the faith from the "ordinary" ministry of those who maintained the church's order and doctrine, and who administered the sacraments. His edition of Mosheim includes a passage distinguishing the "Extraordinary Teachers" who were needed to establish the church, and whom Mosheim identified with the twelve apostles and the seventy disciples, from "ordinary ministers" who enforced and maintained the doctrine taught by the former.[88] Wesley's sermon on "Prophets and Priests" (or "The Ministerial Office") suggests a similar distinction, although it does not limit the "extraordinary" ministers to the apostolic age, as Mosheim had done. In fact, "Prophets and Priests" makes a distinction between "extraordinary" and "ordinary" prophets in the Old Testament, then suggests that the early church reflected a similar distinction between the office of apostles and "evangelists," those authorized "to proclaim glad tidings to all the world," and the office of "Pastor or Bishop," consisting of those authorized "to build up in the faith the congregations that should be founded."[89] He reckoned that the extraordinary ministry of "evangelists" continued in the church until the age of Constantine, when ministerial functions were consolidated in the office of bishop, "in order to engross the whole pay."[90] Because he elsewhere included presbyters and deacons in the same general category with bishops, one must presume that he also thought of presbyters, deacons, and other subordinate clergy as falling under the "ordinary" ministry.[91]

Episcopacy and the Power of Ordination

Anglican studies of the ancient church had focused on the episcopacy, since Anglicans had to defend their own form of church polity against both Puritans and Roman Catholics. John Wesley reflected a similar, conservative attitude toward the ancient episcopate for many years. As late as 27 December 1745 he wrote to his brother-in-law Westley Hall these words:

> We believe it would not be right for us to administer either Baptism or the Lord's Supper unless we had a commission so to do from those bishops whom we apprehend to be in a succession from the apostles. And yet we allow these bishops are the successors of those who were dependent on the Bishop of Rome.[92]

Here Wesley affirmed his belief in the apostolic succession of bishops in such a manner as to question the validity of sacraments administered by clergy not ordained by bishops in that succession. He had expressed the same view in conversations with Spangenberg in Georgia.[93] Up until this point, then, his view of episcopacy (and of the power of ordination) coincided with that of the conservative "Caroline" theologians of the seventeenth century.

Soon after his letter to Westley Hall, however, Wesley's conceptions of the ancient episcopate began to change. His *Journal* for 20 January 1746 records the following:

> I set out for Bristol. On the road I read over Lord King's *Account of the Primitive Church*. In spite of the vehement prejudice of my education, I was ready to believe that this was a fair and impartial draught; but, if so, it would follow that bishops and presbyters are (essentially) of one order, and that originally every Christian congregation was a church independent on all others.[94]

Lord Chancellor Peter King's *Enquiry into the Constitution, Discipline, Unity, and Worship of the Primitive Church* (1712) aimed at a church polity that would comprehend Dissenters as well as Anglicans. As Wesley's *Journal* states, King's work asserted that in the ancient church bishops and presbyters were of the same order (*ordo*), although bishops were a higher "degree" (*gradus*) of presbyters. King's treatise suggested that presbyters had the same inherent right to ordain as bishops did, although it maintained that the ancient presbyters did not exercise this right because of their subordination to the episcopacy.[95] Sometime within the decade following his reading of King (that is, sometime before 1756), Wesley read Edward Stillingfleet's *Irenicum*. Stillingfleet also argued that presbyters had an inherent right to ordain, and went further than King in asserting that ancient presbyters did in fact exercise this right in cases of necessity. Stillingfleet cited the precedent of the ancient church of Alexandria, where (according to Jerome) bishops were elected and ordained by the presbyters, without the assistance of other bishops.[96]

Wesley came to hold opinions on the ancient episcopate similar to the opinions of the Latitudinarians King and Stillingfleet. He continued to believe in a succession of Christian ministers from the apostles through the bishops of the church, but he denied that this was an "uninterrupted" succession. The apostles had chosen bishops to succeed them in various sees, including the see of Rome; but the Roman succession was interrupted at various points.[97] He came to regard bishops and presbyters as being of the same order, as King and Stillingfleet argued they had been in antiquity. His edition of Mosheim includes a passage suggesting that "bishop" came to be used in the first century as a term to denote the presbyter chosen to lead the congregation.[98] Wesley continued to affirm the propriety of episcopal church polity, but not as a fundamental or necessary point of church order:

> As to my own judgment, I still believe "the Episcopal form of church government to be scriptural and apostolical." I mean, well agreeing with the practice and the writings of the apostles. But that it is prescribed in Scripture, I do not believe. This opinion, which I once zealously espoused, I have been heartily ashamed of since I read Bishop Stillingfleet's 'Irenicon.' I think he has unanswerably proved, that 'neither Christ nor his Apostles prescribed any particular form of church government'; and that the plea of divine right for diocesan Episcopacy was never heard of in the primitive church.[99]

As this and others of his writings show, Wesley's conceptions of the office of bishop in the ancient church had changed markedly in the 1740s and 1750s.

This change in Wesley's views of the early Christian episcopate led to a corresponding change in his conception of early Christian ordination. Whereas he had previously believed that only episcopal ordinations were valid, he came to believe that presbyters had the same right as bishops to ordain. He continued to believe that bishops usually performed ordinations in the ancient church, but he held that presbyters could ordain in cases of necessity. Correspondingly, he came to recognize the ministerial orders of non-episcopal churches.[100]

An implication of his new outlook was that Wesley himself had the right or power, as a presbyter, to ordain. Wesley wrote to his brother Charles in 1780,

> Read Bishop Stillingfleet's *Irenicon* or any impartial history of the ancient church, and I believe you will think as I do. I verily believe I have as good a right to ordain, as to administer the Lord's supper. But I see abundance of reasons why I should not use that right, unless I was turned out of the Church. At present, we are just in our place.[101]

But four years later, Wesley's hesitation was at an end. He justified his actions in ordaining Richard Whatcoat and Thomas Vasey as elders, and in consecrating Thomas Coke as "general superintendent," in the following paragraphs from his letter "to Our Brethren in America":

> 2. Lord King's *Account of the Primitive Church* convinced me many years ago that bishops and presbyters are the same order, and consequently have the same right to ordain. For many years I have been importuned from time to time to exercise this right by ordaining part of our traveling preachers. But I have still refused, not only for peace' sake, but because I was determined as little as possible to violate the established order of the National Church to which I belonged.

> 3. But the cause is widely different between England and North America. Here there are bishops who have a legal jurisdiction: in America there are none, neither any parish ministers. So that for some hundred miles together there is none either to baptize or to administer the Lord's supper. Here, therefore, my scruples are at an end; and I conceive myself at full liberty, as I violate no order and invade no man's right by appointing and sending labourers into the harvest.[102]

Wesley found himself in an extraordinary position, an extraordinary position he believed to be like those positions in which the ancient presbyters would have exercised their right to ordain; and so Wesley ordained. The Methodists became committed thereby to their own form of "ordinary" ministry in addition to the "extraordinary" ministry which was their most distinctive note.

Wesley must have discussed with Thomas Coke his reasons for his decision to ordain. Coke and Francis Asbury published a version of the *Doctrines and Discipline of the Methodist Episcopal Church*, with notes defending Methodist beliefs and practices. In their defence of episcopal polity, they wrote:

> St. Jerome, who was as strong an advocate for episcopacy as perhaps any in the primitive church, informs us, that in the church of Alexandria (which was, in ancient times, one of the most respectable of the churches) the college of presbyters not only elected a bishop, on the

decease of the former, but consecrated him by the imposition of their own hands solely, from the time of St. Mark, their first bishop, to the time of Dionysius, which was a space of about two hundred years: and the College of presbyters in ancient times answered to our general conference.[103]

The understanding of episcopacy given here (and the reverence to the Alexandrian precedent) corresponds to Wesley's understanding of the episcopate, especially to that understanding of the episcopate given by Stillingfleet, who also appealed to the Alexandrian precedent. Thus, shocking as Wesley's ordinations were to Anglicans (including his brother Charles), they were consistent with the vision of ancient Christianity that he had come to hold.

Presbyters

Wesley recognized the ancient office of presbyter or elder. He knew that the term "priest" could be used for this office, and did use it in his 1736 manuscript edition of Fleury, but his printed edition of the work omits the term or substitutes "minister" for it.[104] His edition of Cave describes the ancient presbyters as having the right to preach, to consecrate the eucharist, to baptize, and to assist the bishop, although it notes that presbyters did not usually administer the sacraments or preach without the authority of the bishop of the diocese.[105] As the preceding account has shown, he came to believe that the ancient presbyters were regarded as having an inherent power to ordain, even though they only performed ordinations in cases of necessity. His edition of Horneck's "Letter to a Person of Quality" states that the early Christians regarded their ministers as their spiritual parents, expected their ministers to admonish and punish them, and had complete confidence in their ministers' use of the church's treasury in supporting the poor.[106]

One may distinguish some peculiarities in Wesley's treatment of various accounts describing the degree of respect and obedience paid to the clergy of the ancient church. He omitted, for example, passages from Cave elaborating upon the high honor in which bishops in particular and clergy in general were held in the ancient church.[107] Even more notable is the consistent manner in which Wesley omitted passages from the Ignatian epistles which enjoin subjection to the presbyters or the bishops. Wesley omitted passages, for example, asserting that the faithful Christian "is subject unto his bishop as to the Grace of God, and to the Presbytery as to the Law of Jesus Christ" or asserting that to disobey the bishop means to disobey God. There are at least nineteen omissions of this kind of material in his edition of the Ignatian correspondence.[108] Because these passages appear so consistently in the ancient literature, Wesley can hardly have thought of them as incorrectly representing early Christian attitudes towards the clergy. It is more likely, then, that he feared that these passages might be misunderstood by his followers, or used to his disadvantage by his opponents (for example, by insisting that Wesley himself should be obedient to the bishops of his own age). In this case, as in others, Wesley's distortion (by omission) of the ancient text reflects the conditions of conflict between the Methodists and conservative Anglican culture.

Subordinate Ministerial Offices

John Wesley was aware of a number of subordinate offices in the ancient church, among which were deacons, "widows" and deaconesses, and such auxiliary offices as door-keepers, acolytes, and subdeacons. He especially associated deacons with the duties of ministry to the poor and the sick, and distributing the eucharistic elements to them. The edition of Cave asserts that deacons were authorized to preach and to baptize under certain circumstances.[109] He regarded the deaconesses or "widows" of the ancient church as having similar functions, that is, to carry out the church's ministries to the sick and needy, and held up their model as a precedent for the Methodists' "widows" who worked with the poor. He also believed that the ancient deaconesses were required to assist in the baptism of women.[110] Wesley's editions of Mosheim and Cave agree in depicting the early Christian communities as employing the faithful in such roles as doorkeepers (ostiarii), subdeacons, acolytes, readers, and exorcists, from at least the third century.[111]

A Vision of Christian Worship

Both as a religious society within the Church of England and as an independent church, the Methodist discipline focused at many points on worship in the Christian community. Wesley insisted that the Methodists followed ancient Christian worship practices, and believed that they had been called to restore or revive some ancient practices, such as the love-feast and vigils.

Baptism

Wesley's editions of works concerning ancient Christianity tell more about ancient baptismal practices than about ancient beliefs concerning the nature or efficacy of the sacrament. His editions note that sprinkling might have been allowed in the early church, but uniformly represent trine immersion as the normative, ancient mode of baptism for adults and infants alike. These editions mention the use of deaconesses to assist in the baptism of women.[112] Likewise, they represent infant baptism as having been the custom of the early church. Wesley regarded adult baptism as the sign of admission into the number of the faithful and the culmination of the catechetical process for adult believers. He believed that the ancient Christians appointed sponsors for infants who were to be baptized, and that the responsibilities of these sponsors were ". . . to watch over those souls in a peculiar manner, to instruct, admonish, exhort, and build them up in the faith once delivered to the saints."[113]

His version of Cave's and Mosheim's works on early Christianity suggest some further details that he may have associated with baptism in the ancient church. They note that baptisms were usually performed at Easter and Pentecost, and involved the use of the sign of the cross, anointing, and the imposition of the hands of the bishop and the presbytery. Cave elaborated on the white garments given to newly baptized persons as a sign of their new purity in Christ.[114] Wesley included a passage from Cave noting the persistence of the "Novatianist Principle" of postponing baptism until the article of death, but also noted that early Christian writers did not approve of this practice. He omitted from Cave a passage asserting that some (heretical) early Christian groups performed vicarious baptisms on the behalf of the dead.[115]

John Wesley's views of Christian antiquity appear to have influenced his own use of two practices associated with the rite of baptism: the use of baptismal sponsors, and the use of the sign of the cross in baptism. In his "Serious Thoughts concerning Godfathers and Godmothers," Wesley approved of the use of baptismal sponsors, citing his belief noted above that as the ancient baptismal sponsors were committed to the spiritual oversight of minors whom they sponsored, so godfathers and godmothers should concern themselves with the spiritual well-being of their godchildren.[116] As to the other practice, it is interesting to note that Wesley consistently omitted references to the sign of the cross (in his works after 1737), except in the case of baptism. Some copies of the first edition of Wesley's *Sunday Service of the Methodists in North America* (1784) have a rubric instructing the elder to make the sign of the cross on the forehead of persons immediately after their baptism, and gives a prayer to accompany the signing. The second edition of the work (1786), however, omits this rubric and the prayer accompanying it,[117] but it is unclear whether Wesley himself or another early Methodist had come to question the practice.

The Eucharist

Although Wesley, and the works he edited, give numerous details of ancient eucharistic practice, they indicate little of the ancient Christians' understandings of the significance of the eucharist.[118] Although his edition of Mosheim notes that there was considerable variety in the rituals of the early church, this and other works which Wesley edited describe a general pattern for the ancient eucharistic observation, based upon the description given in Justin Martyr's *Apology* and amplified from other sources. These depict the service as having two parts: a preliminary service of prayer, singing, and other acts of worship, which ended with the dismissal of the catechumens (hence this part of the service is referred to as the *missa catechumenorum*), and the eucharistic service proper, including exposition of the Old and New Testament scriptures, episcopal consecration of the eucharistic elements, the distribution of the elements by the deacons, and the blessing or dismissal of the faithful (thus, this second part of the service is referred to as the *missa fidelium*).[119] Wesley acknowledged that water was mixed with wine in the ancient eucharistic observance, and that the consecrated elements were reserved so that they could be carried to the sick by the deacons.[120]

The works Wesley edited, especially that of Cave, suggest more detailed nuances of his conceptions of ancient eucharistic practice. The edition of Cave asserts that in the earliest times the Christians received the sacrament daily, and in later times received it every Sunday.[121] This can be seen as enforcing the Methodist discipline, since according to the "General Rules" attendance at the eucharist was expected of all members of the societies.[122] Although he included Cave's assertion that at first all Christians (including penitents and energumens) partook of the eucharist, he omitted Cave's statement that later only the faithful were admitted. His editions of both Cave and Mosheim represent the sacrament as having been administered to baptized infants.[123] Reflecting a fear of Catholic traditions, he omitted from Cave passages relating how the early Christians would carry about the eucharistic elements, or reserve consecrated elements in their homes, and Wesley omitted Cave's use of the expression "Sacrament of the Altar."[124]

The Lord's Day and the Sabbath

Wesley believed that the early Christians observed the first day of every week in honor of the resurrection as "the Lord's Day," the appointed day when the Christians gathered for prayer and worship.[125] He omitted from Cave a reference to the early Christians' practice of praying standing on the Lord's Day; a practice which he had accepted while under the influence of the Separatist Non-Jurors.[126] He included from Mosheim, but omitted from Cave, passages asserting that the early Christians in some localities continued to observe the Sabbath as well as the Lord's Day.[127] Again, observance of the Lord's day was required by the "General Rules," so that the vision of the ancient observance enforced the Methodist discipline at this point.[128]

In the case of these observances—the Lord's Day, frequent communion, and the use of baptismal sponsors—Wesley may be seen as conforming to the more conventional Anglican culture of his day, however unusual frequent communion may have been (it had been stressed by the Caroline divines). The Anglican liturgy was in fact one of the points at which Wesley held his church to be most in harmony with the apostolic and primitive church. Thus his complex vision of ancient Christianity included certain points that would uphold elements of his own culture. In other points, Wesley's vision offered new and more challenging patterns.

Love Feasts

John Wesley believed that the ancient Christians regularly held a communal meal either before or after the eucharist. At this common meal, termed the *agape* or "love-feast," rich and poor sat down at table together.[129] His edition of Mosheim takes this as a special sign of the equality with which the early Christians regarded each other, and maintains that the love-feasts were suspended in the fifth century, "amidst the decline of that piety which rendered them useful."[130]

Wesley saw the Methodists' celebration of the love-feast as a revival of this ancient Christian communal meal. His comment on the rite in the "Plain Account of the People Called Methodists" is as follows,

> I desired that, one evening in a quarter, all the men in band, on a second, all the women, would meet; and on a third, both men and women together; that we might together "eat bread," as the ancient Christians did, "with gladness and singleness of heart." At these love-feasts (so we termed them, retaining the name, as well as the thing, which was in use from the beginning), our food is only a little plain cake and water.[131]

This particular passage is important, because it makes it explicit that in this case, at least, one of the institutions discussed in the "Plain Account" was intentionally patterned after the early church, and not merely confirmed after its institution by its conformity to ancient Christian practice.

Vigils

Wesley believed that the early Christians sometimes spent entire nights in prayer and celebration. His edition of Horneck refers to these occasions as vigils, and his own writings refer to them as "watch-nights."[132] He held up the ancient practice of observing vigils as a ground for his approval of "watch-nights" among the Methodists. The practice of spending entire nights in prayer began among the Methodists at the Kingswood School. When someone asked Wesley to forbid the practice, he refused, since "upon weighing the thing thoroughly, and comparing it to the practice of the ancient Christians," he wrote, "I could see no cause to forbid it."[133]

Fasts

John Wesley recognized two types of corporate fasts in ancient Christianity. The ancient Christians, he believed, observed the Wednesday and Friday of every week as days of fasting and prayer. This first sort of fasts could be referred to as "stations," "stationary fasts," or "half-fasts" (semijejuniae), since the weekly fasts were observed only until the ninth hour (3:00 p.m.)[134] The second type of fast Wesley recognized in the ancient church was the annual, or Lenten, fast. Wesley believed that the ancient Christians observed the forty days of Lent by vigils, fasting until the twelfth hour (6:00 p.m.) every day, and prayer.[135] Although Wesley included a passage from Horneck's "Letter to a Person of Quality" asserting that a Christian could be recognized by his lean visage, due to his frequent fasting, Wesley omitted from the same work a sentence describing how the early Christians "emaciated" themselves by fasting and other austerities.[136]

Long after his experience in Oxford and Georgia, Wesley continued to hold up the ancient church's observation of Wednesday and Friday fasts as a practice to be followed by the Methodists. The "Large Minutes" suggest observing a fast on Friday mornings, and John Bennett's copy of the minutes of the 1748 Annual Conference records an instruction to lay assistants, that they should fast every Friday until 3:00 p.m.[137] The "Plain Account of the People Called Methodists" notes that the societies met every Friday during "the dinner hour,"[138] and thus they probably omitted the noon meal on that day of the week. His sermon on the "Causes of the Inefficacy of Christianity," written in 1789 (two years before his death) recalls the Oxford Methodists' strict observance of the Wednesday and Friday fasts, and laments the waning of this discipline among the Methodists.[139]

In the cases of the love feast, vigils, and stationary fasts, Wesley's appeals to Christian antiquity conform to the programmatic use of Christianity. These practices were not maintained in Wesley's culture (that is, in his Anglican upbringing; the Moravians had reinstituted a love feast), and his vision of the early church inspired him and the early Methodists to reinstitute them.

Festivals

Wesley also knew of the annual festivals observed by the ancient Christians, especially Easter, Pentecost, and Epiphany. Although he was aware of ancient differences over the date of Easter, he did not think them significant, and suggested that the apostles themselves may have differed over the date of the paschal festival. His editions state that the Holy Week, or octave of Easter, was observed in ancient times as a period of particularly strict fasting. He omitted a passage from Cave representing the ancient Christians as holding a vigil through the night before Easter.[140] He editions recognize the early-Christian observation of Epiphany as the annual festival of Christ's manifestation to the world; but although Wesley included a passage from Mosheim discussing ancient disputes over the date of Christ's nativity, Wesley omitted a similar passage from Cave.[141]

Wesley believed that the early Christians also observed the anniversaries of Christian martyrdoms as days for public prayer. He acknowledged that in the second or third century the eucharist was offered up on behalf of the martyrs, but he felt that this was an abuse of the sacrament.[142] His edition of Mosheim states that in the fourth century the commemorations of the Christian martyrs grew in extravagance and became an occasion for the "indulgence of sinful passions."[143] He omitted from the "Martyrdoms" of Ignatius and Polycarp several passages relating how the early Christians venerated these saints as martyrs and observed the anniversaries of their martyrdoms.[144]

Although there is no evidence that Wesley stressed the annual commemoration of the martyrs or confessors, two entries in his *Journal* in the 1770s indicate that he held up the annual festivals observed in the ancient church as patterns to be emulated among the Methodists. For Christmas Day, 1774, he wrote:

> During the twelve festival days we had the Lord's Supper daily; a little emblem of the Primitive Church. May we be followers of them in all things, as they were of Christ![145]

Similarly, for the festival of the resurrection in 1777, he wrote:

> Sun. 30.-Easter Day was a solemn and comfortable day, wherein God was remarkably present with His people. During the Octave I administered the Lord's Supper every morning, after the example of the Primitive Church.[146]

These passages are important, since they indicate that Wesley's early interests in ancient liturgical practices had not completely died away in his later life.[147]

Individual and Family Devotions

Wesley believed that the early Christians worshipped as individuals and families. He thought that the Jerusalem church observed the third, sixth, and ninth hours of each day, according to Jewish custom, as times of prayer in the Temple, and that individual Christians continued to observe these hours through the third century.[148] His edition of Horneck represents individuals in the early church (laity and clergy) as knowing the Scriptures by heart, even though they did not possess books.[149] His editions of Horneck and Cave agree in portraying early Christian families as gathering for prayer at meals and at other times.[150] Although parallels may not have been explicitly drawn, readers of these editions would have found in their vision of early Christianity support for the Methodists' stress on family and private prayer and scripture study.

In his attempt to link the nascent Methodist movement with "the whole Church in the purest ages," Wesley had followed an idealized vision of ancient Christianity which inspired his ministry of teaching, his practices of evangelization, the institutions he developed for the Methodist fellowship, the church polity which he eventually fostered, and the patterns of worship which he encouraged the Methodists to follow. There was in all of this a certain sense of discovery and excitement: something lost and precious had been found, and the glories of past ages were paralleled in the triumphs of the new evangelistic movement. A new community was being molded on the lines of a vision of the ancient and primitive church.

Chapter 6

CONCLUSION

The cumulative force of the teachings and institutions supported by Wesley (discussed in the last two chapters) should not be missed. Even in his more subtle changes, it is clear that a new cultural matrix was being formed: "priests" had become "elders" or "ministers," the sign of the cross was quietly omitted, and the discipline of the love feast replaced eucharistic discipline. Add to these the less subtle changes, and the force is very strong indeed: presbyters had the right to ordain without bishops, "societies" became central in communal life, religious experience became the focus of evangelistic outreach, and General Councils could be dismissed as "trivial." Altogether, these changes from the culture Wesley had inherited indicate a significant departure from the Catholic and Anglican past, and yet in his enterprise of culture change Wesley appealed to the vision of Christian antiquity.

Previous studies of Wesley's uses of ancient Christian sources have usually attempted to demonstrate his Catholic or Anglican leanings. To refer significantly to ancient doctrines or practices was in itself a reflection of the Catholic past and an indication of Wesley's alignment with conservative Anglicanism—at least, so the argument ran. The grain of truth in this claim is that when Wesley is compared to other Evangelicals of his age (like Howell Harris or George Whitefield), and especially to later British and North American Evangelicals, he comes off appearing relatively "catholic" in comparison. And there were, indeed, many cases in which which Wesley utilized ancient Christian sources as Catholics and conservative Anglicans before him had done.

Held up against the broad background of options in his own age, however, Wesley's vision of Christian antiquity suggests quite a different perspective. In the first place, Wesley's vision of Christian antiquity itself diverged in significant respects from the image of the ancient church handed down by Catholic and Anglican authors. In the second place, his uses of this vision as often challenged Catholic and Anglican beliefs and practices as they upheld them. If anything, this suggests that Wesley stands as a kind of bridge between the older medieval and Reformation traditions and the newer Evangelical traditions which were diverging from the older patterns in Wesley's day.

A Synopsis of Wesley's Uses of Christian Antiquity

The two previous chapters have described and illustrated a variety of ways in which John Wesley expressed and tried to live out his vision of Christian antiquity. We may now consider Wesley's own uses of Christian antiquity in specific comparison to the uses (and configurations of uses) of Christian antiquity that were outlined in chapter two.

To recall the distinctions, "polemical" uses of Christian antiquity called upon early Christian customs or teachings in order to refute the practices or beliefs of the polemicist's opponents. Some Christians of the sixteenth, seventeenth, and eighteenth centuries (Thomas Cartwright, Jean Daillé, the "Tew Circle" in England) used Christian antiquity solely in this manner.

"Conservative" uses of Christian antiquity called upon a vision of Christian antiquity in order to defend customs and teachings of an established church. Anglicans, Gallicans, and Ultramontane Catholics used Christian antiquity in this manner in order to defend institutions such as the episcopacy, and teachings such as the Constantinopolitan doctrine of the Trinity, which, though they did not have explicit warrants in scripture, were seen nevertheless as developments not contradictory to the biblical faith. Typically, those who used some aspects of Christian antiquity in an apologetic manner to defend their own customs and teachings would also use other aspects of Christian antiquity in a polemical manner to refute their opponents' practices and beliefs.

"Programmatic" uses of Christian antiquity called upon a vision of Christian antiquity to find patterns for customs, beliefs, or even virtues which some desired to see restored to the Christianity of their age. Non-Jurors, Latitudinarians, Deists, Pietists, and persons intent on moral reform appealed to Christianity in this manner in Wesley's age. Those who used Christian antiquity in a programmatic manner in order to restore ancient Christian customs, beliefs, or moral standards, also used Christian antiquity in an apologetic manner in order to defend what they perceived as rightly instituted beliefs and practices in their own churches, and in a polemical manner in order to refute their opponents' beliefs and practices.

Our study of John Wesley's appeal to the vision of Christian antiquity shows that his uses conform to the third of our three typical configurations. He utilized his vision of Christian antiquity in a polemical manner in order to refute his opponents, in a conservative manner in order to defend certain Anglican customs and teachings, and in a distinctively programmatic manner in order to restore certain ancient customs, beliefs and moral standards which he felt to be desirable for the church in his age. Specific instances can be related of each of these characteristic uses.

Polemical Uses of Christian Antiquity. John Wesley did use Christian antiquity on several occasions in what could be termed a polemical manner. He published lengthy citations of patristic sources against Roman Catholic teachings and practices in the "Roman Catechism," even though it was not his own composition. He cited Augustine and Chrysostom against the doctrine of predestination. These citations must be considered polemical uses of Christian antiquity, since he did not defend his own, particular views by calling upon these sources, but used them only to refute his opponents' teachings. Similarly, many of his sporadic or incidental references to ancient Christian writers (tabulated in Appendix Two) reflect polemical uses of Christian antiquity.

Conservative Uses of Christian Antiquity. Wesley also used his vision of Christian antiquity in a culturally conservative manner, in order to defend certain Anglican teachings and practices. Just as conservative Anglicans of Wesley's age had defended their church's affirmation of the Nicene (or, more accurately, the Constantinopolitan) doctrine of the Trinity against the challenges of Neo-Arianism, Socinianism, and Deism, so Wesley affirmed the Nicene Creed, including the *filioque* clause, and the teachings of the Athanasian Creed.

Similarly, Wesley's vision of Christian antiquity could serve to uphold certain Anglican practices as well as teachings. He defended the Anglican episcopacy, and what he supposed to be its succession from the apostles, by appeal to patristic precedents; at least, that is, until the 1740s, when his conceptions of the ancient episcopate changed. His general defence of Anglican liturgical traditions shows his affirmation of practices he believed to be consistent with ancient Christian practices.

Programmatic Uses of Christian Antiquity. The distinction between culturally "conservative" and "programmatic" uses of Christian antiquity is not a dichotomy; it is, rather, a continuum between two points. It is a continuum because patterns of belief and practice once accepted fall into desuetude, new patterns replace the old, and often the new patterns become culturally "orthodox" themselves. The use of Christian antiquity as a pattern for the episcopate provides an example of this complex of uses. Conservative Anglicans prior to Wesley had called upon the resources of Christian antiquity, especially the Ignatian epistles, to defend the Anglican episcopate. John Wesley himself reflected this conservative use of Christian antiquity in his discussions with Spangenberg in Georgia, and in his correspondence through the early 1740s. The shift in Wesley's vision of the ancient episcopate in 1744 led to a corresponding shift in his use of those conceptions. After 1744, Wesley used his vision of Christian antiquity in a programmatic manner that challenged Anglican views of the episcopacy. In 1784, he called upon his conceptions of the ancient Christian episcopate to justify the bold step of his ordinations of Whatcoat and Vasey, and his consecration of Thomas Coke. By 1784, however, when Coke and Asbury appealed to the precedent of the Alexandrian church to defend the Methodist episcopate, the cycle had come full round, and their use of Christian antiquity was culturally conservative, in defense of an established church institution. Wesley, then, had a spectrum of uses of Christian antiquity, ranging from those in which conceptions of Christian antiquity were called upon to confirm certain aspects of the Methodist program, to those in which conceptions of Christian antiquity served as intentional patterns for Methodist beliefs and practices.

In some cases, Wesley used Christian antiquity in order to confirm beliefs or practices which the Methodists had espoused in addition to Anglican beliefs and practices. These uses may be considered "programmatic" insofar as they uphold beliefs or practices differing from those of contemporary Anglican culture. Wesley explicitly stated this confirmatory use of Christian antiquity in the introduction to his "Plain Account of the People Called Methodists," where he claimed that Methodist institutions developed in order to meet immediate needs, but were found later to conform to ancient Christian institutions. The Methodist societies and watchnights are depicted in this work as having been designed to meet particular needs, and then later having been found to correspond to the form of the ancient Christian hetaeriae and vigils. The account above shows how Wesley's assertion that the Methodist movement was attested by miraculous signs, his pointing out how the Methodists had been persecuted, and his defence of Montanism and Donatism (in the light of accusations that the Methodists had revived both of these ancient heresies) all tended to confirm Wesley's belief that the Methodist movement represented a revival of primitive Christian religion.

A wider group of Wesley's uses of Christian antiquity can also be considered programmatic in that they uphold Methodist teachings or practices differing from Anglican teachings and practices, although in many of these cases Wesley did not give enough information in order to determine whether he merely called upon Christian antiquity to defend beliefs and practices already instituted among the Methodists, or whether he actually utilized these conceptions as a pattern to be followed by the Methodists, or both. An example would be Wesley's appeal to the ancient Christian practice of commendatory epistles (in the "Plain Account of the People Called Methodists") to justify the Methodists' use of class tickets. Although the introduction to the "Plain Account" asserts that the institutions depicted in the work were not designed to imitate ancient Christian practices, it is certain that Wesley was aware of the ancient practice of commendatory epistles from his reading in Cave and Fleury. Although Wesley did in fact design some of the institutions mentioned in the "Plain Account" after ancient Christian institutions (despite what he says in the introduction), there is not enough evidence to determine whether Wesley consciously designed the use of class tickets after the pattern of the ancient commendatory epistles, or only found the practice later to conform to the ancient practice.

Similarly, there is not sufficient evidence to determine the extent to which Wesley's conceptions of Christian antiquity actually molded the views Wesley advocated with respect to religious experience, faith as "assurance," and sin in, and the repentance of, believers. In each of these cases, it is possible that Wesley's early studies in Christian antiquity may have formed the views he espoused. But in each of these cases it is also possible that Wesley came to his views by way of a number of different sources (Anglican devotionalism, Puritanism, Catholic mysticism, Pietism, and others), and then later called upon ancient Christian views to defend those views.

In other cases, Wesley's uses of Christian antiquity can be demonstrated to have intentionally called upon ancient Christian customs and beliefs as patterns which Wesley wanted to see reinstituted by the Methodists. In these cases we may speak straightforwardly of the direct influence of ancient Christian beliefs and practices on Wesley. Wesley's decision to ordain, as mentioned above, stemmed from his acknowledgement that the ancient presbyters had the right to ordain. Several other Methodist institutions appear to derive, likewise, from Wesley's deliberate imitation of ancient Christian practices. Among these institutions were the following: penitent bands (imitating the ancient discipline of penitents by segregation from the community); visitors of the sick (following the ancient use of deacons and deaconesses to visit the sick); lovefeasts (following the ancient *agapai*); weekly fasts (following the ancient stationary fasts); and annual celebrations (following the ancient observances of Epiphany and Lent). Although the Moravians may have served as a medium for Wesley's knowledge of the lovefeast, he was familiar with the institution since his Oxford reading in Cave. One may also include in this category Wesley's intention to develop a common stock of goods among the Methodists, even though this intention did not come to fruition. In this category we should also place Wesley's understanding of the role of godfathers and godmothers (following the ancient baptismal sponsors as represented by Tertullian), since, although the Anglicans did use godfathers and godmothers, Wesley's understanding of their roles as spiritual counselors to the baptized stands in contrast to contemporary Anglican understandings of their role.

Most prominently, Wesley's uses of Christian antiquity as a vision for the individual Christian life must be seen as programmatic uses. Wesley acknowledged, in his "Letter to Conyers Middleton," in his "Letter to a Roman Catholic," and in later letters explaining his intention in writing "The Character of a Methodist," that he held up the ancient Christians as patterns to be imitated by the women and men of his own age. For church practices, Christian antiquity might be invoked initially as a programmatic pattern, but after those practices were instituted, it would be invoked as an apologetic authority. For individuals, however, the ancient examples were constantly needed as models. Thus Wesley consistently used the resources of Christian antiquity in illustrating the nature and order of religious experience, and in describing the life of virtue to which he believed Christians were called.

In refuting his opponents, in upholding what he believed to be proper Anglican beliefs and practices, and in seeking to change particular aspects of the culture of his age, John Wesley's uses of Christian antiquity were complex indeed, and varied, but conform in general to the programmatic configuration of uses of Christian antiquity that others in his culture had espoused.

Wesley's Uses of Christian Antiquity as Religious Authority

Wesley's conservative and programmatic appeals to the vision of Christian antiquity indicate that he regarded Christian antiquity as having a certain degree of authority for Christian belief and practice.

The authority of tradition had become a critical cultural issue by the end of the seventeenth century. On the one hand, the tendency of scientific and rationalistic thought was to reject tradition as an insufficient ground of human knowledge, especially when compared with observation or reflection. On the other hand, even the most radical advocates of Enlightenment thought appealed, as we have seen, to their vision of classical antiquity.

A spectrum of views on the authority of Christian antiquity emerged in the late seventeenth century. More Radical Protestants tended to reject the use of Christian antiquity as an unnecessary adjunct to scripture. Anglicans and Gallicans had appealed to the "objective" content of ancient Christian tradition against the "active" tradition represented by the Roman papacy, although they used Christian antiquity in support of the "active" traditions of their own communions.[1] A wide variety of persons and groups intent on Christian reform (Jansenists, Latitudinarians, persons intent on moral reform, and others) had called upon Christian antiquity in opposition to the established church orders of even Anglicanism and Gallicanism. Wesley's own uses of Christian antiquity had a similar, programmatic concern, although Wesley did use his conceptions of Christian antiquity in some culturally conservative ways.

Wesley explicitly referred to Christian antiquity as "authority,"[2] and spoke of Christian antiquity in connection with other sources of religious authority. For instance, he appealed to "Scripture, reason, and Christian antiquity" in the preface to the collected edition of his *Works*, and to scripture, the primitive church, and the Church of England in his sermon "On Laying the Foundation of the New Chapel, near the City Road, London."[3] Similarly, when pressed by those who wanted the Methodists to separate from the Church of England in 1789, Wesley wrote,

1. From a child I was taught to love and reverence the Scriptures, the oracles of God; and, next to these, to esteem the primitive Fathers, the writers of the first three centuries. Next after the primitive church, I esteemed our own, the Church of England, as the most scriptural national church in the world. I therefore not only assented to all the doctrines, but observed all the rubric in the Liturgy; and that with all possible exactness, even at the peril of my life.

2. In this judgement, and with this spirit, I went to America, strongly attached to the Bible, the primitive church, and the Church of England. . . . In this spirit I returned . . .[4]

The significance of Christian antiquity as a religious authority for John Wesley, then, should be seen in relation to his views of other sources of religious authority.

Wesley's personal memoir which is generally dated from early 1738 indicates his recognition that, prior to 1737, he had erred in regarding Christian antiquity as a "coordinate" rather than a "subordinate" rule with scripture.[5] Wesley's writings after 1737 indicate that he regarded scripture as having a normative authority over that of Christian antiquity and any other source of religious authority. Scripture could correct even the consensus of ancient Christian opinion; and thus Wesley could regard Montanists and Donatists as representing "scriptural" Christianity in their ages, even though the consensus of ancient Christian teachings had condemned them as heretics.[6] Given this view of scriptural authority, the critical questions with respect to Wesley's views of Christian antiquity are the questions why, if at all, Wesley ascribed a certain religious authority to ancient Christianity, and just what authority he ascribed thereto.

Chapter Three above shows that, after 1737, Wesley's emphasis shifted from an emphasis upon the *consensus* of ancient Christian teaching and practice (so strikingly illustrated by the quotations from the extant parts of Wesley's "Essay upon the Stationary Fasts") to an emphasis upon the *purity* of ancient Christianity, especially its moral purity. It is true that Wesley appealed to the life of "the whole church in the purest ages"[7] (with particular reference to ancient Christianity), and so it must not be denied that he continued to regard the church's unity in antiquity as a particular sign of its virtue; but after 1737 it was often in the context of descriptions of the ancient church's virtue that Wesley mentioned its unity.[8] Wesley's "Letter to Conyers Middleton" states that it was the exceptional virtue of the ancient Christians that made them less susceptible to doctrinal errors.[9]

What effective authority, then, distinct from the authority of scripture, did John Wesley ascribe to Christian antiquity? Several instances may be noted. In the first place, he ascribed a special authority to ancient Christian authors as *interpreters* of scripture. As mentioned above, Wesley felt that their special authority was due to the exceptional merit of the ancient Christians, and perhaps due to a direct oral tradition of interpretation from the apostles.[10] An example of this use of Christian antiquity would be Wesley's response to Bishop Smalbroke in the *Farther Appeal*, where Wesley cited Jerome, Augustine, Chrysostom, and Athanasius in favor of his own interpretation of passages in Romans and I Corinthians.[11]

A second manner in which Wesley called upon Christian antiquity as a religious authority in addition to the authority of scripture was by appealing to the life of the ancient church and the lives of ancient Christians in order to *illustrate* what Wesley believed to be scriptural teachings, practices, and standards of morality. Thus Wesley's poem

"Primitive Christianity" depicts the life of the ancient church as illustrating scriptural virtues of unity and faithfulness, and Wesley's editions of Horneck and Fleury depict the essentially scriptural virtues of individual Christians in the ancient church.[12]

A third instance of the authority Wesley ascribed to Christian antiquity is in the *suggestions* of Christian practices and teachings which Wesley held to be "well agreeing with" the scriptures, though "not prescribed" in scripture.[13] In these cases, Wesley appealed to Christian antiquity not so much to interpret obscure passages of scripture as to authorize practices or teachings about which scripture was simply silent. Wesley could argue that, although these practices and teachings were not prescribed in scripture (and thus were not to be required of Christians), they were nevertheless shown to be truly Christian by their use in the ancient church. Examples of this use of Christian antiquity as a religious authority would be Wesley's approval of episcopal church government and his suggestion of observing Wednesday and Friday fasts, both of which he held to accord with ancient Christian customs, but neither of which he held to be positively prescribed in the Bible.[14]

A fourth respect in which Wesley ascribed a particular religious authority to Christian antiquity is in his appeal to ancient Christian teachings or practices to *confirm* teachings or practices the Methodists had taken up. Wesley's "Plain Account of the People Called Methodists" provides the prime example of this appeal to the authority of Christian antiquity. In this document, he indicated that many of the distinctive Methodist institutions arose out of the circumstances in which the Methodists found themselves, and then were found (in retrospect) to conform to ancient Christian institutions. For example, Wesley stated in the "Plain Account" that the Methodist societies arose out of the desire of individual persons to follow divine grace, and were found later to conform to the catechetical institutions of the ancient church.[15] He took this confirmation by ancient patterns as a special sign of the rightness of Methodist institutions and practices, especially in cases where those institutions had been called into question by Anglican leaders. In these cases, as noted above, what were at one time programmatic appeals to Christian antiquity eventually became conservative appeals, as practices once novel became customary among the Methodists.

In summary, then, Wesley did ascribe an authority to Christian antiquity, not as replacing in any sense the authority of scripture, but as faithfully interpreting and illustrating scriptural truths, and as faithfully suggesting and confirming Christian teachings and practices not specifically enjoined in scripture.

This authority, "subordinate" to Biblical authority, parallels in some respects the authority that Wesley ascribed to the Church of England. He spoke of "the whole Church in the purest ages" on one occasion, and then named "the primitive church" and "the Church of England" as instances thereof.[16] Wesley maintained that the Church of England conformed to both scriptural and primitive Christian precedents: the Church of England was not only "the most scriptural national church in the world,"[17] but followed the primitive church "in most points."[18] It would appear that by "the Church of England" Wesley had in mind the affirmation of the constitutional documents (Articles, Homilies, Prayer Book) of the Church more than its present governors. It was the Church of England "as appears from all her authentic records, from the uniform tenor of her Liturgy, and from numberless passages in the Homilies,"[19] and elsewhere defined as

> that body of people, nominally united, which profess to uphold the doctrine contained in the Articles and *Homilies*, and to use Baptism, the Lord's Supper and Public Prayer, according to the Common Prayer Book.[20]

He expressed reservations, however, about adding a clause entailing submission to the present governors of the church to this definition.[21] In fact, Wesley could cite "the Church of England" against Anglican leaders of his own age, as he did (citing the Articles and Homilies) in his *Farther Appeal, Part I*.[22] Wesley thus appealed to the "objective tradition" of the Church of England against the "active tradition" represented by contemporary Anglican church leadership. In this respect, especially, his appeal to the Anglican tradition bears a close parallel to his culturally programmatic appeal to Christian antiquity.

Seen from the perspective of his own culture's views of religious authority, then, Wesley's conceptions of the authority of Christian antiquity were delimited by the following criteria: a) on the one hand, he ascribed a certain authority to Christian antiquity in addition to the authority of scripture, and thus he should not be classed among those more radical Protestants who rejected the use of Christian antiquity as a religious authority; and b) on the other hand, he appealed to Christian antiquity as "objective tradition" often in contention with the "active tradition" represented by the Church of England in his age, and thus he should not be classed with those Catholics (both Gallican and Ultramontane) and Anglicans who in one way or another appealed to Christian antiquity most characteristically in defence of their own active traditions. Wesley's understanding of the authority of Christian antiquity conforms most nearly to that of late seventeenth-century and early eighteenth-century Christians intent on church reform and renewal who appealed to the ancient church as a model or paradigm for church renewal in their own age.

Some Broader Issues

These conclusions are relevant to some of the broader issues in the field of Wesley studies. We may now observe how a study of Wesley's vision of Christian antiquity is relevant to the specific issues of Wesley's church-party loyalties, of Wesley's radicalism, and of Wesley's place within the Christian tradition.

Wesley's Church-Party Loyalties

For the last century Wesley studies have been dominated by a concern to identify Wesley's loyalties among the various parties in the Christendom of his age. A series of monographic studies was initiated in the late nineteenth century over the question of Wesley's "High-Church" as opposed to "Protestant" leanings. Interpreters who wanted to demonstrate Wesley's Anglican and Catholic loyalties tended to stress the years of Wesley's life in Epworth, London, and Oxford, as a formative period in which his church-party loyalties developed. Interpreters who wanted to show Wesley's connections with either Magisterial or Pietistic Protestantism tended to stress the Georgia encounter and the subsequent Aldersgate Street experience as the watershed from which Wesley's mature theological views developed. Further studies explored Wesley's connections with Puritanism, Roman Catholic mysticism, and the Radical Reformation.[23] Insofar as this work focuses on Wesley's relationship to a particular aspect of the Christian tradition (Christian antiquity), it follows the pattern of these earlier monographic studies. It does not, however, attempt to demonstrate that Wesley's principal loyalty lay with any one of these particular parties, but tries to show the complexities of Wesley's relationships to each of them, as indeed some more recent works in the field of Wesley studies have done.[24]

Fidelity to Christian antiquity was a crucial religious issue in Wesley's age, and the various parties of Christendom held distinctive conceptions of Christian antiquity and employed those conceptions in distinctive manners. Neither Wesley's conceptions nor his uses of Christian antiquity conforms precisely to the patterns maintained by any one of these parties. While it is the case that Wesley's early conceptions and uses of Christian antiquity conform to those of the Manchester Non-Jurors to whom he was attached, this cannot of itself

113

identify him with "High Church" loyalties, as some nineteenth-century interpreters thought.[25] Although the Non-Jurors were understood to be precursors of Oxford Movement High Churchmanship by these interpreters, the Non-Jurors to whom Wesley was attached were a peculiar sect (the Manchester group), as shown by their fondness for the Baptist William Whiston. Despite the Manchester Non-Jurors' keen interests in the ancient liturgies, they did not conform to nineteenth-century conceptions of High Churchmanship. And most importantly, Wesley repudiated their views in 1737.

On the other hand, what Wesley repudiated in 1737 was not the vision of Christian antiquity as a pattern for community or individual life, but certain particular conceptions of Christian antiquity, especially those grounded in the Apostolic Canons and Apostolic Constitutions, stressed by the Manchester Non-Jurors.[26] Although his conceptions of Christian antiquity may have changed after 1737, his programmatic uses continued. In some respects, for instance in his use of the Macarian homilies, Wesley's conceptions and uses of Christian antiquity after 1737 conform to the Pietists' conceptions and uses of Christian antiquity. In other respects, for example in his continued stress on the stationary fasts and the observation of Lent and Easter according to ancient Christian precedents, his views and uses differed even from those of the Pietists.

Our study of Wesley's vision of Christian antiquity suggests more the particularity of Wesley's relationships to various church parties than his clear identification with any one of them. The conventional view that Wesley was "actually a High Churchman," and that his use of ancient Christian sources demonstrates his High-Church inclinations, comprehends neither the complexity of attitudes towards Christian antiquity in Wesley's day, nor the significant shifts that occurred in Wesley's own vision of Christian antiquity. Wesley was, it should be argued, a very unique Evangelical who had an unusual commitment to Christian tradition (especially ancient tradition), and he therefore remains as a challenge (and hopefully a resource) to Evangelicals, who too often in the past have jettisoned Christian tradition as irrelevant to the on-going lives of individual Christians and to the life of the Christian community.

Wesley's Radicalism

In recent decades, efforts have been made to appropriate certain aspects of Wesley's life and thought which have been found relevant to contemporary Christian movements for social and cultural transformation. Wesley has been examined by Liberation theologians, who have pointed out his identification with the poor, and his communalistic intentions.[27] Theologically conservative Wesleyans have also found in John Wesley a precedent for Christian approaches to social and cultural reform.[28] Making a case for Wesley's radicalism is not a uniformly easy task, however, given Wesley's conservative attitudes towards political events and towards the Enlightenment.

Our study of Wesley's vision of Christian antiquity, however, does show a sense in which Wesley can be considered a cultural "radical." Wesley's was a radicalism that challenged his cultural inheritance by appeal to its own distinctively Christian roots (its *radices*). Wesley's communalism, for instance, was grounded in his conviction that the "primitive" Christians had practiced a community of possessions that flowed from their love for one another. The challenge that Wesley's communalism lay before his own culture lay in his claim that his culture's attachment to possessions and commitment to surplus accumulation were a degradation of its own best roots. This is the case, not only with respect to Wesley's communalistic intentions, but with many of the ancient Christian beliefs and practices and ideals of virtue which he wanted to see restored to the church.

Wesley's Place in the Christian Tradition

The issues of Wesley's church-party loyalties and of his radicalism are both embraced by a larger issue that is perhaps the constitutive issue, at least of the historical component, of Wesley studies, namely, the issue of Wesley's place in the Christian tradition.[29] The issue of Wesley's church-party loyalties examines but one aspect of the larger issue, that is, Wesley's relationships to the various parties which represented various strands of the Christian tradition in Wesley's age and place. Where can we place Wesley within the scope of the Christian tradition in such a way as to account for his relationships to his own Anglican tradition and to the other Christian traditions to which he was exposed? The issue of Wesley's radicalism also examines an aspect of the larger issue, namely, Wesley's radical challenge to the nominally Christian culture of his age. Where can we place Wesley within the Christian tradition in such a way as to account for both his conservative reaction against Enlightenment thought and his own radical critique of a nominally Christian society?

Consider other Christian leaders who have held idealistic visions of the Christian past and who have attempted to bring about reform or renewal in the church based on their visions. Early Christian monasticism, for example, appealed to the example of Jesus (as an ascetic) and to a vision of the church during the age of persecution in their efforts to renew the Christian community.[30] The early Franciscans appealed to their distinctive vision of the "poor Christ," and their vision of the poverty of the early Christian community, in their own efforts to follow a radical Christian lifestyle.[31] The Anabaptists of the sixteenth century (who may have indirectly influenced Wesley) held pre-Constantinian Christianity to be a heroic age in which believers held their possessions in common.[32] Finally, the Pietists, who directly influenced Wesley, developed a conception of ideal Christianity blended from the New Testament and the early post-apostolic church, as the second section of Spener's *Pia Desideria* shows.[33]

Both Wesley's vision of Christian antiquity as an age in which an ideal of Christian corporate and individual life was realized and his uses of this vision to challenge the nominally Christian cultural patterns of his age place him within a *genus* that includes the leaders of other Christian renewal movements who held structurally similar conceptions of the Christian ideal as realized in a particular time in the past (the apostolic age, perhaps extending into the early Christian centuries), and who used their conceptions in order to challenge their own nominally Christian cultures. Seen from the perspective of the Christian tradition as a whole, and from the perspective of his own attitudes toward that tradition, Wesley "fits" in the *genus* of distinctively Christian renewal movements.

But within this *genus* Wesley's conceptions and uses of Christian antiquity suggest some *differentiae specificae* that distinguish his intentions for Christian renewal from the intentions of other leaders of renewal movements. The first and principal *differentia specifica* which distinguishes Christian renewal movements one from another is the particular cultural context within which, and, to some extent, against which, each has operated. Wesley's movement was distinguished by its development within the particular Anglican culture of the early eighteenth century in the context of which it arose. But beyond this principal *differentia*, Wesley's intentions for Christian renewal may be distinguished by some more particular *differentiae*, some of which the present study has pointed out. Wesley's conceptions of Christian antiquity, for example, are distinguished by his growing recognition of corruptions within the pre-Constantinian church, a recognition which I have yet to find in Anabaptist or Pietist descriptions of the pre-Constantinian church. Wesley's uses of Christian antiquity, to take a further example, are distinguished from others' uses of Christian antiquity by Wesley's conservative uses of Christian antiquity to defend such a traditional Anglican practice as the Friday fast. Our research has tentatively suggested that examinations of Wesley's conceptions and uses of scriptural Christianity and the faith of the English Reformation might point to further evidence of both his identification within the *genus* of leaders of Christian renewal movements, and of the particular manners in which his intentions for church renewal differed from those of other leaders of Christian renewal movements.

Although conventional interpretations of John Wesley have focused on his relationships to the Christian parties of his age, some of Wesley's interpreters, especially those who have had the opportunity to see him from the perspective of the broad sweep of Christian history, have in fact placed Wesley's movement within the *genus* of Christian renewal movements. The Anglican historian Henry Wakefield, in the context of a general history of the Church of England, referred to Wesley as "the St. Francis of the eighteenth century."[34] Similarly, Herbert Brook Workman, a Methodist historian whose principal area of research was ancient and medieval asceticism, drew a series of parallels between Wesley's movement and early monasticism, Franciscanism, and the Society of Jesus.[35] The Roman Catholic scholar Maximin Piette concluded his study of *John Wesley in the Evolution of Protestantism* by pointing out parallels between Wesley and St. Benedict, St. Dominic, St. Francis, and Ignatius Loyola.[36] Finally, the Lutheran historian Martin Schmidt summarized one chapter of his theological biography of Wesley in these terms,

> John Wesley introduced into the main stream of history the attempt to make the spiritual impetus of primitive Christianity fruitful for the present by giving it an appropriate external form. This tradition extended from the coenobitic monasticism of the Eastern Church, through the whole of Western monasticism, to the Waldensians, Hussites, Anabaptists, and from them to the Pietists and their precursors in the mystical spiritualists. In each case the ideal was understood somewhat differently, and so the attempts were always tackled in different ways.[37]

Our research substantiates these observations by pointing to more particular parallels between Wesley's conceptions and uses of Christian antiquity and the manners in which leaders of other Christian renewal movements conceived of, and used their visions of, the Christian ideal.

This placement of Wesley within the Christian tradition may illuminate the issues of Wesley's church-party loyalties and of Wesley's radicalism. It suggests that Anglicanism provided for Wesley *both* the immediate cultural context out of which his movement arose, *and* a source for his conceptions of the Christian ideal. It suggests, further, that scripture (and, above all, Christ) provided the basis for Wesley's conception of the Christian ideal, and that ancient Christianity provided for Wesley powerful conceptions of that ideal as realized (and thus realizable!) in the church.

117

Our placement of Wesley within the general range of leaders of Christian renewal movements goes some way, in the second place, towards explaining Wesley's "radicalism." Wesley does fit a certain pattern of Christian radicalism. It is not the radicalism of Origen or of Immanuel Kant, whose radicalism lay in their attempts to test the credibility of Christianity in the light of cultural and ideological patterns external to Christianity (for Origen, the inheritance of Platonic thought; for Kant, the thought of the Enlightenment). Rather, Wesley's was more like the radicalism of Francis of Assisi or of Philipp Jakob Spener, whose radicalism lay in their critique of contemporary Christianity by questioning its appropriateness to the apostolic faith itself.

Towards an Explanation

Is it at all possible to explain why Wesley should have taken up an idealized vision of Christian antiquity, and why he should have appealed to this particular vision as the basis for his challenge to English religious culture? Historical explanations are always partial—always, if you will, educated guesses—but in this case some elements of an explanation can be offered.

Why John Wesley himself should have become a visionary in the first place will have to remain unexplained, at least here. Perhaps his genius grew out of the harsh contrast between the material poverty of his family's life and their rich educational, cultural, and religious heritage. Perhaps it grew more from his parents' own senses of religious vocation. For whatever reason, we must take it for granted that John Wesley emerged early in life with a consistent sense of the failure of contemporary Christianity and with a correspondingly visionary sense of the possibilities for reform or renewal.

Taking it for granted, then, that John Wesley was to seek to change English religious culture, the question (one which we are far better qualified to answer) becomes, why did he take up the particular vision that guided him? In some respect, the answer must be that by certain historical accidents he encountered first the Manchester Non-Jurors, with their distinctive understanding of ancient Christianity, and then the Salzburger and Moravian Pietists who were in Georgia, whose vision of ancient Christianity forced him to rethink his vision of the primitive church. Wesley then took up his particular vision of Christian antiquity as a result of his encounters with these earlier views, and by his own further reflection on them.

But we may also seek a somewhat broader explanation than this. The leader of a movement for culture change, religious or not, must have a guiding vision, what anthropologist Anthony F. C. Wallace calls the "cultural mazeway" by which persons live, and which is reformulated by leaders of cultural revitalization movements.[38] Within the various alternative sources for a guiding vision (for example, Wallace mentions "cargo cults" which import cultural visions from another culture), only two appear with some regularity in Christian history, namely, the vision of an apocalyptic end to history seen as imminently arriving, or the vision of a golden age in the Christian past whose purity is to be renewed or revived. The apocalyptic vision, however, had been discredited in the sixteenth century by the activities of the Anabaptist groups associate with Thomas Münzer and the Peasants Revolt, then by the tragic circumstances of the siege of Münster. In seventeenth-century England, moreover, apocalyptic hopes had again been discredited by the failure of the Cromwellian Revolution and the plethora of millenarian sects it engendered. By the beginning of the eighteenth century, apocalyptic visions were not a serious option for culture change. Although Johann Albrecht Bengel and John Wesley speculated on the second advent of Christ, they agreed in placing their speculative date well beyond their own deaths.

The failure of apocalyptic vision, then, left eighteenth-century Christian visionaries with the quest for a golden age in the past, and this concurred well with what we have already described as the eighteenth century's passion for "classical revival" of various forms. For the most radical Protestants, this might mean return to the vision of the church in the New Testament age alone. But at this point Wesley's Anglican heritage became critical, since most Anglicans had not perceived the stark break in Christian history at the end of the "apostolic age" that more radical Protestants had posited. What one might expect, then, of a distinctively Anglican visionary would be a vision of New Testament Christianity in continuity with the church of the earliest centuries, but a vision that nevertheless stood as a clear challenge to contemporary Anglicanism. Our researches into Wesley's vision of Christian antiquity have shown him to have held just such a vision.

John Wesley's vision of Christian antiquity, then, emerged not only as a result of his encounters with Manchester Non-Jurors and Continental Pietists, but also from the particular circumstances of his development as a visionary leader within a particular religious tradition that had stressed the continuity of ancient Christianity with the faith of the apostolic age. Wesley, we might say, was a distinctively Anglican religious visionary.

Not far from the magnificent structure of St. Paul's Cathedral, past Aldersgate Street and across Bunhill Fields, on City Road, there is a small chapel, the floor-plan of which resembles that of the most ancient Christian churches, even as they were conceived in the eighteenth century. It is nearly square, with two rows of columns running from front to back, dividing its area roughly into thirds. In the front of it is a semicircular apse within which an altar was located, and on whose wall the sanctus is inscribed.

Just outside this eighteenth-century basilica, past altar and apse, is a tomb, the beginning of whose inscription[39] reads as follows:

> To the Memory of
> THE VENERABLE JOHN WESLEY, A.M.
> Late Fellow of Lincoln College, Oxford.
> This GREAT LIGHT arose
> (by the Singular Providence of God)
> To Enlighten THESE NATIONS
> and to revive, enforce, and defend
> The Pure Apostolical DOCTRINES and PRACTICES of
> THE PRIMITIVE CHURCH

Appendix 1

The following is a transcription of a manuscript found in Wesley's third Georgia Diary (which covers the period from 12 February 1737 through 31 August 1737). This manuscript was begun in a book later reversed and used for the Georgia Diary. Its binding suggests that it was purchased and bound in 1732. A list of John Wesley's purchases of (blank) books shows that one of five volumes, numbered 11–15, was purchased for the writing of a "Genesis." Elsewhere Wesley indicated (probably in 1732) that he intended to write a "Genesis on Fasting." The third Georgia Diary has the number "11" in the inside back cover—where the present manuscript begins. This manuscript therefore most probably dates from the period 1732–1734, when Wesley was under the influence of the Separatist Non-Jurors, and was engaged in the writing of his "Essay on the Stationary Fasts," part of which Thomas Deacon included in *A Compleat Collection of Devotions*. This manuscript is in all likelihood an earlier draft of that essay.

The essay which John Wesley began in this manuscript is incomplete. Judging from the outline he gave in its second paragraph, the manuscript contains only the first of two (or possibly three; the third is underlined, perhaps for omission) intended parts of the essay. The portion given bears relevance because Wesley's intention in it was to demonstrate that all particular Christian communions are obligated to follow the customs of the universal church, especially (as appears from the substance of the essay) its customs expressed by the church in its supposedly undivided, primitive state. Almost all of this manuscript after the first sentence of the third paragraph is a fairly direct translation from a Latin comment on I Corinthians 11:16 in Bishop William Beveridge's *Thesaurus Theologicus* (given in volume 10 of Beveridge's works in the Library of Anglo-Catholic Theology edition, pp. 473–489). The *Thesaurus* is a systematic treatment of theology

121

based on selected scripture passages, and the passage treated in this comment falls under the heading "On Ecclesiastical Rites."

In this transcription I have followed as closely as possible Wesley's spelling and punctuation. The manuscript includes numerous revisions, which are given either in superscript characters or on the facing page and indicated by a carat. I have included the revisions in brackets, but I have not included portions which Wesley scored through. I have placed in italics some other passages that appear underlined in the manuscript, and it is unclear whether Wesley intended for them to be simply underlined or struck out; in fact the latter seems likely.

Of the Weekly Fasts of the Church

By the Church I here mean, The Catholick Church, or, The Whole Body of Christians, united in Christ their Head; By the Weekly Fasts of this Church, the Wednesday and Friday of each Week, which were [antiently] observed as such by All its Members: What I propose to enquire concerning These, is Whether the observing them Now, be the Duty of its present Members or no.

In order to this, it will be abundantly sufficient to examine, First, Whether it be Our Duty to obey the Antient Injunctions of the Catholic Church, Secondly, Whether the Church did injoin these Fasts, *Thirdly, Whether this injunction binds Us.*

First, We are to examine, Whether [it be Our Duty to obey] *the Antient* Injunctions of the Catholic Church *bind its members now militant.** "The [one] Catholic Church, as we may observe, consist's of All the Particular Churches which have ever been constituted from the time of our Lord's Passion, and not of Those only which subsist together at Any One Period of Time. All those Churches which constitute the One Universal, have always agreed in the Articles of Faith; But as for Rites, Some have been Peculiar to Particular Churches, Some Common to All. The Rites Peculiar to Any Particular Church may be either retained or abrogated by that Church: as they may either be admitted or rejected by Others. For they receive their whole Power of binding from That Church, by whose Authority they are established. But the Rites of the Church Universal, ought to be observed by All Particular Churches. For it is not in the Power of Any Particular Church, to reject what is establisht by the Church Universal. By so doing, it would become schismatical, disjoining itself from the Body of Christ."

"This may be [fully] prov'd [without going any further than] By [*sic*] those words of S. Paul to the Corinthians, 1 Cor. 11.16, If any man be contentious, we have no such Custom, neither the Churches of GOD. (The Church, some copies have it, which is the same thing, seeing All the Churches put together make up the One.) When the Apostle writ This, Some men were endeavoring to introduce a New Rite into the Church of Corinth. Against the Admission of this he uses several Arguments, the last and Chief whereof is This; We have no Such Custom, neither the Churches of GOD; as if he had said, That which is contrary to the Custom of All Other Churches, Ought not to be received in that of Corinth. But That is contrary to the Custom of All Other Churches: Therefore This Ought not to be received in that of Corinth."

"If the Church of Corinth was not obliged to observe the Customs [How much more the *Injunctions*] of the Catholic Church, the Apostle's Argument is of no force. But that it is of force, there can be no question, seeing it was dictated to him by the Spirit of GOD: so that here is no possibility of Fallacy; and consequently, we have the Utmost Assurance, that every Particular Church, is obliged to conform to Every Custom, which is injoined by the Church Universal. If Any do's not, it may be convicted of Error and Schism, by this Infallible Argument. Since GOD himself dictated this to the Apostle, it necessarily follow's, That it is the Will of GOD, That all Particular Churches observe the Customs [and much more the Injunctions] of the Universal Church; And that we should have this Argument taught by himself, ready upon all occasions, to determine Every Controversy."

"Accordingly, by This, the Christians of All, but *especially* the Earliest Ages, have determin'd Every Controversy. Whenever any Dispute arose, concerning any Custom of a Particular Church, the Appeal was ever made to the Custom of the Church Universal, and according to That, sentence past. To bring only One Instance. The Primitive Church was long divided concerning the time of celebrating Easter. The Church of Asia, observing it, like the Jews, on the 14th day of the Month, whether it were Sunday or no. But all the other Churches kept it on the Sunday following that day. The Point was at length refer'd to the General Council at Nice, where it was prov'd, that All the Churches, beside that of Asia, had been accustom'd to celebrate the Feast on Sunday. And for this reason (*toutou heneken*) All the Fathers there assembled, determined, That the Asian Church should keep it on the same Day. Whence it appears that These Holy Men used the same Argument against the Church of Asia, which S. Paul had done against that of Corinth: Which S. Cyprian uses against Novatian, S. Augustine against the Donatists, and Epiphanius against All

Hereticks and Schismatics of all kinds; by which he proves All those to be without Excuse, who either in Doctrine or Discipline had departed from the Catholic Church."

*What follows on this head is translated from Bishop Beveridge.

Appendix 2

References to Ancient Christian Works
In John Wesley's Works

The following list of references to patristic authors and works in John Wesley's works is based principally on my own study of key works by John Wesley (such as his "Letter to Conyers Middleton") in which patristic references are likely to occur, and on a careful study of the indices to major editions of Wesley's works (Jackson, Telford, Sugden, Curnock, etc.). The list is organized according to patristic author and patristic work. The second line of each entry gives the locus of the reference in John Wesley's works, with volume number and pagination in a printed edition given in parentheses. For the sake of space, I haved had to use the following abbreviations in this list for Wesley's works:

AC	"An Address to the Clergy"
AF	Wesley's edition of the *Apostolic Fathers* (preface)
DPF	"A Dialogue between a Predestinarian and his Friend"
FA	*A Farther Appeal to Men of Reason and Religion*
LCM	"A Letter to the Reverend Dr. Conyers Middleton"
LRDH	"A Letter to the Reverend Dr. Horne"
PPCC	"Popery Calmly Considered"
RC	"A Roman Catechism, with a Reply Thereto"
STGG	"Serious Thoughts on Godfathers and Godmothers"
TN	"Thoughts on Necessity"

Other abbreviations utilized in this list are explained in the list of abbreviations for the work as a whole.

Apostolic Constitutions
   (General Reference)
      LCM II:9 (Jackson 10:28)

Arnobius
  Adversus Nationes
    LCM [C]:13 (Jackson 10:13)
    LCM I:14 (Jackson 10:23)

Athanasian Creed
  Journal 1750/08/17 (Jackson 3:30, Curnock 3:491)
  Sermons 55:3 (Jackson 6:200; Outler 2:377)

Athanasius
  Contra Arianos
    FA:V:22 (Jackson 8:99)
  (General Reference)
    Letters 1738/01/02 (Telford 1:367)
  (unidentified)
    Sermons 55:5 (Jackson 6:201; Outler 2:379)

Athenagoras
  Legatio
    LCM IV:IV:12 (Jackson 10:51)

Augustine
  Confessions
    Sermons 103:II:4 (Jackson 7:170; Outler 3:459)
    Letters 1781/04/12 (Telford 7:58)
    Sermons 3:II:5 (Jackson 5:29, Sugden 1:76; Outler 1:148)
    Sermons 37:28–29 (Jackson 5:475–476, Sugden 2:100; Outler 2:57)
    Sermons 67:26 (Jackson 6:323; Outler 2:548)
    Sermons 51:I:5 (Jackson 6:138, Sugden 2:466; Outler 2:285)
    Letters 1745/12/30 (Jackson 12?67, Telford 2:60)
    Letters 1746/06/25 (Jackson 12:37, Telford 2:70–71)
  Contra Adamantium
    RC, Qu. 63 (Jackson 10:118–119)
  Contra Petil.
    RC, QU 6 (Jackson 10:90–91)
  De Fide et Symbolo
    RC, Qu 47 (Jackson 10;111)
  De Sermone Domini in Monte
    RC, Qu. 12 (Jackson 10:93)
  De Unitate Ecclesiae
    RC, Qu. 13 (Jackson 10:94)
  Epistola ad Januarium

RC, Qu. 52 (Jackson 10:113)
Epistles
RC, Qu. 63 (Jackson 10:113)
Quaestiones Evangelicae
RC, Qu. 25 (Jackson 10:100–101)
Sermons
   Sermons 63:12 (Jackson 6:281; Outler 2:490)
   Sermons 85:III:7 (Jackson 6:513; Outler 3:208)
(General References)
   Journal 1746/03/09 (Jackson 2:9, Curnock 3:236)
   AC I:2 (Jackson 10:256)
   DPF (Jackson 10:256)
   Letters 1729/12/19 (Jackson 12:1)
   Letters 1756/03/12 (Telford 3:170–171)
   Letters 1775/08/18 (Telford 6:175)
   LRDH 3 (Jackson 9:113, Telford 4:176, Cragg 454)
   Sermons 68:9 (Jackson 6:328–329; Outler 2:556)
   TN IV:1 (Jackson 10:469)
(Unidentified References)
   PPCC IV:1 (Jackson 10:149)
   PPCC IV:10 (Jackson 10:154)

Barnabas (Pseudo-)
   Epistle
      LCM I:06 (Jackson 10:19)

Basil
   (General References)
      AC I:2 (Jackson 10:424)
      Sermons 112 (132 in Jackson) :II:3 (Jackson 7:424; Outler 3:586)

Chrysostom
   In Epistolam ad Romanos
      FA–I V:16, 18 (Jackson 8:92, 94–95; Cragg 155–159)
   In Joannem
      FA–I V:16, 18 (Jackson 8:92, 94–95; Cragg 155–159)
   (General References)
      AC I:2 (Jackson 10:484)
      Letters 1747/03/25 (Jackson 12:86; Telford 2:92)
      Letters 1747/07/10 (Jackson 12:92; Telford 2:100)
      Letters 1747/07/10 (Jackson 12:97; Telford 2:105)
      LRDH 3 (Jackson 9:113; Telford 4:176; Cragg 454)
      Sermons 112 (132 in Jackson) :II:3 (Jackson 7:424; Outler 3:586)

(Unidentified References)
  DPF (Jackson 10:256)
  LCM [A]:4 (Jackson 10:1–2)
  LCM [C]:3 (Jackson 10:9)
  Letters 1747/03/25 (Jackson 12:89)
  Sermons 40:II:16 (Jackson 6:12; Sugden 2:165; Outler 2:113)

Clement of Alexandria
  Stromateis
    RC, Qu. 13 (Jackson 10:94)
    LCM III:7 (Jackson 10:31–32)
    Journal 1767/03/04 (Jackson 3:273; Curnock 5:197)
    Letters 1774/11/30 (Jackson 12:297–298)
  (General Reference)
    AC II:1:6 (Jackson 10:492)

Clement of Rome
  I Clement
    LCM I:7 (Jackson 10:20)
  (General References)
    AC II:1:6 (Jackson 10:492
    AF (CL) Preface (Jackson 14:223–226)
    LCM VI:III:11 (Jackson 10:79)
    Letters 1755/07/25 (Jackson 12:468; Telford 3:137)
    Sermons 112 (132 in Jackson) :III:3 (Jackson 7:424; Outler 3:586)

Cyprian
  Ad Demetrianum
    RC, Qu. 22 (Jackson 10:99)
  De Idolorum Vanitate
    LCM I:14 (Jackson 10:23)
  De Immortalitate
    RC, Qu. 21 (Jackson 10:98)
  De Lapsis
    LCM IV:IV:15 (Jackson 10:52)
  Epistles
    LCM V:8 (Jackson 10:64)
    LCM I:14 (Jackson 10:22–23)
    LCM IV:IV:4–8 (Jackson 10:48–49)
  (General References)
    AC II:1:6 (Jackson 10:492)
    Journal 1738/01/09 (Jackson 1:73; Curnock 1:416)
    Journal 1754/08/05 (Jackson 3:314; Curnock 4:97)

LCM II:2, 9 (Jackson 10:24, 27)
LRDH 3 (Lackson 9:113; Telford 4:176)
Sermons 61:25 (Jackson 6:261; Outler 2:461–462)
Sermons 104:14 (Jackson 7:178; Outler 3:469–470)
Sermons 112 (132 in Jackson) :II:3 (Jackson 7:424; Outler 3:586)
(Unidentified References)
 Journal 1739/08/27 (Jackson 1:220; Curnock 2:263)
 LCM [C]:3 (Jackson 10:9)
 Letters 1739/06/23 (Jackson 12:106)
 Letters 1755/06/20 (Jackson 12:117)
 Sermons 40:II:16 (Jackson 6:12; Sugden 2:165; Outler 2:113)
 Sermons 54:10 (Jackson 6:193; Outler 2:364)
 Sermons 84:III:13 (Jackson 6:504; Outler 3:196–197)
 Sermons 102:17 (Jackson 7:164; Outler 3:450)
 Sermons 103:II:3 (Jackson 7:170; Outler 3:458–459)

Dionysius of Alexandria
 (General References)
  LCM II:4, 9 (Jackson 10:25, 27)
  LCM IV:IV:9 (Jackson 10:49–50)

Dionysius the Areopagite (Pseudo-)
 Mystical Divinity
  Journal 1740/07/16 (Jackson 1:281; Curnock 2:365)

Ephraem Syrus
 Exhortations
  Journal 1736/10/12 (Jackson 1:42; Curnock 1:279)
  Journal 1747/04/04 (Jackson 2:47–48; Curnock 3:284)
 (General References)
  AC I:2 (Jackson 10:484)
  Sermons 112 (132 in Jackson) :II:3 (Jackson 7:424; Outler 3:586)
 (Unidentified Reference)
  Journal 1761/05/21 (Jackson 3:56–59; Curnock 4:457–459)

Epiphanius
 Adversus Haereses
  LCM IV:IV:11 (Jackson 10:50)
  Sermons 27:I:6 (Jackson 5:347; Sugden 1:454; Outler 1:596–597)
  Sermons 122 (116 in Jackson) :14 (Jackson 7:288; Outler 4:94)
  RC, Qu. 40 (Jackson 10:107)
 Contra Catharos
  RC, Qu., 23 (Jackson 10:99)

Expositio Fidei
    Sermons 27:I:6 (Jackson 5:347; Sugden 1:454; Outler 1:596–597)

Eusebius
    Historia Ecclesiastica
        Journal 1741/11/19 (Jackson 1:347; Curnock 2:515)

Gregory of Nazianzen
    Orations
        RC, Qu. 21 (Jackson 10:99)

Hermas
    Shepherd
        LCM I:10 (Jackson 10:21)

Ignatius of Antioch
    Ephesians
        LCM I:3 (Jackson 10:18)
    (General References)
        AC II:1:[6] (Jackson 10:492)
        LCM I:2 (Jackson 10:18)
        LCM I:6 (Jackson 10:19)
        LCM VI:III:11 (Jackson 10:79)
        Letters 1755/07/25
    (Unidentified References)
        Sermons 112 (132 in Jackson) :II:3 (Jackson 7:424; Outler 3:586)
        Journal 1743/01/24 (Jackson 1:412; Curnock 3:65)

Irenaeus
    Adversus Haereses
        LCM [C]:3 (Jackson 10:8)
        LCM I:11 (Jackson 10:21–22)
        LCM III:11 (Jackson 10:33)
        LCM III:16 (Jackson 10:35)
        LCM III:16 (Jackson 10:38)
        LCM IV:I:1 (Jackson 10:39)
        LCM IV:VI:1–2 (Jackson 10:54)
    (General Reference)
        LCM III:22 (Jackson 10:38)

Jerome
    Commentary on Galatians
        RC, Qu. 23 (Jackson 10:99–100)

Commentary on Haggai
    RC, Qu. 7 (Jackson 10:91)
Commentary on Joel
    RC, Qu. 23 (Jackson 10:100)
(General References)
    AC I:2 (Jackson 10:484)
    FA–I V:17 (Jackson 8:39; Cragg 156)
(Unidentified References)
    LCM [C]:3 (Jackson 10:9)
    LCM [C]:11 (Jackson 10:9)
    Sermons 40:II:16 (Jackson 6:12; Sugden 2:165; Outler 2:113)

Justin Martyr
    First Apology
        LCM III:14 (Jackson 10:33)
        LCM [C]:3 (Jackson 10:9)
        LCM III:7 (Jackson 10:31–32)
        LCM III:9 (Jackson 10:32)
        LCM III:14 (Jackson 10:34)
        LCM V:5 (Jackson 10:62)
        Letters 1789/06/12 (Telford 8:143)
    Second Apology
        LCM I:11 (Jackson 10:21)
        LCM III:6 (Jackson 10:31)
        Sermons 70:II:6 (Jackson 6:357; Outler 2:596)
    Cohortatio ad Graecos
        LCM III:8 (Jackson 10:32)
        LCM IV:IV:13 (Jackson 10:51)
    Dialogus cum Tryphone Judaeo
        LCM I:11 (Jackson 10:21)
        LCM III:2 (Jackson 10:29–30)
        LCM III:5 (Jackson 10:30–31)
        LCM III:15 (Jackson 10:53)
    (General References)
        AC II:1:[6] (Jackson 10:492)
        LCM II:2, 4, 9 (Jackson 10:24–25, 27)
        LCM III:22 (Jackson 10:38)
        LCM IV:IV:4 (Jackson 10:48)
    (Unidentified References)
        LCM III:4 (Jackson 10:30)

Lactantius
    Divinae Institutiones

LCM I:14 (Jackson 10:23)

Macarius (Pseudo-)
Spiritual Homilies
Sermons 43:I:7 (Jackson 6:45–46; Outler 2:159)
(General Reference)
Sermons 112 (132 in Jackson) :II:3 (Jackson 7:424; Outler 3:586)

Minucius Felix
Octavius
LCM I:12 (Jackson 10:22)

Origen
Contra Celsum
FA–I V:21 (Jackson 8:97; Cragg 161);
LCM [C]:3 (Jackson 10:13)
LCM I:13 (Jackson 10:22)
LCM II:6 (Jackson 10:25–26; Telford 2:336–337)
LCM II:9 (Jackson 10:27)
RC, Qu. 37 (Jackson 10:105)
Contra Marcionem
RC, Qu. 63 (Jackson 10:118)
De Oratione
FA–I V:17 (Jackson 8:93; Cragg 156–157)
FA–I V:20 (Jackson 8:96; Cragg 159–160)
De Principiis
FA–I V:16–17 (Jackson 8:93; Cragg 156–157)
In Exodum
FA–I V:20 (Jackson 8:96; Cragg 159–160)
In Librum Jesu Nave
FA–I V:20 (Jackson 8:97; Cragg 156)
(General References)
AC II:1:[6] (Jackson 10:492)
Letters 1747/03/25 (Telford 2:91)
Letters 1747/03/25 (Telford 2:92)
Letters 1747/07/10 (Telford 2:100)
Letters 1747/07/25 (Telford 2:105)
Letters 1755/07/25 (Jackson 12:468; Telford 3:137)
Sermons 112 (132 in Jackson) :II:3 (Jackson 7:424; Outler 3:586)
(Indirect Reference)
Sermons 5:II:2 (Jackson 5:56; Sugden 1:119–120; Outler 1:187–188)
(Unidentified Reference)

LCM IV:III:7 (Jackson 10:43)

Polycarp
   Martyrdom of Polycarp
      LCM I:9 (Jackson 10:20)
   Phillipians
      LCM I:3 (Jackson 10:18)
   (General References)
      AC II:1:[6] (Jackson 10:492)
      LCM I:8 (Jackson 10:20)
      LCM VI:III:11 (Jackson 10:79)
      Letters 1755/07/25 (Jackson 12:468; Telford 3:137)
      Sermons 112 (132 in Jackson) :II:3 (Jackson 7:424; Outler 3:586)

Tertullian
   Adversus Marcionem
      LCM IV:IV:13 (Jackson 10:51)
   Apologeticus
      LCM I:12 (Jackson 10:22)
      Letters 1738/07/06 (Telford 1:250)
      Sermons 49:III:5 (Jackson 6:123–124; Outler 2:262)
   Contra Hermogenem
      RC, Qu. 5 (Jackson 10:90)
   De Anima
      LCM IV:IV:2 (Jackson 10:47)
   De Ieiuniis
      Sermons 27:I:3 (Jackson 5:346; Sugden 1:452–453; Outler 1:595)
   De Praescriptione Haereticorum
      LCM II:9 (Jackson 10:28)
   De Pudicitia
      Sermons 40:II:16 (Jackson 6:12; Sugden 2:165; Outler 2:113)
   De Spectaculis
      LCM IV:III:5 (Jackson 10:42–43)
   (General References)
      AC II:1:[6] (Jackson 10:492)
      Sermons 61:24 (Jackson 6:261; Outler 2:461)
      Sermons 112 (132 in Jackson) :II:3 (Jackson 7:424; Outler 3:586)
   (Unidentified References)
      LCM [C]:3 (Jackson 10:9)
      STGG 1 (Jackson 10:506)

Theodoret
   (Unidentified Reference)

RC, Qu. 33 (Jackson 10:104)

Theophilus of Antioch
Ad Autolycum
LCM I:11 (Jackson 10:22)
LCM IV:I:4 (Jackson 10:39–40)

Notes

The following abbreviations designating standard reference works and series are utilized in the notes:

ANF: Alexander Roberts, James Donaldson, and A. Cleveland Coxe, eds., *The Ante-Nicene Fathers*. 10 vols. New York: Charles Scribner's Sons, 1885–1887.
BMC: Trustees of the British Museum, *The British Museum Catalogue of Printed Books*.
CBTEL: John McClintock and James Strong, eds., *Cyclopedia of Biblical, Theological, and Ecclesiastical Literature*. 12 vols. New York: Harper and Brothers, 1891.
CL¹: John Wesley, ed., *A Christian Library*. First edition. 50 vols. Bristol: Felix Farley, 1749–1755.
DNB: Leslie Stephen and Sidney Lee, eds., *Dictionary of National Biography*. 28 vols. Oxford: Clarendon Press, 1921–1922.
NSHERK: Samuel MacAuley Jackson, ed., *The New Shaff-Herzog Encyclopedia of Religious Knowledge*. 12 vols. New York and London: Funk and Wagnalls Company, 1908–1912.
NUC: *National Union Catalog: Pre-1956 Imprints*. 685 vols. London: Mansell, 1968–1980.
ODCC²: F. L. Cross and E. A. Livingstone, eds., *The Oxford Dictionary of the Christian Church*. Second edition, revised. Oxford: Oxford University Press, 1974.
PL: Jean-Paul Migne, ed., *Patrologiae Cursus Completus: Series Latina*. 221 vols. Paris: 1878–1890.

Preface

1. My article "Is It Just Nostalgia? The Renewal of Wesleyan Studies" (*Christian Century* 107:13 [18 April 1990], pp. 396–398) gives a sketch of contemporary work in Wesleyan Studies that grows out of a concern for renewal in the Wesleyan traditions.
2. Cf. Outler's introduction to *John Wesley* (A Library of Protestant Thought; New York: Oxford University Press, 1964), pp. 9–10, and especially the lengthy footnote on p. 9.

Chapter 1

1. John Wesley, sermon "On Laying the Foundation of the New Chapel, near the City-Road, London" II:1–4 (in Thomas Jackson, ed., *The Works of the Reverend John Wesley, A.M.* [London: Wesleyan Conference Office, 14 volumes, 1872], hereafter cited as "Jackson," 7:423–424; and in Albert C. Outler, ed., *Sermons* [4 vols., The Bicentennial Edition of

the Works of John Wesley; Nashville: Abingdon Press, 1984–1987], hereafter cited as "Outler," 3:585).

2. John Wesley, Preface to *Sermons on Several Occasions*, par. 5 (Outler 1:105; Jackson 5:3).

3. On Wesley's views and uses of Scripture, cf. William Arnett, "John Wesley: Man of One Book" (Ph.D. dissertation, Drew University, 1954), Thowald Kaellstad, *John Wesley and the Bible: A Psychological Study* (Upsalla: Upsalla University, 1974), Wilbur H. Mullen, "John Wesley's Method of Biblical Interpretation" (*Religion in Life* 47 [Spring 1978]: 99–108), R. M. Casto, "Exegetical Method in John Wesley's *Explanatory Notes on the New Testament*" (Ph.D. dissertation, Duke University, 1977), and George Allen Turner, *The More Excellent Way: The Scriptural Basis of the Wesleyan Message* (Winona Lake, IN: Light and Life Press, 1952). On Wesley and the Church of England, cf. David Baines-Griffiths, *Wesley the Anglican* (London: MacMillan and Co., Ltd., 1919), Frank Baker, *John Wesley and the Church of England* (Nashville: Abingdon Press, 1970), and R. Denny Urlin, *The Churchman's Life of Wesley* (London: SPCK, 1880).

4. Sermon "On Laying the Foundation of the New Chapel," II:1 (Jackson 7:423; Outler 3:585).

5. In Wesley's own time, something like this this appeared in the accusation that he was a Jesuit! From the late nineteenth century, cf. R. Denny Urlin, *John Wesley's Place in Church History* (London: Rivington's, 1870), pp. 59–86, and his *Churchman's Life of Wesley*; William F. Slater, *Methodism in the Light of the Early Church* (London: T. Woolmer, 1885); and in the same vein, though from early in this century, David Baines-Griffiths, *Wesley the Anglican* (London: The MacMillan Co., Ltd., 1919).

6. Maximin Piette, *John Wesley in the Evolution of Protestantism* (New York: Sheed and Ward, 1937; originally published in 1925 as *John Wesley: Sa Réaction dans l'Evolution du Protestantisme*); cf. the literature cited in the previous note, and Albert C. Outler, *Theology in the Wesleyan Spirit* (Nashville: Tidings, 1975), pp. 1–22. In a somewhat different vein are two more recent dissertations: Luke L. Keefer, "John Wesley, Disciple of Early Christianity" (Ph.D. dissertation, Temple University, 1982), and Arthur C. Meyers, "John Wesley and the Church Fathers" (Ph.D. dissertation, St. Louis University, 1985). The work by Meyers catalogs Wesley's patristic sources and seems to be inspired by the enterprise (mentioned in the text) of linking Methodism to its Catholic roots; Keefer's work traces the general theme of revivalism—both of the New Testament Church and the Church of the first few centuries—in Wesley.

7. Victor Turner, "Metaphors of Anti-Structure in Religious Culture," in Alan W. Eister, ed., *Changing Perspectives in the Scientific Study of Religion* (New York: John Wiley and Sons, 1974), pp. 63–84.

8. The critical term "Christian antiquity" denoted for Wesley and Christians of his age an historical period which might include the events described in the New Testament canon, but most characteristically included only events after the canonical age, roughly through the fifth century. "Christian antiquity," then, is in the first place a designation of an historical age or epoch, and in the second place a term for a particular source of religious authority. The definition of the later end of Christian antiquity (especially when considered as an authoritative period for Christian thought and practice) was much debated, but was often defined so as to include Augustine and the Council of Chalcedon, and so the term roughly denotes Christianity in the second through mid-fifth centuries.

9. See, for instance, the conclusion of Wesley's "Letter to Conyers Middleton" VI (Jackson 10:67–79).

10. "Culture" is understood as denoting the inheritance of humanly conceived structures (to which I may also refer as "patterns" or even "models") by which conduct and belief are guided.

11. I do not mean to imply that Wesley's own vision was determinative of the cultural shifts that Evangelicalism brought about, since there were numerous other leaders of the Evangelical Revival.

Chapter 2

1. The relationship of Wesley's thought, and that of English Evangelicals more broadly, to their contemporary culture, especially that of the Enlightenment, has been the subject of a number of recent studies: cf. Frederick Dreyer, "Faith and Experience in the Thought of John Wesley" (*American Historical Review* 88 [1983], pp. 12–30); Rex Dale Matthews, "'Religion and Reason Joined': A Study in the Theology of John Wesley" (Ph.D. dissertation, Harvard University, 1986); Richard E. Brantley, *Locke, Wesley, and the Method of English Romanticism* (Gainesville: University of Florida Press, 1984); D. W. Bebbington, *Evangelicalism in Modern Britain: A History from the 1730s to the 1980s* (London: Unwin Hyman, 1989), pp. 20–74; and Henry Rack, *Reasonable Enthusiast* (Philadelphia: Trinity Press International, 1989).

2. Cf. Herbert Pothorn, *Architectural Styles* (New York: The Viking Press, 1971), pp. 88–90.

3. Leslie Stephen and Sidney Lee, eds., *Dictionary of National Biography* (Oxford: Oxford University Press, 1921–1922; 28 vols.; hereafter cited as "DNB"), s.v. "Temple, William"; William Temple, *The Works of Sir William Temple, Bart.* (Edinburgh: G. Hamilton et al., 1754; 4 vols.), 2:141–181.

4. Temple, 2:181 (italicized in original).

5. Peter Gay, *The Enlightenment: An Interpretation*, vol. 1: *The Rise of Modern Paganism* (New York: Alfred A. Knopf, 1966), pp. xi, 31–58; quotation is on p. 31.

6. Cf. Schmidt, 1:70–71; Bebbington, pp. 67–69; John Wesley's Latin and Greek grammars are given in the fourteenth volume of the Jackson edition of his *Works*.

7. John Pearson, *An Exposition of the Creed* (New York: D. Appleton and Co., 1851), dedication (no pagination given).

8. Stanley Lawrence Greenslade, *The English Reformers and the Fathers of the Church* (Oxford: Clarendon Press, 1960), pp. 9–10; William P. Haugaard, "Renaissance Patristic Scholarship and Theology in Sixteenth-Century England," *Sixteenth-Century Journal* 10 (1979): 37–60; Norman Sykes, *From Sheldon to Secker* (Cambridge: Cambridge University Press, 1959), p. 107; Ted A. Campbell, "John Wesley's Conceptions and Uses of Christian Antiquity (Ph.D. dissertation, Southern Methodist University, 1984), appendix 1, "Some British Editions and Translations of the ante-Nicene Fathers Prior to 1800," pp. 317–320; Sykes, pp. 106–107; Greenslade, p. 13; Norman Sykes, *William Wake* (Cambridge: Cambridge University Press, 1957; 2 vols.), 1:63; Peter Meinhold, *Geschichte der kirchlichen Historiographie* (Munich: Verlag Karl Albert Freiburg, 1967; 2 vols.), 2:11–14.

9. On Cave, cf. DNB, s.v. "Cave, William"; William Cave, *Scriptorum Ecclesiasticorum Historia Literaria* (London: Richard Chiswell, 1688–1698; 2 vols.), *passim*.

10. Sykes, *From Sheldon to Secker*, pp. 107–111; DNB, s.v. "Pearson, John"; Sykes, *William Wake*, 1:62–69.

11. Glanmor Williams, *Reformation Views of Church History* (Richmond, Virginia: John Knox Press, 1970), pp. 7–21.

12. Yves M. J. Congar, *Tradition and Traditions* (New York: The Macmillan Co., 1967), pp. 139–145, 153–155.

13. See John Leith, ed., *Creeds of the Churches*, second edition (Atlanta: John Knox Press, 1973), pp. 403–405.

14. John K. Luoma, "Who Owns the Fathers? Hooker and Cartwright on the Authority of the Primitive Church," *Sixteenth-Century Journal* 8 (1977): 48–53.

15. John [i.e., Jean] Daillé, *A Treatise concerning the Right Use of the Fathers* (London: John Martin, 1651; trans. Thomas Smith), *passim*; see especially the "Designe of the whole Work," pp. v-viii. This edition has a list of approbations from English divines Lucius Cary (Viscount Falkland), George Digby, Jeremy Taylor, and Andrew Rivet (pp. ix-x); cf. Henry R. McAdoo, *The Spirit of Anglicanism* (New York: Charles Scribner's Sons, 1965), p. 316; Paul A. Welsby, *Lancelot Andrewes, 1555–1626* (London: SPCK, 1958), pp. 156–157.

16. Loc. not given; cited in Greenslade, pp. 8–9.

17. McAdoo, pp. 319–320; McAdoo refers to Hooker's *Ecclesiastical Polity*, book 5, chs. 6–8; Luoma, pp. 53–58.

18. Lancelot Andrewes, *Opuscula quaedam posthumata* (Oxford: John Henry Parker, 1852; Library of Anglo-Catholic Theology edition), p. 91; cited in McAdoo, p. 320; cf. McAdoo, pp. 317–318; Welsby, pp. 154–157.

19. Cited in McAdoo, p. 318.

20. Luoma, pp. 49–50, n. 29; McAdoo, p. 320.

21. McAdoo, pp. v-vii and *passim*; Gerald R. Cragg, *Freedom and Authority* (Philadelphia: The Westminster Press, 1975), pp. 118–124.

22. Pearson, *Exposition*, dedication (no pagination given).

23. DNB, s.v. "Pearson, John"; Pearson, *Exposition*, dedication (no pagination given).

24. William Wake, trans., *The Genuine Epistles of the Apostolical Fathers* (London: Richard Sare, fourth edition, 1693), [1:]175. There are two sequences of pagination in this book, one for Wake's preliminary materials, the other for his translations. In this and subsequent references I have indicated the sequence by a "1" or "2" in square brackets.

25. William Reeves, trans., *The Apologies of Justin Martyr, Tertullian, and Minucius Felix in Defence of the Christian Religion* (2 vols., London: A. and J. Churchill, 1709), pp. i-ii.

26. Ibid., pp. iii-iv.

27. John Pearson, *Vindiciae Epistolarum S. Ignatii* (Oxford: John Henry Parker, 1852; 2 vols.), *passim*; Sykes, *From Sheldon to Secker*, pp. 107–111; DNB, s.v. "Pearson, John."

28. Reeves, pp. xxii-xxxiv; quotation is on p. xxxii.

29. Ibid., p. iii.

30. Sykes, *From Sheldon to Secker*, pp. 111–113.

31. Robert Nelson, *A Companion to the Festivals and Fasts of the Church of England* (London: SPCK, 1845), *passim*; DNB, s.v. "Nelson, Robert."

32. Reeves, pp. xvii-xviii.

33. George Bull, *Defensio Fidei Nicaenae: A Defence of the Nicene Creed, out of the Extant Writings of the Catholick Doctors, who Flourished during the First Three Centuries of the Christian Church* (Oxford: John Henry Parker, 1851; 2 vols.), 1:vi-vii, 5–12; idem, *The Judgement of the Catholic Church on the Necessity of Believing that our Lord Jesus Christ is very God* (Oxford: John Henry Parker, 1855), *passim*; DNB, s.v. "Bull, George"; Sykes, *From Sheldon to Secker*, pp. 140–142.

34. [John Edward] Christopher Hill, *The World Turned Upside Down* (New York: Penguin Books, 1976), *passim*.

35. Meinhold, 1:357–363. The expression *traditio quinsecularis* is not from Calixtus himself, but is a later description of his teaching.

36. Edward Stillingfleet, *The Irenicum: or, Pacificator* (Philadelphia: M. Sorin, 1842), *passim*.

37. Peter King, *An Enquiry into the Constitution, Discipline, Unity and Worship of the Primitive Church* (New York: P. P. Sandford, 1841), pp. 13–14, 17–18.

38. Ibid., pp. 62–79.

39. Sykes, *From Sheldon to Secker*, p. 141.

NOTES TO PAGES 17–27

40. Duffy, p. 299; DNB, s.v. "Whiston, William"; Sykes, *From Sheldon to Secker*, pp. 165–167; Cragg, pp. 136–137.

41. William Beveridge, ed., *Synodikon, sive Pandectae Canonum Ss. Apostolorum et Conciliorum Ecclesia Graeca Receptorum* (Oxford: William Wells and Robert Scott, 1672; 2 vols.), *passim*; cf. ODCC^2, s.v. "Apostolic Canons."

42. William Beveridge, *Codex Canonum Ecclesiae Primitivae Vindicatus ac Illustratus* (Oxford: John Henry Parker, 1847; 2 vols.), *passim*, esp. 1:xxviii-xxxvii.

43. Ibid., 1:xvi-xxv; quotation is 1:xxiv-xxv; Meinhold, 1:363–369.

44. Nathaniel Marshall, *The Penitential Discipline of the Primitive Church* (Oxford: John Henry Parker, 1844), *passim*; Duffy, pp. 296–297. Marshall was also known for a translation of Cyprian.

45. Congar, pp. 185–186.

46. William Cave, *Primitive Christianity: or, the Religion of the Ancient Christians in the First Ages of the Gospel* (London: Thomas Tegg, 1840), p. iii.

47. Ibid., p. iv.

48. Cited in DNB, s.v. "Cave, William."

49. I have had access to two English translations (both anonymous) of Fleury's work: *An Historical Account of the Manners and Behaviour of the Christians* (London: Thomas Leigh, 1698) and *The Manners of the Christians* (Oxford: A. R. Mowbray, 1872); cf. ODCC^2, s.v. "Fleury."

50. Philipp Jakob Spener, *Pia Desideria*, trans. Theodore G. Tappert, (Philadelphia: Fortress Press, 1964), pp. 39, 40–41, 44, 49, 81–85, 104, 111–112.

51. Ernst Benz, *Die protestantische Thebais: Zur Nachwirkung Makarios des Ägypters im Protestantismus der 16. und 17. Jahrhunderts in Europa und Amerika* (Wiesbaden: Verlag der Akademie der Wissenschaften und der Literatur in Mainz, 1963), *passim* and esp. pp. 129–131; Johannes Quasten, *Patrology* (Westminster, Maryland: Newman Press, 1960; 3 vols.), 3:162.

52. Anthony Horneck, *The Happy Ascetick: or, the Best Exercise* (London: Henry Mortlock, 4th edn., 1699), "Epistle Dedicatory" (no pagination).

53. Ibid., pp. 553–603; list of early Christian writers is on p. 602.

Chapter 3

1. Samuel Wesley, *Dissertationes in Librum Jobi* (London: William Bowyer, 1736) *passim*. Most editions of this work have a new title-page with the date 1736, although it was published in 1735; cf. BMC, s.v. "Wesley, Samuel," etc.

2. [Samuel Wesley,] *The Young Student's Library* (London: John Dunton, 1692), p. iv.

3. Samuel Wesley, *Advice to a Young Clergyman, in a Letter to Him* (London: C. Rivington, 1735), pp. i, 22–42.

4. Ibid., pp. 46–50.

5. Ibid., p. 56.

6. Samuel Wesley, letters to John Wesley 1725/01/26 and 07/14 (in Baker 1:158, 171).

7. Diaries 1726/09/23 (Ms. Colman I [The first volume of the Oxford diaries is unnumbered in the Colman Collection. I shall refer to it as "Ms. Colman I"]:78), 1726/11/15 (Ms. Colman I:91, 1726/12/12 (Ms. Colman I:95), 1730/08/20–09/22 (Ms. Colman 3:54–58), 1730/09/10–10/25 (Ms. Colman 3:56–61).

8. Cited in Wesley, Letters 1733/06/13 (Baker 1:350–351).

9. The beginnings of the Wednesday and Friday fasts are reported in the following loci: 1) a letter to Richard Morgan, Sr., which appears as the introduction to published editions of Wesley's *Journal* under the title "The Rise and Design of Oxford Methodism"

(Baker 1:343; Nehemiah Curnock, ed., *The Journal of The Reverend John Wesley, A.M.* [8 vols.; New York: Eaton and Mains, 1938; hereafter cited as "Curnock"], 1:101; W. Reginald Ward and Richard P. Heitzenrater, eds., *Journals and Diaries* [The Bicentennial Edition of the Works of John Wesley; Nashville: Abingdon Press, 1988ff.; hereafter cited as "Ward and Heitzenrater"], 1:131–132); 2) a review of Wesley's life which precedes the account of his Aldersgate Street experience in the *Journal* 1738:05:24 (Curnock 1:468; Ward and Heitzenrater 1:245); and 3) a sermon on the "Causes of the Inefficacy of Christianity" (Jackson 7:288; Outler 4:94).

10. Nelson, p. 362. There is a reference at this point to Tertullian, *De Ieiuniis* 2 (PL 2:1007). Wesley's readings in Nelson are noted in his diary for 1731/09/17 (Ms. Colman 3:100).

11. Heitzenrater, "John Wesley and the Oxford Methodists," p. 163, note 2; cf. Wesley, diaries 1732/06 (Ms. Colman 3:100). Both John Wesley and Benjamin Ingham observed the sixteenth day of the month as a fast, apparently following an ancient Christian institution reported in a pamphlet entitled *The Penitential Office for the Sixteenth Day of the Month.* Unfortunately, we have been unable to locate an extant copy of this work, and the ancient origin of the fast on the sixteenth remains an unsolved mystery; cf. Richard P. Heitzenrater, ed., *Diary of an Oxford Methodist: Benjamin Ingham, 1733–1734* (Durham, NC: Duke University Press, 1985), p. 15 and note 17, and p. 198, note 128.

12. Letters 1733/06/13 (Baker 1:350–351), 1734/01/15 (Baker 1:367).

13. *Fog's Weekly Journal* 9 December 1732; cited in Heitzenrater, "John Wesley and the Oxford Methodists," pp. 189–190.

14. Diaries 1732/06/20–21 (Ms. Colman 9:1), 1733/08 (Ms. Colman 9b:9), 1732/08/09 (Ms. Colman 9:12), 1732/08/11 and 25 (Ms. Colman 9:13 and 15), 1733/06/13 (Ms. Colman 9:137).

15. See the discussion of the Manchester Non-Jurors and their attachment to the Apostolic Canons and Constitutions in chapter one.

16. Diaries (Ms. Colman 2:166; cited in Heitzenrater, "John Wesley and the Oxford Methodists," p. 161, n. 2, pp. 429–430).

17. *Journal* 1732/08 (Curnock 1:101); diaries 1732/08/11 and 25 (Ms. Colman 9:13, 15).

18. ODCC², s.v. "Non-Jurors."

19. Thomas Lathbury, *A History of the Non-Jurors* (London: William Pickering, 1845), pp. 309–361.

20. Charles Edward Mallet, *A History of the University of Oxford* (New York: Longmans, Green, and Co., 1924; 3 vols.), 3:33–43.

21. Baker, *John Wesley and the Church of England*, p. 31; Green, *The Young Mr. Wesley*, pp. 81–82.

22. Lathbury, pp. 492–496; cf. Schmidt, 1:102–103. Schmidt distinguishes between the Non-Jurors who used the 1549 Prayer Book and those who used Deacon's work, but gives no evidence for this distinction, and cites Lathbury. Lathbury, by contrast, does distinguish the "Usagers" from other Non-Jurors, but does not distinguish between those Usagers who preferred the 1549 Prayer Book and those who utilized Deacon's book. I suspect that Schmidt was simply confused on this point, and that the Usagers originally used the 1549 Prayer Book, then, with the publication of Deacon's *Compleat Collection of Devotions*, began to use the latter.

23. Wesley ms. cited in Heitzenrater, "John Wesley and the Oxford Methodists," pp. 160, 339; cf. Ward and Heitzenrater, 1:212

24. Lathbury, pp. 277–303.

25. Lathbury, pp. 496–501.

26. Letter from John Clayton to John Wesley, 1735/09 (given in Baker 1:433); cf. Wesley's diary 1735/10/18 (Ward and Heitzenrater 1:313).

27. Cited in Wesley, Letters 1733/07/[25] (Baker 1:352); on Wesley's visit to Manchester, cf. Baker, *John Wesley and the Church of England*, p. 31.

28. Cited in Wesley, Letters 1733/09/10 (Baker 1:355–356).

29. Cited in Wesley, Letters 1733/08/02 (Baker 1:392).

30. Ibid.

31. Wesley ms. cited in Baker, *John Wesley and the Church of England*, pp. 40–41; passages italicized are struck through in the original.

32. Baker, *John Wesley and the Church of England*, pp. 350–354.

33. Diaries 1733/03 (Ms. Colman 9b:38), 1733/06/07 (Ms. Colman 9:80), 1733/09/25 (Ms. Colman 9b:50), 1733/10/04 (Ms. Colman 10:1), 1734/07 (Ms. Colman 10b:23); cf. Heitzenrater, "John Wesley and the Oxford Methodists," pp. 508, 510, 512, 523; ODCC², s.v. "Vincent of Lérins."

34. Diaries 1734/03/08 (Ms. Colman 10:91), 1734/03/17 (Ms. Colman 10:100), 1734/09/18 (Ms. Colman 16:12), 1734/12/02 (Ms. Colman 16:86), 1735/02/25 (Ms. Colman 16:170); cf. Heitzenrater, "John Wesley and the Oxford Methodists," pp. 497, 500, 507, 516.

35. Cited in Wesley, Letters 1733/09/10 (Baker 1:355–356).

36. Diaries 1733/04/15, 18 (Ms. Colman 9:66–67); 1733/07/2, 5.

37. Wesley, ms. given in Appendix 1 of this book.

38. Deacon, title page.

39. Given in Deacon, pp. 72–74.

40. Wesley ms. cited in Heitzenrater, "John Wesley and the Oxford Methodists," p. 259.

41. Benjamin Ingham, diary for 1734/05/04 (Heitzenrater, ed., *Diary of an Oxford Methodist*, p. 185; cf. Heitzenrater, "John Wesley and the Oxford Methodists," pp. 270–271).

42. Benjamin Ingham, diary for 1734/04/25 (Heitzenrater, ed., *Diary of an Oxford Methodist*, pp. 204–205; cf. "John Wesley and the Oxford Methodists," pp. 270–271).

43. Cited in Wesley, Letters 1735/09 (Baker 1:438).

44. Letters 1735/09/30 (Baker 1:438).

45. Cited in Baker, *John Wesley and the Church of England*, p. 40.

46. Diaries 1735/10/25–28 (Ms. Colman 1:4–7; Curnock 1:114–115; Ward and Heitzenrater 1:315–316), and 1736/01/26 (Ms. Colman 1:93; Curnock 1:143; Ward and Heitzenrater 1:345).

47. Schmidt, 1:152.

48. Cited in Schmidt, 1:138, n. 6.

49. Norman Sykes, *From Sheldon to Secker* (Cambridge: Cambridge University Press, 1959), p. 138.

50. Cited in Schmidt, 1:138, n. 6.

51. Diaries 1736/03/16–04/02 (Ms. Colman 11:142–157; Curnock 1:183–191; Ward and Heitzenrater 1:369–374); cf. DNB, s.v. "Echard, Laurence"; Laurence Echard, *A General Ecclesiastical History* (London: W. Bowyer for Jacob Jonson, 1702), sig. "b," pp. 1–3, p. 183, and *passim*.

52. Diaries 1736/04/24 (Easter Eve, 1739; Ms. Colman 11:170; Curnock 1:198; Ward and Heitzenrater 1:379); 1736/09/19 (Emory University ms., p. 126; hereafter cited as Georgia Diary II; Curnock 1:276; Ward and Heitzenrater 1:424); 1736/10/05 (Georgia Diary II:141; Curnock 1:279; Ward and Heitzenrater 1:428); 1736/10/10 and 16 (Georgia Diary II:146; Curnock 1:279; Ward and Heitzenrater 1:429, 432; cf. *Journal* 1736/10/16 (Curnock 1:283; Ward and Heitzenrater 1:172).

53. Diaries 1737/03/08 and 07/07 (Curnock 1:328; Ward and Heitzenrater 1:482); 1737/07/11 (Curnock 1:368; Ward and Heitzenrater 1:526); 1737/05/13 (Curnock 1:356; Ward and Heitzenrater 1:507).

54. References to Wesley's study of Fleury are given in the diaries for the following dates: 1736/04/24, 28–29, 05/04, 09/13, 18, 10/25, 1737/03/13, 05/18, 07/18, 28–29 (Curnock 1:198, 202, 210, 275, 276, 288, 338, 343, 356–357, 370–371; Ward and Heitzenrater 1:379, 380, 382, 422, 423, 435, 488, 509, 529, 530), and in the *Journal* 1736/10/25, 1737/10/23 (Curnock 1:289, 397; Ward and Heitzenrater 1:435, 567). The mss. of Wesley's abridgements of Fleury's *Catéchisme historique* and *Moeurs des Chrétiens* are in Ms. Colman 15, in the Methodist Archives, the John Rylands University Library, Manchester. I have utilized a photocopy of the mss., and I have compared them against both of the English translations of Fleury mentioned in chapter two, note 44.

55. Ms. Colman 15:1–54, *passim*.

56. *Journal* 1736/02/21 (Curnock 1:166–167; Ward and Heitzenrater 1:150).

57. *Journal* 1737/09/11, reflecting Wesley's actions on 1736/03/10 (Curnock 1:393; Ward and Heitzenrater 1:563–564).

58. *Journal* 1736/02/28 (Curnock 1:170–171; Ward and Heitzenrater 1:151); cf. Schmidt, 1:156.

59. DNB, s.v. "Deacon, Thomas."

60. *Journal* 1736/09/13 (Curnock 1:274–275; Ward and Heitzenrater 1:171–172; bracketed portions deleted in one ms.).

61. Ibid., diary section.

62. Diaries 1736/09/21 (Curnock 1:277; Ward and Heitzenrater 1:425); perhaps Wesley's statement in the *Journal* account for 13 September mistakenly reflects his consideration of the *Synodikon* after 21 September.

63. *Journal* 1736/09/20 (Curnock 1:276–278; Ward and Heitzenrater 1:424; bracketed portions are omitted in one ms.).

64. Beveridge, *Codex Canonum Ecclesiae Primitivae Vindicatus ac Illustratus* (London: Robert Scott, 1678; reprint by University Microfilms International), pp. 158–159 (cf. Library of Anglo-Catholic Theology edition, 1:205–207).

65. *Journal* 1736/09/21–10/04 (Curnock 1:277–279; Ward and Heitzenrater 1:425–428).

66. Wesley ms. cited in Baker, *John Wesley and the Church of England*, p. 357, n. 75.

67. Cited in Outler, *John Wesley*, p. 46; Heitzenrater, "John Wesley and the Oxford Methodists," p. 531.

68. *Journal* 1738/05/24 (Curnock 1:465–477; Ward and Heitzenrater 1:242–251); 1738/06/14–09/16 (Curnock 2:3–63; Ward and Heitzenrater 1:255–297 [the Ward and Heitzenrater edition leaves off at 14 August); 1738/11/12 (Curnock 2:101); 1739/04/02 (Curnock 2:172–173); and 1740/07/16, 20, 23 (Curnock 2:365–366, 369–371); cf. Baker, *John Wesley and the Church of England*, pp. 52–57, 74–77.

69. Eamon Duffy asserts that in 1738 Wesley gave up his pursuit of "primitive Christianity": "Primitive Christianity Revived: Religious Renewal in Augustan England," in Derek Baker, ed., *Renaissance and Renewal in Christian History* (Studies in Church History, no. 14; Oxford: Basil Blackwell, 1977), pp. 299–300.

70. See Appendix 2, where I have listed references to these works.

71. See the material cited below in this chapter, as well as the next two chapters.

72. Cyprian: *Journal* 1738/01/09 (Jackson 1:73; Curnock 1:416; Ward and Heitzenrater 1:209); Pseudo-Dionysius: *Journal* 1741/11/7–15 (Jackson 1:347; Curnock 2:515); 1741/11/19 (Jackson 1:347; Curnock 2:515); on Turrettini, cf. NSHERK, s.v. "Turrettini" and NUC, s.v. "Turrettini."

73. Poem "On Clemens Alexandrinus's Description of a Perfect Christian," in John and Charles Wesley, *Hymns and Sacred Poems* (1739), given in George Osborn, ed., *The Poetical Works of John and Charles Wesley* (13 vols.; London: Wesleyan Conference Office, 1868), 1:37–38.

74. A note in a biography of John Gambold indicates his fondness for ancient Christian mystical writers: in *The Works of the Late Reverend John Gambold, A.M.* (Bath: S. Hazard, 1789), pp. iii-iv.

75. *Journal* 1767/03/05 (Jackson 3:273, Curnock 5:197).

76. Specific teachings common to the two are: hope of immortality, "Character of a Methodist" 7 (Jackson 8:342–343) vs. *Stromateis* 7:13 (ANF 2:547a); prayer without ceasing, "Character of a Methodist" 8 (Jackson 8:343) vs. *Stromateis* 7:12 (ANF 2:544a); love of neighbor, "Character of a Methodist" 9 (Jackson 8:343) vs. *Stromateis* 7:12 (ANF 2:544b-545a); obedience to God's commandments, "Character of a Methodist" 12 (Jackson 8:344) vs. *Stromateis* 7:12 (ANF 2:546b); and freedom from worldly desires, "Character of a Methodist" 15 (Jackson 8:345) vs. *Stromateis* 7:12 (ANF 2:545b).

77. *Farther Appeal, Part I*, V:15–23 (Cragg, pp. 154–166).

78. Cf. Frank Baker, note on Wesley, Letters 1745/05 (from "John Smith"; Baker, 2:138, n. 18); cf. Outler, *John Wesley*, p. 3. The following is the catena of five interchanges, noting the specific parts of the letters referring to the patristic period: "Smith," 1746/08/11, par. 7 (Baker 2:211); Wesley, 1747/03/25, par. 7 (Baker 2:223–233); "Smith," 1747/04/27, par. 7 (Baker 2:240); Wesley, 1747/07/10, par. 6–7 (Baker 2:246–248); "Smith," 1747/08/21, par. 8 (Baker 2:260).

79. *Journal* 1746/01/20 (Jackson 2:6–7, Curnock 2:232).

80. John Telford, introduction to "A Plain Account of the People Called Methodists" (Telford 2:292).

81. "Plain Account of the People Called Methodists," introduction, par. 2 (Jackson 8:248, Telford 2:292).

82. Ibid., I:10 (Jackson 8:251, Telford 2:294–295).

83. Cf. Baker, *John Wesley and the Church of England*, pp. 106–136.

84. Leslie Stephen, article in DNB, s.v., "Middleton, Conyers" (13:343–348); idem, *History of English Thought in the Eighteenth Century* (third edition, 1902; reprint edition of Harcourt Brace, and World, Inc., Harbinger Books, New York, 1962), 1:213–230; Conyers Middleton, *A Free Inquiry into the Miraculous Powers, Which are Supposed to have Subsisted in the Christian Church from the Earliest Ages* (London: R. Manby and H. S. Cox, 1749 [sic]; reprint edition, New York and London: Garland Publishing, Inc., 1976). Cf. Ted A. Campbell, "John Wesley and Conyers Middleton on Divine Intervention in History," *Church History* 55:1 (March 1986): 39–49.

85. ODCC[2], s.v. "Fleury, Claude" (p. 518); Wesley's manuscript is ms. Colman 15, cf. pp. 16, 20, 21, and 38–45. The ODCC[2] article errs in its assertion that Wesley's edition of Fleury appeared in the *Christian Library*.

86. Campbell, "John Wesley's Conceptions and Uses of Christian Antiquity," pp. 118–121.

87. *Christian Library*[1] 1:i-iv.

88. Wesley had read in Macarius while in Georgia: Diaries 1736/07/30 (Curnock 1:254; Ward and Heitzenrater 1:405); on the translator of *Primitive Morality*, cf. Campbell, "John Wesley's Conceptions and Uses of Christian Antiquity," pp. 121–124.

89. Anthony Horneck, *The Happy Ascetick, or, the Best Exercise*, pp. 553ff.; the 1660 Latin letter is that of Jean Fronteau, *Epistola ad ... Franc. de Harlay ... in qua de Moribus et Vita Christianorum in Primis Ecclesiae Saeculis Agitur* (Paris: C. Savreux, 1660); cf. Campbell, "John Wesley's Conceptions and Uses of Christian Antiquity," pp. 124–126.

90. Cave, *Primitive Christianity*[4], passim and [1:xiii]; *Christian Library*[1] 31:149–298.

91. ODCC[2], s.v. "Mosheim, Johann Lorenz von,"; Wesley, ed., *A Concise Ecclesiastical History*. Wesley adds paragraphs or notes in the first volume concerning Montanus (par. XI, p. 114), the representation of Origen as a "mystic" theologian (note "a," p. 133), Novatian (par. following par. XI, p. 145), Pelagius (note "a," p. 248), and Muhammad (par. III, pp. 282–283).

92. "An Address to the Clergy" (Jackson 10:480–500); Wesley's suggestions for reading in ancient Christian writers appear at I:2:[6] and II:[6] (Jackson 10:484, 492).

93. "Letter to Conyers Middleton," [B]:12 (Jackson 10:7); cf. ibid. [C]:15 (Jackson 10:14).

94. *Sermons* 132:II:3 (Jackson 7:424; Outler 3:586).

95. [Fleury], *Manners of the Ancient Christians*, ed. Wesley, 1:1 (1798 edn., p. 3); similarly, Wesley's edn. of Horneck's "Letter to a Person of Quality" describes early Christianity as having all of its perfections in its infancy (CL^1 29:112–114).

96. "Letter to Conyers Middleton" [C]:10 (Jackson 10:11); Horneck, "Letter to a Person of Quality" in *Happy Ascetick*^{4}, p. 555 (cf. CL^1 29:112).

97. "An Address to the Clergy" I:2 (Jackson 10:484). For references to the persistence of miraculous powers in the pre-Constantinian church, see below under "Inspiration and Miraculous Gifts among the Early Christians." On the anonymous saints of the pre-Constantinian church, cf. "Letter to Conyers Middleton" IV:VI:3–6 (Jackson 10:54–55).

98. "Letter to Conyers Middleton" [C]:15 (Jackson 10:14); cf. ibid, II:9 (Jackson 10:27) and IV:VI:15 (Jackson 10:59); Letters 1782/02/22 (to J. Benson; Telford 7:105); "An Address to the Clergy" II:1:[7] (Jackson 10:493).

99. [Fleury], *Manners of the Ancient Christians*, ed. Wesley, 3:3 (1798 edn., p. 10).

100. Ibid. 2:3 (1798 edn., p. 8).

101. Ibid. 2:2, 2:6 (1798 edn., pp. 7, 9); [Mosheim], *A Concise Ecclesiastical History*, ed. Wesley, I:II:III:3 (1781 edn., 1:64) and I:II:V:7 (1781 edn., 1:75–76).

102. "An Address to the Clergy" II:1:[6] (Jackson 10:492); on Wesley's inclusion of the Apostolic Fathers in the second century, see Wesley's *Sermons* 132:II:3 (Jackson 7:424; Outler 3:586).

103. [Mosheim], *A Concise Ecclesiastical History*, ed. Wesley, I:II:II:9 (1781 ed., 1:60–61). That Wesley was aware of corruptions in the biblical texts appears from his alteration of a passage in Ignatius' Epistle to the Philadelphians, ch. 8. Here Ignatius asserts that Jesus Christ is the principal monument to which Christians appeal, and argues against those who asserted that if something did not "appear" in the biblical texts, they would not believe it. Wake renders the expression "that it does not appear," and Wesley alters it to "what [did not] lay before them in their corrupt manuscripts," a fairly elaborate expansion, the intent of which seems to be to move the issue from that of scriptural authority to particular scriptural texts: Wake [2]: 183; C11 1:57; cf. the note on this difficult passage in the LCL edition of the Apostolic Fathers, 1:247. The passage from I Clement referred to in the text (using the legend of the Phoenix) is ch. 25; Wesley's comments on it come in his "Letter to Conyers Middleton" I:7 (Jackson 10:20).

104. Cave, *Primitive Christianity*, ed. Wesley, I:VI:3 (CL^1 31:180).

105. Cf. the account of persecutions and martyrdoms in Cave, *Primitive Christianity*, ed. Wesley, II:II:VII:1–12 (CL^1 31:248–255); on the persistence of miraculous gifts to aid the church in persecutions and in propagating the faith, cf. "Letter to Conyers Middleton" [B]:11–12 (Jackson 10:6–7).

106. Horneck, "Letter to a Person of Quality" (*Happy Ascetick*^{4}, p. 567; cf. CL^1 29:119); Ignatius, Romans 5 (Wake [2]:164; cf. CL^1 1:52); "Martyrdom of Polycart" 7 (Wake [2]:237; cf. CL^1 1:74); Cave, *Primitive Christianity* (1682 edn., II;192ff.; cf. CL^1 31:259).

107. "An Address to the Clergy" II:I:[6] (Jackson 10:492); *Sermons* 112:II:3 (Jackson 7:424; Outler 3:586): cf. "Letter to Conyers Middleton" VI:VIII:II (Jackson 10:79).

108. See references under these writers in Appendix Two.

109. "Letter to Conyers Middleton" [C]:11 (Jackson 10:12); *Sermons* 102:17 (Jackson 7:164; Outler 3:450–451).

110. *Journal* 1754/08/05 (Jackson 2:314; Curnock 4:96–97); to this one may compare Voltaire's ridicule of the councils under "Councils" (*conciles*) in the *Encyclopédie philosophique*.

111. *Sermons* 104:14 (Jackson 7:178; Outler 3:469–470).

112. *Sermons* 102:15–16 (Jackson 7:163–164; Outler 3:449–450); cf. DNB, s.v. "Newton, Thomas" (14:403–405).

113. *Sermons* 89:2 (Jackson 7:26–27; Outler 3:263–264); 102:15–16 (Jackson 7:163–164; Outler 3:449–450); [Fleury], *Manners of the Ancient Christians*, ed. Wesley, 8:7 (1798 edn., p. 24).

114. [Mosheim], *A Concise Ecclesiastical History*, ed. Wesley, IV:I:I:4–5, IV:I:II:1 (1781 edn., 1:164–166).

115. *Sermons* 89:2 (Jackson 7:26–27; Outler 263–264), 115:7–8 (Jackson 7:275–276; Outler 4:77–78); "The Origin of Image-Worship" (Jackson 10:175–177). On the cessation of miraculous powers in the fourth century, see under "Inspiration and Miraculous Powers among the Early Christians"; on the elaboration of rituals after the fourth century, see under "Customs of the Early Christians."

116. "Address to the Clergy" I:2"[6] (Jackson 10:484).

117. *Sermons* 132:II:3 (Jackson 7:424; Outler 3:586); "Letter to Conyers Middleton" VI:III:11 (Jackson 10:79).

118. See the entries under Augustine and Jerome in Appendix Two; for Wesley's scathing criticisms of Augustine, see below under "Teachings and Heresies of the Early Church."

119. *Sermon* 132, "On Laying the Foundation . . .," II:1 (Jackson 7:423; Outler 3:585).

120. Ibid., II:3 (Jackson 7:424; Outler 3:586).

121. Letters 1784/09/10, to "Our Brethren in America," par. 6 (Outler, *John Wesley*, p. 84).

122. Coke and Asbury, *The Doctrines and Discipline of the Methodist Episcopal Church in America, with Explanatory Notes* (Philadelphia: Henry Tuckniss, 1798), pp. 45–46.

123. *Sermons* 61 (Jackson 6:253–267; Outler 2:451–470), especially pars. 23–28 (Jackson 6:260–262; Outler 2:460–464).

124. *Sermons* 102 (Jackson 7:157–166; Outler 3:440–453), especially pars. 15–17 (Jackson 7:163–164; Outler 3:449–451).

125. *Sermons* 115 (Jackson 7:273–281; Outler 4:72–84); cf. *Journal* 1789/03/30 and 04/12 (Jackson 4:449 and 451, Curnock 7:482–483 and 486).

Chapter 4

1. A critical presupposition of this and the next chapter is that it is possible to discern how Wesley utilized his conceptions of Christian antiquity, based on available sources. The historical evidence for John Wesley's uses of Christian antiquity varies according to the explicitness with which he expressed his intentions for those uses. One might rank it in the following manner: (a) passages in which Wesley explicitly stated his intentions(s) in using conceptions of Christian antiquity (for example, a passage in which Wesley stated that the ancient Christians exhibited true Christianity, in contrast to the Christians of Wesley's own age); (b) passages in which Wesley cited ancient authorities in favor of his own beliefs and practices, or against beliefs and practices to which he was opposed (for example, a passage in which Wesley cited Epiphanius in favor of Wednesday and Friday fasts); (c) passages in which Wesley upheld particular beliefs and practices conformable to, but not specifically referenced to, his conceptions of Christian antiquity (for example, a passage in which Wesley suggests that the Methodists ought to work towards a community of possessions); and (d) passages from works which Wesley edited which either include references to ancient beliefs and practices to which Wesley's beliefs and practices conformed, or omits references to ancient beliefs or practices which Wesley opposed. All of

these forms of evidence must be treated with caution, but especially the last two. In cases where Wesley did not refer explicitly to ancient Christian precedents, one must ask whether the beliefs and practices he advocated do not conform more directly to his conceptions of New Testament Christianity, or to precedent Anglican or other forms of Christianity.

2. See above under "A Vision of Christian Teaching"; "Letter to Conyers Middleton" VI:II:1–12 (Jackson 10:72–75).

3. Wesley's understanding of the *ordo salutis* respecting the individual Christian life is discussed in standard works treating Wesley's thought: Outler, *Theology in the Wesleyan Spirit, passim*; Williams, *John Wesley's Theology Today, passim*.

4. Letters 1771/04/14 (to Miss March; Telford 5:237).

5. Wesley, preface to [Mosheim], *Concise Ecclesiastical History*, ed. Wesley, 6–7 (1781 edn., 1:v-vi).

6. [Fleury], *Manners of the Ancient Christians*, ed. Wesley, 2:1 (1798 edn., p. 7).

7. Ibid. 1:1 (1798 edn., p. 3).

8. Cave, *Primitive Christianity*, preface (1682 edn., p. xii).

9. Ibid.

10. Horneck, "Letter to a Person of Quality," ed. Wesley, *passim* (CL[1] 29:109–138).

11. "Letter to Conyers Middleton" VI:III:12 (Jackson 10:79).

12. "Character of a Methodist," inscription (Jackson 8:339).

13. Ibid., preface, par. 4 (Jackson 8:339).

14. *Earnest Appeal* 6–7 (Cragg, pp. 46–47).

15. *Sermons* 18 (Jackson 5:212–223; Sugden 1:280–297; Outler 1:415–430).

16. Letters 1745/12/30 (to "John Smith," par. 13; Telford 2:64; Baker 2:182).

17. "John Smith," letter to John Wesley, 1747/04/25, pars. 7–8 (Baker 2:240).

18. Letters 1747/07/10 (to "John Smith," par. 7; Baker 2:247).

19. *Farther Appeal*, Part I V:16–22 (Cragg, pp. 156–163).

20. Ibid. V:18 (Cragg, pp. 157–159).

21. Ibid. V:22 (Cragg, p. 163).

22. "John Smith," letter to John Wesley, 1746/08/11, par. 7 (Baker 2:211).

23. Idem, letter to John Wesley, 1747/04/25, pars. 7–8 (Baker 2:240).

24. Letters 1747/07/10 (to "John Smith," par. 11; Baker 2:251).

25. Ibid. (par. 7; Baker 2:247).

26. *Sermons* 110 and 113 (Jackson 7:231–238, 256–264; Outler 4:28–38, 48–59). In these two sermons Wesley laid out in some detail his views of faith as a "sense" of the soul, the epistemological ground of religious belief.

27. *Farther Appeal*, Part I V:1 (Cragg, p. 139).

28. Ibid. V:4 (Cragg, p. 141).

29. Ibid. V:15–23 (Cragg, pp. 154–166).

30. "John Smith," letter to John Wesley, 1747/074/25, pars. 7–8 (Baker 2:240).

31. Letters 1747/07/10 (to "John Smith," par. 11; Baker 2:251).

32. Cited in Cragg, p. 354.

33. "Letter to the Author of 'The Enthusiasm of Methodists and Papists Compar'd'" 17–18 (Jackson 9:6–8; Telford 3:264–265; Cragg, pp. 367–368).

34. The *via* or *ordo salutis* can be seen, in brief, in Wesley's sermon on "The Scripture Way of Salvation" (Jackson 6:43–54; Sugden 2:442–460; Outler 2:152–169), but appears throughout the sermons, particular ones of which deal with specific stages of the *ordo salutis* ("Justification by Faith," "Christian Perfection," "The Wilderness State," etc.). Williams's *John Wesley's Theology Today* and Outler's *Theology in the Wesleyan Spirit* describe Wesley's thought using the *ordo salutis*.

35. Cf. Campbell, "John Wesley's Conceptions and Uses of Christian Antiquity," Appendix 4, Table 5.

36. Cave, *Primitive Christianity* II:11:1 (CL^1 31:229).

37. Homily 2 (*Primitive Morality*, pp. 107–109; cf. CL^1 1:91); 2 (*Primitive Morality*, p. 111; cf. CL^1 1:92); 12 (*Primitive Morality*, pp. 193–205); and 16 (*Primitive Morality*, p. 255; cf. CL^1 1:111).

38. Homily 19 (*Primitive Morality*, p. 286; CL^1 1:120); other examples are tabulated in Campbell, "John Wesley's Conceptions and Uses of Christian Antiquity," Appendix 4.

39. Homily 4 (*Primitive Morality*, pp. 117–121; cf. CL^1 1:93); Homily 14 (*Primitive Morality*, pp. 209–211); other examples are tabulated in Campbell, "John Wesley's Conceptions and Uses of Christian Antiquity," Appendix 4.

40. I Clement 30 (CL^1 1:13; cf. Wake [2]:43).

41. "Dialogue between a Predestinarian and His Friend" (Jackson 10:265).

42. My translation. The quotation is from Augustine, Sermon 169 xi (13). Wesley, *Sermons* 85:III:7 (Jackson 6:513; Outler 3:208).

43. The view that earlier Christian teachers maintained the freedom of humans to do good, and the Augustine himself espoused this view at least through the time of the writing of his *Confessions*, has been demonstrated by William S. Babcock, "Grace, Freedom, and Justice: Augustine and the Christian Tradition" (*Perkins School of Theology Journal* 27:1 [Summer 1973]: 1–15); although Wesley does not seem to have been aware of the nuance that it was freedom to do the good (not human freedom in general) that Augustine denied when he took up the notion of predestination.

44. Letters 1729/12/19 (to his father; Jackson 12:1; Telford 1:45; Baker 1:241).

45. "Thoughts on Necessity" I:2 and II:1 (Jackson 10:457–458).

46. Letters 1744/06 (to John Bennet; Telford 2:23; Baker 2:107).

47. [Mosheim], *Concise Ecclesiastical History*, ed. Wesley, V:II:V:18 (1781 edn., 1:248, note "a").

48. Letters 1761/07/07 (to Alexander Coates; Jackson 12:240; Telford 4:158).

49. *Sermons* 68:9 (Jackson 67:328–329; Outler 2:556).

50. Letters 1775/08/18 (to John Fletcher; Telford 6:175).

51. Letters 1755/08/18 (to John Fletcher; Telford 6:175).

52. Epistle of Polycarp 10 (Wake [2]:94; cf. CL^1 1:30).

53. I Clement 11 (Wake [2]:21; cf. CL^1 1:8).

54. E. H. Sugden, preface to Wesley, *Sermons* 10 (Sugden 1:199–202).; Williams, *John Wesley's Theology Today*, pp. 102–114.

55. Homily 1 (CL^1 1:90), 20 (CL^1 1:123–124), 27 (CL^1 1:137).

56. Letters 1755/07/25 (to R. Tompson; Jackson 12:468); 1756/02/05 (to R. Tompson; Telford 3:159).

57. "On Clemens Alexandrinus's Description of a Perfect Christian," *passim* (*Hymns and Sacred Poems* [1739], pp. 37–38; Osborn 1:34–36).

58. See passages tabulated in Campbell, "John Wesley's Conceptions and Uses of Christian Antiquity," Appendix 4, Table 3.

59. Two examples are the following: a passage describing the Christian's warfare with Satan (Homily 26; *Primitive Morality*, p. 329; CL^1 1:129–130); and a passage asserting that Christians can fall from grace (Homily 15; *Primitive Morality*, p. 225; CL^1 1:109). Other passages asserting the teaching of sin in believer's are tabulated in Campbell, "John Wesley's Conceptions and Uses of Christian Antiquity," Appendix 4. The passage asserting the need for believer's repentance is from Homily 1 (*Primitive Morality*, p. 106; CL^1 1:90).

60. *Journal* 1763/03/28 (Jackson 3:130; Curnock 5:10).

61. *Sermons* 13:2 (Jackson 5:144–145; Sugden 2:361; Outler 1:317).

62. I Clement 32 (Wake [2]:45; CL^1 1:14).

63. Ignatius, Ephesians 14 (Wake [2]:116; CL^1 1:38).

64. "Martyrdom of Ignatius 2 (Wake [2]:220; CL¹ 1:67); see also the assertion of Ignatius, that "I am not yet made perfect in Jesus Christ" Ephesians 3 (Wake [2]:108; CL¹ 1:34).

65. "On Clemens Alexandrinus' Description of a perfect Christian," I (*Hymns and Sacred Poems* [1739 edn.], p. 37; Osborn 1:34).

66. Horneck, "Letter to a Person of Quality," ed. Wesley (CL¹ 29:125).

67. Letters 1756/03/12 (to W. Dodd; Telford 3:170).

68. Wesley, "Thoughts on Christian Perfection," in Outler, *John Wesley*, p. 287.

69. Homily 26 (*Primitive Morality*, p. 321; cf. CL¹ 1:129); cf. ODCC², s.v. "apotheosis" (p. 77).

70. Doing good by "violence": Homily 29 (*Primitive Morality*, p. 285; CL¹ 1:120); "Degrees of Perfection": Homily 8 (*Primitive Morality*, p. 164; CL¹ 1:103).

71. Homily 10 (*Primitive Morality*, p. 178; CL¹ 1:107).

72. Homily 27 (*Primitive Morality*, p. 353; CL¹ 1:133).

73. Homily 43 (*Primitive Morality*, p. 431; CL¹ 1:140). It is interesting that Wesley let this passage stand, since he himself did not use the language of Spirit baptism to describe (entire) sanctification (although John Fletcher did). The expression passed from Fletcher to Methodist Holiness circles, and thence to modern Pentecostalism. Cf. Laurence W. Wood, *Pentecostal Grace* (Wilmore, Kentucky: Frances Asbury Press, 1980), pp. 198–239.

74. A tabulation of passages dealing with holiness and perfection included in Wesley's edition of the Macarian homilies is given in Campbell, "John Wesley's Conceptions and Uses of Christian Antiquity," Appendix 4. Benz, Wakefield, and Outler all point to the influence of the Macarian literature on Wesley's conceptions of holiness and perfection: Benz, pp. 121–127; Outler, *John Wesley*, p. 9, and esp. n. 26; Wakefield, p. 165.

75. Preface to Macarian homilies, par. 7 in Wesley's edition (CL¹ 1:83; cf. *Primitive Morality*, p. 33).

76. The examples mentioned are as follows: Cave, *Primitive Christianity*, (1682 edn., 2:108–128, 2:55–63, 1:95–96; cf. CL¹ 31:243, 236, 174). Other examples are tabulated in Campbell, "John Wesley's Conceptions and Uses of Christian Antiquity," Appendix 4.

77. Horneck, "Letter to a Person of Quality," ed. Wesley (CL¹ 29:128–129); Cave, *Primitive Christianity*, ed. Wesley, II:II:1–8 (CL¹ 31:230–234); [Fleury], *Manners of the Ancient Christians*, ed. Wesley, 8:5 (1798 edn., p. 23); cf. "Character of a Methodist" 5, 15 (Jackson 8:341, 345).

78. Cave, *Primitive Christianity*, ed. Wesley, II:VI:1–6, 13–18 (CL¹ 31:244–247, 255–259); "Letter to Conyers Middleton" V:6–10 (Jackson 10:63–65); "Letter to the Author of 'The Enthusiasm of Methodists and Papists Compared'" 17–18 (Jackson 9:6–8; Telford 3:264–265).

79. Cave, *Primitive Christianity*, ed. Wesley, III:III:2–8 (CL¹ 31:279–283); Horneck, "Letter to a Person of Quality," ed. Wesley (CL¹ 29:114–115); Wesley's poem "Primitive Christianity" I:5–6, II:23 (Cragg, pp. 91, 93).

80. Horneck, "Letter to a Person of Quality," ed. Wesley (CL¹ 29:123–124); cf. Wesley, "Letter to Conyers Middleton" V:14 (Jackson 10:66).

81. Cave, *Primitive Christianity*, ed. Wesley, II:V:1–6 (CL¹ 31:240– 243); Horneck, "Letter to a Person of Quality," ed. Wesley (CL¹ 29:115).

82. For example, Wesley omits Macarius's use of the image of marital love to explain fidelity to Christ: Homily 4 (*Primitive Morality*, pp. 129–130; cf. CL¹ 1:94). Similar passages omitted are in Homilies 16, 18, and 28 (*Primitive Morality*, pp. 253–254, 280, 362; cf. CL¹ 1:110, 116–117, 135–136).

83. Cave, *Primitive Christianity*, ed. Wesley, II:IV:1–4, II:III:1–5 (CL¹ 31:237–240, 234–237); Horneck, "Letter to a Person of Quality," ed. Wesley (CL¹ 29:127–128).

84. Cave, *Primitive Christianity*, ed. Wesley, II:I:1–4 (CL¹ 31:226– 229); Wesley, *Sermons* 22:I:2 (Jackson 5:262; Sugden 1:335–336; Outler 1:489); preface to the Apostolic

Fathers, par. 12 (CL^1 1:[iv]). The latter is part of the paragraph which Wesley added to Cave's prefatory materials, and is therefore original to Wesley.

85. "Character of a Methodist" 9, 16 (Jackson 8:343, 346); Cave, *Primitive Christianity*, ed. Wesley, III:II:2–15 (CL^1 31:266–277); Horneck, "Letter to a Person of Quality," ed. Wesley (CL^1 29:119, 122–124, 130).

86. Cave, *Primitive Christianity*, ed. Wesley, III:I:1–7 (CL^1 31:262–265); the following are omissions of references to the early Christians' "subjection" to the civil government: 1682 edn., 2:208, 321, 322–324, 327, 347 (cf. CL^1 31:262, 284, 285, 286, 288); Wesley does not retain the term "subjection" in the title of Pt. III, ch. 4 (CL^1 31:283) and does include passages asserting that the ancient Christians obeyed civil authorities.

87. Poem "Primitive Christianity" (Jackson 8:43–45; Cragg, pp. 90–94).

88. "Letter to Conyers Middleton" VI:I:1–15, VI:III:II (Jackson 10:67–72, 79)

89. "Letter to a Roman Catholic" 15 (Jackson 10:84–85; Telford 3:12).

90. Horneck, "Letter to a Person of Quality," ed. Wesley, concluding paragraph (CL^1 29:138).

91. I Clement 12 (Wake [2]:22–23; cf. CL^1 1:9); Ignatius, Philadelphians 6 (Wake [2]:181; cf. CL^1 1:56).

92. In fact, the term "Law" is not used in the Greek text, but appears in Wake's translation, where "the Jewish Law" renders *Ioudaismon*.

93. Campbell, "John Wesley's Conceptions and Uses of Christian Antiquity," ch. 5 under "Virtues of the Early Christians," and the references tabulated in Appendix 4, Tables 7 and 8.

94. Wesley, preface to Mosheim, *Concise Ecclesiastical History*, ed. Wesley, par. 10 (1781 edn., 1:vii-viii).

Chapter 5

1. "Plain Account of the People Called Methodists," preface, par. 2 (Jackson 8:248).

2. Ibid. I:10 (Jackson 8:250–251).

3. Ibid. VII:3 and XI:4 (Jackson 8:260, 263).

4. "Letter to Conyers Middleton" [C]:15 (Jackson 10:14).

5. Letters 1782/02/22 (to Jos. Benson; Telford 7:105)

6. Wesley ms. cited in Outler, *John Wesley*, p. 50; cf. Baker, *John Wesley and the Church of England*, p. 46; Heitzenrater, "John Wesley and the Oxford Methodists," p. 531.

7. Wake, prefatory material to the Apostolic Fathers, ed. Wesley (CL^1 1:i).

8. Ibid.

9. *Farther Appeal*, Part III 28 (Cragg, p. 310; Jackson 8:233).

10. Preface to 1771 [Pine] edn. of Wesley's *Works*, par. 4 (given in Jackson 1:iv).

11. *Farther Appeal*, Part I V:15 (Cragg, p. 154)

12. The particular expression is from Wesley's edition of Mosheim, *A Concise Ecclesiastical History* I:II:II:9 (1781 edn., 1:60–61), and I would take it to be confirmed by Wesley's familiarity with, e.g., the epistles of Ignatius, in which New Testament writings are frequently cited as authoritative.

13. "Address to the Clergy" I:2 (Jackson 10:484).

14. [Fleury], *Manners of the Ancient Christians*, ed. Wesley, 2:2 (1798 edn., p. 8).

15. On Irenaeus' reliance on oral tradition, see the "Letter to Conyers Middleton" III:16 (Jackson 10:35); on the ancient Christians' allegorical interpretations of scripture, ibid. IV:V:2 (Jackson 10:53).

16. "Address to the Clergy" I:2:[6] (Jackson 10:484).

17. *Farther Appeal,* Part I V:15–23 (Jackson 8:91–101; Cragg, pp. 154–166); Letters 1756/03/12 (to Wm. Dodd; Telford 3:170)

18. "Letter to Conyers Middleton" [C]:15 (Jackson 10:14); Horneck, "Letter to a Person of Quality," ed. Wesley (CL[1] 29:131–132).

19. "Letter to Conyers Middleton" [C]:11 (Jackson 10:12).

20. Arianism (see chapter two) had been revived, in various forms, by William Whiston and Samuel Clarke. *Sermons* 20:II:14 (Jackson 5:242; Sugden 2:435; Outler 1:459–460), 117:5 (Jackson 7:292; Outler 4:100); *Journal* 1756/01/14 (Jackson 2:352–353; Curnock 4:145–146); Letters 1756/07/03 (to the Rev. Mr. Clarke; Jackson 13:211; Telford 3:182), 1756/10/05 ("to the Monthly Reviewers"; Jackson 13:386), 1765/04/24 (to Dr. Erskine; Telford 4:296), 1774/09/16 "to a Member of the Society"; Jackson 12:296; Telford 6:113), 1780/06/08 (to Chas. Wesley; Jackson 12:147; Telford 7:21–22), 1788/09/17 (to Jos. Benson; Telford 8:89–90); "The Question, 'What is an Arminian?' Answered" 4 (Jackson 10:358–359).

21. *Journal* 1779/04/22 (Jackson 4:149; Curnock 6:230–231).

22. *Sermons* 63:12 (Jackson 6:281; Outler 2:493), 85:III:7 (Jackson 6:513; Outler 3:208–209); "Dialogue between a Predestinarian and his Friend" (Jackson 10:265).

23. "The Question, 'What is an Arminian:' Answered" 4 (Jackson 10:358–359).

24. John Downes, letter to John Wesley; cited in Wesley, Letters 1759/11/17 (to John Downes: Telford 4:329).

25. Wesley, Letters 1759/11/17 (to John Downes; Telford 4:329).

26. Cf. [Mosheim,] *Concise Ecclesiastical History,* ed. Wesley, III:II:V:1 (1781 edn., 1:145); *Journal* 1750/08/15 (Jackson 2:204; Curnock 3:490).

27. Letters 1756/07/03 (to the Rev. Mr. Clarke; Jackson 13:211; Telford 3:182).

28. *Journal* 1754/08/05 (Jackson 2:324; Curnock 4:96–97); cf. Wesley's comments on Eutychianism and Nestorianism in his Letters 1780/06/08 (to Chas. Wesley; Jackson 12:147; Telford 7:21–22).

29. [Mosheim], *A Concise Ecclesiastical History,* ed. Wesley, I:II:III:3 (1781 edn., 1:64); on Wesley's adherence to the Nicene Creed, *Notes* John 15:26 (1976 edn., p. 370); on Wesley's adherence to the Chalcedonian formula, see John Deschner, *Wesley's Christology: An Interpretation* (Dallas: Southern Methodist University Press, 1960), p. 15; on Wesley's general approval of the teaching of the Athanasian Creed, *Journal* 1760/12/20 (Jackson 3:30; Curnock 4:424); *Sermons* 55:3 (Jackson 6:200). The eighth Article of Religion is cited from the Book of Common Prayer.

30. *The Sunday Service of the Methodists in North America* (London: [Strahan], 1784, pp. 306–314).

31. Letters 1760/12/20 (given in Jackson 3:30; Curnock 4:424).

32. Ibid.

33. "Letter to Conyers Middleton" VI:II:1–12 (Jackson 10:72–75).

34. *Sermons* 55:3 (Jackson 6:200; Outler 2:376–377); 55:5 (Jackson 6:201; 2:378–379); cf. *Notes* I John 5:7 (1976 edn., p. 917). The Johannine Comma is now almost universally recognized as a later addition to the Vulgate text of I John 5:7, possibly made under the pressure of Arian teachings; cf. ODCC[2], s.v. "Johannine Comma" (pp. 741–742).

35. Wesley omits references to the "ruling powers of the soul" in Homily 1 (*Primitive Morality,* p. 97; cf. CL[1] 1:86), and to the "Five Senses of the Soul" in Homily 4 (Wesley's number 2; *Primitive Morality,* pp. 122–129; cf. CL[1] 1:94). My research has identified a dozen such omissions.

36. *Sermons* 55:5 (Jackson 6:201; Outler 2:378–379).

37. *Sermons* 117:5 (Jackson 7:292; Outler 4:100).

38. "The Question, 'What is an Arminian?' Answered" 4 (Jackson 10:358–359); cf. *Sermons* 20:II:14 (Jackson 5:242; Sugden 2:435; Outler 1:459–460); Letters 1756/07/03 (to Mr. Clarke; Jackson 13:211; Telford 3:182); ibid. 1756/10/05 (to the Monthly Reviewers";

Jackson 13:386). More recent research on Arianism has indeed identified the issue as "the doctrine of the relation between God and the divine in Christ" (Jaroslav Pelikan, *The Christian Tradition: A History of the Development of Doctrine*, vol. 1, *The Emergence of the Catholic Tradition (100–600)* [Chicago and London: University of Chicago Press, 1971], p. 195) as Wesley seems to have done; but more recent scholarship has stressed the Arians' continuity with earlier Christological motifs and with the thought of Origen and Dionysius of Alexandria, and has pointed out the Arians' worship of, and directing prayers to, Christ (ibid., pp. 191–200).

39. Letters 1774/09/16 ("to a Member of the Society"; Jackson 12:296; Telford 6:113); 1765/04/24 (to Dr. Erskine; Telford 4:296); *Journal* 1756/01/14 (Jackson 2:352–353; Curnock 4:145–146).

40. *Journal* 1779/04/22 (Jackson 4:149; Curnock 6:230–231).

41. Letters 1780/06/08 (to Chas. Wesley; Jackson 12:147; Telford 7:21–22); cf. Letters 1788/09/17 (to Joseph Benson; Telford 8:89–90), where Wesley warns that the book in question might indeed lead a believer into Arianism, or Socinianism.

42. All of the following passages from Ignatius' epistles are omitted by Wesley: Ephesians 20 (Wake [2]:120–121; cf. CL^1 1:40); Trallians 9–10 (Wake [2]:151; cf. CL^1 1:48); Romans 7 (Wake [2]:166; cf. CL^1 1:53); Smyrnaeans 2–3 (Wake [2]:194–195; cf. CL^1 1:60); Smyraneans 5 (Wake [2]:197; cf. CL^1 1:60); and Smyrnaeans 7 (Wake [2]:198–199; cf. CL^1 1:60– 61).

43. Deschner, pp. 14–44.

44. Cave, *Primitive Christianity*, ed. Wesley, (CL^1 31:193–194).

45. [Fleury], *Manners of the Ancient Christians*, ed. Wesley, 3:3 (1798 edn., p. 10).

46. The title of vol. 1 of Gay's *The Enlightment*.

47. *Earnest Appeal* 26–27 (Jackson 8:10–11; Cragg, pp. 54–55).

48. "Doctrine of Original Sin," Part I:II (Jackson 9:208–238).

49. *Sermons* 63:1–7 (Jackson 6:277–279; Outler 2:485–488).

50. "Plain Account of the People Called Methodists" I:10 (Jackson 10:250–251).

51. [Fleury], *Manners of the Ancient Christians* 3:4 (Ms. Colman 15:18; cf. 1798 edn., p. 10); 4:3 (Ms. Colman 15:22; cf. 1798 edn., p. 13).

52. *Sermons* 115:9–18 (Jackson 7:276–280; Outler 4:78–83); "Plain Account of the People Called Methodists" I:10 (Jackson 8:250–251); Letters 1789/06/12 (to the printer of the *Dublin Chronicle*; Telford 8:143).

53. These passages do appear in the (1736) ms. version of Fleury, *Manners of the Ancient Christians*, ed. Wesley, 3:4 (Ms. Colman 15:18; cf. 1798 edn., p. 10), 4:3 (Ms. Colman 15:22; cf. 1798 edn., p. 13).

54. Letters 1756/03/12 (to Wm. Dodd; Telford 3:170–171).

55. See ch. 4, under "Virtues of the Ancient Christians."

56. Cf. Campbell, "John Wesley and Conyers Middleton," p. 46.

57. "Letter to Conyers Middleton" [D] (Jackson 10:16).

58. Ibid. IV:VI (Jackson 10:54–59).

59. Homilies 10 and 26 (CL^1 1:107, 130); [Fleury], *Manners of the Ancient Christians*, ed. Wesley (1798 edn., p. 17).

60. "Letter to Conyers Middleton" IV:IV:3, 11–12 (Jackson 10:47, 50–51).

61. *Journal* 1750/08/15 (Jackson 2:204; Curnock 3:490). The book to which Wesley refers is *The General Delusion of Christians, touching the way of God's revealing himself to and by prophets, evinc'd from Scripture and primitive antiquity* (London: S. Keimer, 1713), supposed to have been the work of John Lacy (b. 1664, d. after 1737), one of the "French Prophets." Cf. DNB, s.v. "Lacy, John" (11:382–383); CBTEL, s.v. "Lacy, John" (5:190).

62. Letters 1761/02/17 (to the editor of the London Magazine; Telford 4:133): *Sermons* 68:9 (Jackson 6:328; Outler 2:555); "Real Character of Montanus," *passim* (Jackson 11:485–

486; *Arminian Magazine* 8 [1785]:35); [Mosheim], *Concise Ecclesiastical History*, ed. Wesley, II:II:V:11 (1781 edn., 1:114).

63. [Fleury], *Manners of the Ancient Christians*, ed. Wesley, 1:3, 3:4 (1798 edn., pp. 3, 11); Wesley, "Letter to Conyers Middleton" [B]:11– 12 (Jackson 10:6–7).

64. "Letter to Conyers Middleton" IV:VI:3–6 (Jackson 10:54–55).

65. [Mosheim], *Concise Ecclesiastical History*, ed. Wesley, II:I:II:8–9 (1781 edn., 1:80–81).

66. "Letter to Conyers Middleton" [A]:3–4 (Jackson 10:1–2).

67. Ibid. [C]:6 (Jackson 10:10). Other references to the cessation of the miraculous powers in the age of Constantine are the following: [C]:3, [C]:15, IV:II:5, and IV:VI:10–11 (Jackson 10:8, 14, 41, 57).

68. Cave, *Primitive Christianity*, ed. Wesley (1682 edn., 1:51 [n.b., second occurrence of this page number]; cf. CL^1 31:167).

69. *Sermons* 89:2 (Jackson 7:26–27; Outler 3:263–264).

70. *Journal* 1739/09/28 (Curnock 2:283).

71. See the numerous instances catalogued in the index to Curnock, under "Prayer, notable answers to," and "Providence, interpositions of" (Curnock 8:442, 443).

72. "The Principles of a Methodist Farther Explained: V (Jackson 8:460); repeated verbatim in "A Letter to the Lord Bishop of Gloucester: (Jackson 9:155).

73. "Letter to Conyers Middleton" II:9 (Jackson 10:27).

74. "John Smith," letter to John Wesley, 1747/08/21, pars. 8–10 (Baker 2:260–261); Wesley, *Farther Appeal*, Part III 28 (Jackson 8:233–234; Cragg, p. 310); "Letter to the Lord Bishop of Gloucester" (Jackson 9:155–163).

75. "Letter to the Lord Bishop of Gloucester": (Jackson 9:118–125; Cragg, pp. 468–475).

76. Wesley uses the term in his *Farther Appeal, Part I* VII:3 (Cragg 188–189); his edition of Cave's *Primitive Christianity* applies it to the early Christian communities on the authority of Pliny, II:IV:6 (CL^1 31:288). For this reason I regard Pliny's letter as a more likely source for Wesley's use of the term than John of Damascus or later Greek writers, as Cragg suggested. Cf. A. N. Sherwin-White, ed., *Fifty Letters of Pliny* (Oxford: Oxford University Press, 1969), pp. 70–177.

77. "The Nature, Design, and General Rules of the United Societies" 4 (Jackson 8:270).

78. "Plain Account of the People Called Methodists" IV:3 (Jackson 8:257).

79. Cave, *Primitive Christianity*, ed. Wesley III:V:13 (CL^1 31:298).

80. See the comments and notes on Marshall's work in chapter 1.

81. "Plain Account of the People Called Methodists" VII:3 (Jackson 8:260).

82. [Fleury], *Manners of the Ancient Christians*, ed. Wesley, 1:9 (1798 edn., p. 6).

83. Cave, *Primitive Christianity*, ed. Wesley, I:VI:8 (CL^1 31:184).

84. Horneck, "Letter to a Person of Quality," ed. Wesley (CL^1 29:115, 126–127); cf. [Fleury], *Manners of the Ancient Christians*, ed. Wesley, 2:4 (1798 edn., p. 8); Wesley, "Plain Account of the People Called Methodists" XV:6 (Jackson 8:268).

85. Minutes 1744/06/28 (Publications of the Wesley Historical Society 1 [London, 1896]:14).

86. "Plain Account of the People Called Methodists" XI:4 and XIII:3 (Jackson 8:263, 265).

87. Letters 1784/09/10 (to "Our Brethren in America"; Telford 7:239).

88. Mosheim, *Concise Ecclesiastical History*, ed. Wesley, I:II:II:1–3 (1781 edn., 1:55–56); but cf. [Fleury], *Manners of the Ancient Christians*, ed. Wesley, 1:10 (1798 edn., p. 6), where the apostles and the seventy are simply distinguished from the laity as those "set apart for ministry in public."

89. *Sermons* 115:6–7 (Jackson 7:275–276; Outler 4:76–77).

90. Ibid., par. 8 (Jackson 7:276; Outler 4:77–78).

91. Cave's *Primitive Christianity* distinguishes two groups of clergy: those appointed to acts of worship (bishops, priests, and deacons), and those appointed to "the more mean and common Services of the Church" (I:VIII:3; CL[1] 31:198). I may note at this point two interesting omissions: Wesley omitted the latter part of ch. 42 and all of ch. 43 from his version of I Clement. These chapters assert Christ's establishment of the offices of bishop, priest, and deacon, and draw a parallel between Christian clergy and the leaders of Israel (Wake [2]:58–60; cf. CL[1] 1:18). Similarly, he omitted from his 1736 ms. of Fleury a chapter describing the orders of ministry in the ancient church (Ms. Colman 15:44–45). Nevertheless, that Wesley continued to affirm the antiquity and propriety of the orders of bishop, presbyter, and deacon is evident (cf. the text and notes following).

92. Letters 1745/12/27 (to Westley Hall; Telford 2:55; Baker 2:173; also given in Curnock 3:229–230).

93. Spangenberg's diary; cited in Schmidt, 1:138, n. 6.

94. *Journal* 1746/01/20 (Jackson 2:6–7; Curnock 3:232).

95. King, pp. 62–79; cf. Edgar W. Thompson, *Wesley: Apostolic Man* (London: Epworth Press, 1957), pp. 23–30.

96. The first indication of Wesley's reading in Stillingfleet comes in his Letters 1756/07/03 (Jackson 13:211; Telford 3:182); Stillingfleet, pp. 402–405 (ordination by presbyters), pp. 297–300 (precedent in Alexandrian church); cf. Thompson, pp. 31–33.

97. Letters 1761/02/19 (to the editor of the *London Chronicle*; Telford 4:139–141; also given in Curnock 4:438–439); [Fleury], *Manners of the Ancient Christians*, ed. Wesley, 2:2 (1798 edn., p. 7); cf. I Clement 44 (Wake [2]:60–61; CL[1] 1:18–19).

98. Letters 1784/09/10 (to "Our Brethren in America"; Telford 7:238); 1789/06/12 (to the printer of the *Dublin Chronicle*; Telford 8:143); [Mosheim], *Concise Ecclesiastical History* I:II:II:6–7 (1781 edn., 1:57–59). Wesley's edition of Cave does include a passage representing the ancient episcopate as an order distinct from that of presbyters, and omits Cave's acknowledgement of contemporary questions about the ancient distinction of the orders: Cave, *Primitive Christianity* I:VIII:4 (1684 edn., I:221; CL[1] 31:195–196).

99. Letters 1756/07/03 (to the Rev. Mr. Clarke; Jackson 13:21; Telford 3:182).

100. Letters 1761/04/10 ("to a friend"; Jackson 13:235–236; Telford 4:150); 1780/06/08 (to Chas. Wesley; Jackson 12:147; Telford 7:21); 1784/09/10 (to "Our Brethren in America"; Jackson 13:251; Telford 7:238); 1785/04/19 (to an anonymous clergyman; Jackson 13:253). Wesley's edition of Cave includes a discussion of ordination in the ancient church which holds that ordinations were performed by the imposition of hands, by all the bishops of a province, or at least by two of them, if all the rest gave their consent in writing: *Primitive Christianity* I:VIII:9 (CL[1] 31:198–199). Wesley's acknowledgement of the ministerial orders of the European Reformed churches comes in the Minutes of the Annual Conference of 1747, as recorded in John Bennet's copy (*Publications of the Wesley Historical Society* 1 [London, 1896]: 48).

101. Letters 1780/06/08 (to Chas. Wesley; Jackson 12:147; Telford 7:21).

102. Letters 1784/09/10 (to "Our Brethren in America"; Telford 7:238).

103. Thomas Coke and Francis Asbury, *The Doctrines and Discipline of the Methodist Episcopal Church in America, with Explanatory Notes* (Philadelphia: Henry Tuckniss, 1798), pp. 45–46.

104. [Fleury], *Manners of the Ancient Christians*, ed. Wesley, 3:8 (Ms. Colman 15:19; cf. 1798 edn., p. 12); 8:4 (Ms. Colman 15:31; cf. 1798 edn., p. 23).

105. Cave, *Primitive Christianity*, ed. Wesley, I:VIII:5 (CL[1] 31:196).

106. Horneck, "Letter to a Person of Quality," ed. Wesley (CL[1] 29:125–126).

107. Cave, *Primitive Christianity*, ed. Wesley (1682 edn., I:222, 248–250; cf. CL[1] 31:195, 200).

108. The two examples cited are from the Epistle to the Magnesians, chs. 2 and 3 (Wake [2]:128–129; cf. CL^1 1:42). Other examples are tabulated in Campbell, "John Wesley's Conceptions and Uses of Christian Antiquity," Appendix 4.

109. "Plain Account of the People Called Methodists" IX:4 (Jackson 8:263); Cave, *Primitive Christianity*, ed. Wesley, I:VIII:6 (CL^1 31:196–197).

110. "Plain Account of the People Called Methodists" XI:4 and XIII:3 (Jackson 8:263, 265); Horneck, "Letter to a Person of Quality," ed. Wesley (CL^1 29:115, 120); Cave, *Primitive Christianity*, ed. Wesley, I:VIII:11 (CL^1 31:199–200).

111. [Mosheim], *Concise Ecclesiastical History*, ed. Wesley, III:II:II:4 (1781 edn., 1:130–131); Cave, *Primitive Christianity*, ed. Wesley, I:VIII:7–8 (CL^1 31:197–198).

112. Ibid. I:X:6–7 (CL^1 31:211–215); [Fleury], *Manners of the Ancient Christians*, ed. Wesley, 3:8 (1798 edn., p. 12); [Mosheim], *Concise Ecclesiastical History*, ed. Wesley, I:II:IV:8 (1781 edn., 1:71).

113. "Serious Thoughts concerning Godfathers and Godmothers" 1 (Jackson 10:506); Cave, *Primitive Christianity*, ed. Wesley, I:X:2 and 7 (CL^1 31:203, 212); [Fleury], *Manners of the Ancient Christians*, ed. Wesley, 3:8 (1798 edn., p. 12). The authority generally given for the use of baptismal sponsors is Tertullian.

114. Cave, *Primitive Christianity*, ed. Wesley, I:X:4 and 7 (CL^1 31:209, 213–215); [Mosheim], *Concise Ecclesiastical History*, ed. Wesley, II:II:III:9 (1781 edn., 1:106–107).

115. Cave, *Primitive Christianity*, (1682 edn., 1:310–311; cf. CL^1 31:210).

116. "Serious Thoughts concerning Godfathers and Godmothers," *passim* (Jackson 10:506–509).

117. *Sunday Service* (1784 edn., p. 142; 1788 edn., p. 145).

118. Wesley omitted from his edition of the Macarian homilies a passage explaining the spiritual presence of Christ in the eucharistic elements (Homily 27; *Primitive Morality*, p. 353), but this would appear too isolated to indicate much of how Wesley understood ancient beliefs about the eucharist.

119. [Mosheim], *Concise Ecclesiastical History*, ed. Wesley, I:II:IV:4, II:II:III:8 (1781 edn., 1:69, 106); Cave, *Primitive Christianity*, ed. Wesley, I:XI:1 (CL^1 31:216–217).

120. Both of these observations are based upon Justin Martyr's account: "Letter to Conyers Middleton" [C]:3, IV:IV:4 (Jackson 10:8–9, 48); Cave, *Primitive Christianity*, ed. Wesley, I:XI:6 (CL^1 31:223); Wesley, Letters 1789/06/12 (to the printer of the *Dublin Chronicle*; Telford 8:143).

121. Cave, *Primitive Christianity*, ed. Wesley, I:XI:2 (CL^1 31:217).

122. Horneck, "Letter to a Person of Quality," ed. Wesley (CL^1 29:134); [Mosheim], *Concise Ecclesiastical History*, ed. Wesley, II:II:III:4 (1781 edn., 1:103); Cave, *Primitive Christianity*, ed. Wesley, I:VII:1–3 (CL^1 31:185–187). The passage from Cave regards the observation of Lord's Day as being of apostolic origin.

123. Ibid. (1682 edn., 1:333–334; cf. CL^1 31:216–217); [Mosheim], *Concise Ecclesiastical History*, ed. Wesley, II:II:III:8 (1781 edn., 1:106).

124. Cave, *Primitive Christianity*, ed. Wesley (1682 edn., 1:335–337, 342; cf. CL^1 31:217, 219).

125. Cf. *Explanatory Notes on the New Testament*, note on Rev. 1:10 (London: Epworth Press, 1976; p. 939); Cave, *Primitive Christianity*, ed. Wesley, I:VII:1–3 (CL^1 31:185–187).

126. Cave, *Primitive Christianity* (1682 edn., 1:163–164; cf. CL^1 31:185). See comments on the practice in Chapter 3.

127. Ibid. (1682 edn., 1:173–179); [Mosheim], *Concise Ecclesiastical History*, ed. Wesley, II:II:III:4 (1781 edn., 1:103).

128. "Plain Account of the People Called Methodists" VI:5–6 (Jackson 8:258–259; Telford 2:302); [Fleury], *Manners of the Ancient Christians*, ed. Wesley, 2:6 (1798 edn., p. 9); Horneck, "Letter to a Person of Quality," ed. Wesley (CL^1 29:130); Cave, *Primitive Chris-*

tianity, ed. Wesley, I:XI:5 (CL[1] 31:219–220); [Mosheim], *Concise Ecclesiastical History*, ed. Wesley, I:II:IV:7 (1781 edn., 1:71).

129. [Fleury], *Manners of the Ancient Christians*, ed. Wesley, 2:6 (1798 edn., p. 9); Horneck, "Letter to a Person of Quality," ed. Wesley (CL[1] 29:130); Cave, *Primitive Christianity*, ed. Wesley, I:XI:5 (CL[1] 31:219–220).

130. [Mosheim], *Concise Ecclesiastical History*, ed. Wesley, I:II:II:5, V:II:IV:3 (1781 edn., 1:57, 232).

131. "Plain Account of the People Called Methodists" VI:5 (Jackson 8:258–259; Telford 2:302).

132. "Plain Account of the People Called Methodists" III:1 (Jackson 8:255); Horneck, "Letter to a Person of Quality," ed. Wesley (CL[1] 29:134–135).

133. Ibid. III:1 (Jackson 8:255).

134. *Sermons* 27:I:6 (Jackson 5:347; Sugden 1:454; Outler 1:596–597); [Fleury], *Manners of the Ancient Christians*, ed. Wesley, 5:1 (1798 edn., p. 14); Horneck, "Letter to a Person of Quality," ed. Wesley (CL[1] 29:134); Cave, *Primitive Christianity*, ed. Wesley, I:VII:4 (CL[1] 31:187); [Mosheim], *Concise Ecclesiastical History*, ed. Wesley, I:II:IV:10 (1781 edn., 1:72). Mosheim regarded the Wednesday and Friday fasts as being of first-century, if not apostolic, origin.

135. *Sermons* 27:I:6 (Jackson 5:347; Sugden 1:454; Outler 1:596–597); [Fleury], *Manners of the Ancient Christians*, ed. Wesley, 3:6 and 5:1 (1798 edn., pp. 11 and 14); Cave, *Primitive Christianity*, ed. Wesley, I:VII:5 (CL[1] 31:187–188).

136. Horneck, "Letter to a Person of Quality," ed. Wesley (CL[1] 29:118, 130; cf. *Happy Ascetick*[4], p. 586).

137. "Large Minutes," Qu. 35 (Jackson 8:316–317); Minutes 1748/06/05 (*Publications of the Wesley Historical Society* 1[1896]:56).

138. "Plain Account of the People Called Methodists: I:8 (Jackson 8:250).

139. *Sermons* 116:14 (Jackson 7:288–289; Outler 4:94).

140. "Letter to Conyers Middleton" I:8 (Jackson 10:20); [Mosheim], *Concise Ecclesiastical History*, ed. Wesley, II:II:III:5 (1781 edn., 1:103–104); Cave, *Primitive Christianity*, ed. Wesley, I:VII:609 (CL[1] 31:188–191).

141. [Mosheim], *Concise Ecclesiastical History*, ed. Wesley, IV:II:IV:5 (1781 edn., 1:186); Cave, *Primitive Christianity*, ed. Wesley, I:VII:7–9 (CL[1] 31:189–191; cf. 1682 edn., pp. 195–197).

142. "Letter to Conyers Middleton" [C]:3, 5 (Jackson 10:9–10); Cave, *Primitive Christianity*, ed. Wesley, I:VII:10 (CL[1] 31:191); Horneck, "Letter to a Person of Quality," ed. Wesley (CL[1] 29:134).

143. [Mosheim], *Concise Ecclesiastical History*, ed. Wesley, IV:II:IV:5 (1781 edn., 1:186).

144. "Martyrdom of Ignatius" 13–15 (Wake [2]:228–229; cf. CL[1] 1:71); "Martyrdom of Polycarp" 17–19, 21 (Wake [2]:248–249, 251; cf. CL[1] 1:77, 78).

145. *Journal* 1774/03/30 (Jackson 4:38; Curnock 6:54).

146. Ibid. 1777/03/30 (Jackson 4:95; Curnock 6:54).

147. R. Denny Urlin cited both passages as examples of Wesley's continuing interest in ancient Christian liturgy (*John Wesley's Place in Church History*, p. 68, n. 1).

148. [Fleury], *Manners of the Ancient Christians*, ed. Wesley, 2:5 (1798 edn., p. 9); Cave *Primitive Christianity*, ed. Wesley, I:VI:2 and I:IX:2 (CL[1] 31:180, 202); [Mosheim], *Concise Ecclesiastical History*, ed. Wesley, II:II:IV:4 (1781 edn., 1:137).

149. Horneck, "Letter to a Person of Quality," ed. Wesley (CL[1] 29:132).

150. Ibid. (29:117, 129–130); Cave, *Primitive Christianity*, ed. Wesley, I:IX:1 (CL[1] 31:201).

Chapter 6

1. The terms are those of Congar, p. 185.
2. *Farther Appeal, Part I* V:15 (Cragg, p. 154).
3. Preface to Pine edition of *Works*, par. 4 (given in Jackson 1:iv); *Sermons* 132:II:1–4 (Jackson 7:423–425; Outler 3:585).
4. "Farther Thoughts on Separation from the Church" 1–2 (Jackson 13:272–274).
5. Given in Outler, *John Wesley*, p. 46.
6. [Mosheim,] *Concise Ecclesiastical History*, ed. Wesley, III:II:V:1 (1781 edn., 1:145); *Journal* 1750/08/15 (Jackson 2:204; Curnock 3:490).
7. *Sermons* 132:II:3 (Jackson 7:424; Outler 3:586).
8. For example, in the poem "Primitive Christianity," I:9–10 (Cragg, p. 91).
9. "Letter to Conyers Middleton" C:10 (Jackson 10:11).
10. Preface to Apostolic Fathers in CL^1 1:i.
11. *Farther Appeal, Part I* v:15–23 (Cragg, pp. 154–166).
12. [Fleury,] *Manners of the Ancient Christians*, ed. Wesley, *passim*; Horneck, "Letter to a Person of Quality," ed. Wesley, *passim*.
13. Letters 1756/07/03 (to the Rev. Mr. Clarke; Jackson 13:211; Telford 3:182).
14. Ibid., "Large Minutes," qu. 35 (Jackson 8:316–317); *Minutes* 1748/06/05 (*Publications of the Wesley Historical Society* 1 [1896]: 56); "Plain Account of the People Called Methodists" I:8 (Jackson 8:250).
15. "Plain Account of the People Called Methodists" I:1–10 (Jackson 8:249–250).
16. *Sermons* 132:II:3–4 (Jackson 7:424–425; Outler 3:586).
17. "Farther Thoughts on Separation from the Church" 1–2 (Jackson 13:272–274).
18. *Sermons* 13:I:3 (Jackson 5:145; Sugden 2:361; Outler 1:317–318).
19. *Sermons* 132:II:4 (Jackson 7:425; Outler 3:586).
20. Ms. "Ought We to Separate from the Church of England?" in Baker, *John Wesley and the Church of England*, p. 327.
21. Ibid., pp. 327–328.
22. *Farther Appeal, Part I*, II:1–9, IV:3–5, V:24–26 (Cragg, pp. 108–116, 133–137, 166–170).
23. Kenneth D. Rowe, "The Search for the Historical Wesley," in Kenneth D. Rowe, ed., *The Place of Wesley in the Christian Tradition* (Metuchen, New Jersey: Scarecrow Press, 1976), pp. 1–10. Albert C. Outler's plenary address at the 1982 Oxford Institute of Methodist Theological Studies referred to the last century of monographic studies attempting to place Wesley with respect to particular aspects of the Christian tradition as "stage two" Wesley studies ("stage one" was the period in the nineteenth century when Wesley was portrayed as a Methodist folk-hero): Outler, "A New Future for Wesley Studies: An Agenda for 'Phase III,'" in M. Douglas Meeks, ed., *The Future of the Methodist Theological Traditions* (Nashville: Abingdon Press, 1985), pp. 34–52.
24. An example would be Frank Baker's study of *John Wesley and the Church of England* (1970).
25. Urlin, *John Wesley's Place in Church History* and *Churchman's Life of Wesley, passim*.
26. Eamon Duffy, for instance, asserted that in 1738 Wesley abandoned the ideal of "primitive" Christianity for that of "real" Christianity: pp. 299–300.
27. Theodore M. Runyon, ed., *Sanctification and Liberation* (Nashville: Abingdon Press, 1981); cf. especially the editor's introduction, pp. 9–48).
28. Howard A. Snyder, *The Radical Wesley and Patterns for Church Renewal* (Downer's Grove, Illinois: InterVarsity Press, 1980).
29. In his plenary address at the 1982 Oxford Institute for Methodist Theological Studies (see note 67 above), Professor Outler proposed a "Phase III" of Wesley studies in

which Wesley would be understood with respect to the Christian tradition as a whole; Outler, "A New Future for Wesley Studies," *passim.*

30. Cf. Benedicta Ward, trans., *Sayings of the Desert Fathers* [*Apothegmata Patrum*] (Oxford: Mowbrays, 1975), p. 24; Athanasius, *The Life of Anthony and the Letter to Marcellinus* [the former work is the *Vita Antonii* referred to in the text], trans. Robert C. Gregg (New York: Paulist Press, 1980); Jacques Lacarriére, *Men Possessed by God: The Story of the Desert Monks of Ancient Christendom* (Garden City, New York: Doubleday, 1964).

31. M. D. Lambert, *Franciscan Poverty: The Doctrine of the Absolute Poverty of Christ and the Apostles in the Franciscan Order, 1210–1323* (London: SPCK, 1961), esp. chs. 1 and 2.

32. Franklin H. Littell, *The Origins of Sectarian Protestantism* (New York: The Macmillan Co., revised edition, 1964; originally published in 1952 as *The Anabaptist View of the Church*), pp. 46–78.

33. Spener, pp. 76–86.

34. Henry Offley Wakefield, *An Introduction to the History of the Church of England* (London: Rivington's, 8th edn., 1919), pp. 438–440.

35. Herbert Brook Workman, *The Place of Methodism in the Catholic Church*, 2nd edn. (London: Epworth Press, 1921), pp. 61–75.

36. Piette, p. 480.

37. Schmidt, *John Wesley: A Theological Biography*, 2/1:125–126.

38. Anthony F. C. Wallace, "Revitalization Movements," *American Anthropologist* 58 (1956), pp. 268–275.

39. Transcribed from photograph.

Bibliography

Andrewes, Lancelot. *Opuscula qaedam posthumata*. Library of Anglo-Catholic Theology. Oxford: John Henry Parker, 1852.

Athanasius. *The Life of Anthony and the Letter to Marcellinus*. Translated by Robert C. Gregg. Classics of Western Spirituality. New York: Paulist Press, 1980.

Ayling, Stanley. *John Wesley*. Cleveland and New York: William Collins Publishers, 1979.

Babcock, William S. "Grace, Freedom, and Justice: Augustine and the Christian Tradition." *Perkins School of Theology Journal* 27:1 (Summer 1973): 1–15.

Baines-Griffiths, David. *Wesley the Anglican*. London: Macmillan and Co., Ltd., 1919.

Baker, Frank. *John Wesley and the Church of England*. Nashville: Abingdon Press, 1970.

_____. *A Union Catalogue of the Publications of John and Charles Wesley*. Durham, North Carolina: Duke University Press, 1966.

Bebbington, D. W. *Evangelicalism in Modern Britain: A History from the 1730s to the 1980s*. London: Unwin Hyman, 1989.

Benz, Ernst. *Die protestantische Thebais: Zur Nachwirkung Makarios des Ägypters im Protestantismus der 16. und 17. Jahrhunderts in Europa und Amerika*. Wiesbaden: Verlag der Akademie der Wissenschaften und der Literatur in Mainz, 1963.

Beveridge, William. *Codex Canonum Ecclesiae Primitivae Vindicatus ac Illustratus*. London: Robert Scott, 1678; reprint ed., University Microfilms English Books 1641–1706 series, reel 808.

_____. Library of Anglo-Catholic Theology. Oxford: John Henry Parker, 1847.

_____. *Synodikon, sive Pandectae Canonum Ss. Apostolorum et Conciliorum Ecclesia Graeca Receptorum.* Oxford: William Wells and Robert Scott, 1672.

_____. *Thesaurus Theologicus.* Library of Anglo-Catholic Theology. Oxford: John Henry Parker, 1847.

Bowmer, John. *The Sacrament of the Lord's Supper in Early Methodism.* Westminster: The Dacre Press, 1951.

Brightman, Robert Sheffield. "Gregory of Nyssa and John Wesley in Theological Dialogue on the Christian Life." Ph.D. dissertation, Boston University, 1969.

British Museum Catalogue of Printed Books. London: Trustees of the British Museum, 1965–1966. 263 volumes.

Bull, George. *Defensio Fidei Nicaenae: A Defence of the Nicene Creed out of the Extant Writings of the Catholick Doctors, who Flourished during the First Three Centuries of the Christian Church.* Library of Anglo-Catholic Theology. 2 vols. Oxford: John Henry Parker, 1851.

_____. *The Judgement of the Catholic Church on the Necessity of Believing that our Lord Jesus Christ is Very God.* Library of Anglo-Catholic Theology. Oxford: John Henry Parker, 1855.

Campbell, Ted A. "John Wesley and Conyers Middleton on Divine Intervention in History." *Church History* 55:1 (March 1986): 39–49.

_____. "John Wesley's Conceptions and Uses of Christian Antiquity." Ph.D. dissertation, Southern Methodist University, 1984.

Cave, William. *Primitive Christianity: or, the Religion of the Primitive Christians in the First Ages of the Gospel.* Ed. Henry Cary. London: Thomas Tegg, 1840.

_____. *Scriptorum ecclesiasticorum Historia literaria.* 2 vols. London: Richard Chiswell, 1688 and 1698.

Chitty, Derwas J. *The Desert a City: An Introduction to the Study of Egyptian and Palestinian Monasticism under the Christian Empire.* Oxford: Basil Blackwell, 1966.

Coke, Thomas, and Francis Asbury. *The Doctrines and Discipline of the Methodist Episcopal Church in America, with Explanatory Notes.* Philadelphia: Henry Tuckniss, 1798.

Colie, Rosalie. *Light and Enlightenment: A Study of the Cambridge Platonists and the Dutch Arminians.* Cambridge: Cambridge University Press, 1957.

Congar, Yves M. D. *Tradition and Traditions.* New York: The Macmillan Co., 1967.

Cotelier, Jean Baptiste, ed. *Ss. Patrum qui Temporibus apostolicis floruerunt . . . Opera.* Antwerp: "Huguetanorum sumptibus," 1698.

Cragg, Gerald R. *The Church in the Age of Reason, 1648–1789.* Grand Rapids, Michigan: William B. Eerdmans Publishing Co., 1960.

_____ . *Freedom and Authority: A Study of English Thought in the Early Seventeenth Century.* Philadelphia: Westminster Press, 1975.

Cross, F. L., ed. *The Oxford Dictionary of the Christian Church.* Oxford: Oxford University Press, second edition, revised, 1976.

_____ . *Patristic Study at Oxford.* Presidential Address to the Oxford Society of Historical Theology. Oxford: Basil Blackwell, 1948.

Daillé, John [i.e., Jean]. *A Treatise concerning the Right Use of the Fathers, in the Decision of the Controversies that are at this Day in Religion.* Translated by Thomas Smith (?). London: John Martin, 1651.

[Deacon, Thomas.] *A Compleat Collection of Devotions, both Publick and Private: Taken from the Apostolical Constitutions, the Ancient Liturgies, and the Common Prayer Book of the Church of England.* London: printed for the author, 1734.

Deschner, John. *Wesley's Christology: An Interpretation.* Dallas: Southern Methodist University Press, 1960.

Dreyer, Frederick. "Faith and Experience in the Thought of John Wesley." *American Historical Review* 88 (1983), pp. 12–30.

Duffy, Eamon. "Primitive Christianity Revived: Religious Renewal in Augustan England." In Derek Baker, ed. *Renaissance and Renewal in Christian History.* Studies in Church History, no. 14. Oxford: Basil Blackwell, 1977. Pp. 287–300.

Echard, Laurence. *A General Ecclesiastical History, from the Nativity of our Blessed Saviour to the First Establishment of Christianity by Humane Laws under the Emperor Constantine the Great.* London: W. Bowyer for Jacob Jonson, 1702.

Evans, Arthur C. "John Wesley and the Church Fathers" (Ph.D. dissertation, St. Louis University, 1985).

[Fleury, Claude.] *An Historical Account of the Manners and Behaviour of the Christians.* London: Thomas Leigh, 1698; reprint ed., University Microfilms International, English Books 1641–1707 series, reel 184.

_____ . *The Manners of the Ancient Christians.* Edited by John Wesley. Bristol: Felix Farley, 1749.

_____ . _____ . Based upon the French edition of the *Bibliothèque des Écoles.* Oxford: A. R. Mowbray, 1872.

Fronteau, Jean. Epistola ad . . . Franc. de Harlay . . . In qua de Moribus et Vita Christianorum in primis Ecclesiae Saeculis agitur. Paris: C. Savreux, 1660.

Gambold, John. *The Works of the Reverend John Gambold, A.M.* Bath: S. Hazard, 1789.

Gay, Peter. *The Enlightenment: An Interpretation.* New York: Alfred Knopf, 1966. Vol. 1, *The Rise of Modern Paganism.*

Green, Richard. *The Works of John and Charles Wesley: A Bibliography.* London: Kelly, 1896.

Green, Vivian H. H. *The Young Mr. Wesley: A Study of John Wesley and Oxford.* London: Epworth Press, 1963.

Greenslade, Stanley Lawrence. *The English Reformers and the Fathers of the Church.* Oxford: Clarendon Press, 1960.

Haaugaard, William P. "Renaissance Patristic Scholarship and Theology in Sixteenth-Century England." *Sixteenth-Century Journal* 10 (1979):37–60.

Heitzenrater, Richard P., ed. *Diary of an Oxford Methodist: Benjamin Ingham, 1733–1734.* Durham, NC: Duke University Press, 1985.

_____. "John Wesley and the Oxford Methodists, 1725–1735." Ph.D. dissertation, Duke University, 1972.

Herbert, Thomas Walter. *John Wesley as Editor and Author.* Princeton Studies in English, no. 17. Princeton, New Jersey: Princeton University Press, 1940.

Hill, [John Edward] Christopher. *The World Turned Upside Down.* New York: Penguin Books, 1976.

Horneck, Anthony. *The Happy Ascetick: or, the Best Exercise.* London: Henry Mortlock, fourth edition, 1699.

Keefer, Luke L. "John Wesley, Disciple of Early Christianity." Ph.D. dissertation, Temple University, 1982.

King, Peter. *An Inquiry into the Constitution, Discipline, Unity, and Worship of the Primitive Church that Flourished within the First Three Hundred Years after Christ.* New York: G. Lane and P. Sandford, 1841.

Lacarriére, Jacques. *Men Possessed by God: The Story of the Desert Monks of Ancient Christendom.* Translated by Roy Monckom. Garden City, New York: Doubleday, 1964.

Lambert, M. D. *Franciscan Poverty: The Doctrine of the Absolute Poverty of Christ and the Apostles in the Franciscan Order, 1210–1323.* London: SPCK, 1961.

Lathbury, Thomas. *A History of the Non-Jurors.* London: William Pickering, 1845.

Leith, John, ed. *Creeds of the Churches*. Second edition. Atlanta: John Knox Press, 1973.

Lindström, Harald. *Wesley and Sanctification*. London: Epworth Press, 1950.

Littell, Franklin H. *The Origins of Sectarian Protestantism*. Second edition (formerly published as *The Anabaptist View of the Church*). New York: The Macmillan Co., 1964.

Lovejoy, Arthur O., and George Boas. *Primitivism and Related Ideas in Antiquity*. Originally published in 1935; reprint ed., New York: Octagon Books, 1965.

Luoma, John K. "Who Owns the Fathers? Hooker and Cartwright on the Authority of the Primitive Church." *Sixteenth-Century Journal* 8 (October 1977):45–59.

Macarius [pseudo-]. Primitive Morality: or, the Spiritual Homilies of St. Macarius the Egyptian. London: W. Taylor and J. Innys, 1721.

McAdoo, Henry R. *The Spirit of Anglicanism: A Survey of Anglican Theological Methodology in the Seventeenth Century*. New York: Charles Scribner's Sons, 1965.

McIntosh, Lawrence D. "The Nature and Design of Christianity in John Wesley's Early Theology: A Study in the Relationship of Love and Faith." Ph.D. dissertation, Drew University, 1966.

_____. "The Place of John Wesley in the Christian Tradition: A Selected Bibliography." In Kenneth Rowe, ed. *The Place of Wesley in the Christian Tradition*. Metuchen, New Jersey: The Scarecrow Press, 1976, pp. 134–159.

Mallett, Charles Edward. *A History of the University of Oxford*. 3 vols. New York: Longmans, Green, and Co., 1924.

Marshall, Nathaniel. *The Penitential Discipline of the Primitive Church for the First Four Hundred Years after Christ*. Library of Anglo-Catholic Theology. Oxford: John Henry Parker, 1844.

Matthews, Rex Dale. "'Religion and Reason Joined': A Study in the Theology of John Wesley." Ph.D. dissertation, Harvard University, 1986.

Meinhold, Peter. *Geschichte der kirchlichen Historiographie*. Munich: Verlag Karl Albert Freiburg, 1967.

Meyers, Arthur C. "John Wesley and the Church Fathers." Ph.D. dissertation, St. Louis University, 1985.

Middleton, Conyers. *A Free Inquiry into the Miraculous Powers which are Supposed to have Subsisted in the Christian Church through Several Successive Centuries*. London: R. Manby and H. S. Cox, 1749; reprint ed., New York: Garland Publishing Co., 1976.

Moorman, John. *A History of the Franciscan Order: From its Origins to the Year 1517*. Oxford: Clarendon Press, 1968.

Mosheim, John Lawrence [i.e., Johann Lorenz von]. *An Ecclesiastical History*. Translated by Archibald MacLaine. 4 vols. London: Thomas Tegg et al., 1826.

National Union Catalog: Pre–1956 Imprints. 685 vols. London: Mansell, 1968–1980.

Nelson, Robert. *A Companion to the Festivals and Fasts of the Church of England*. London: SPCK, 1845.

Newton, Thomas. *Dissertations on the Prophecies*. London: J. F. Dove (no date given).

Niebuhr, H. Richard. *Christ and Culture*. New York: Harper and Row, 1951.

Outler, Albert C. *John Wesley*. A Library of Protestant Thought. New York: Oxford University Press, 1964.

_____ . "John Wesley's Interests in the Early Fathers of the Church." *The Bulletin* (Committee on Archives and History of the United Church of Canada) 29 (1983 [1980–1982]): 5–17.

_____ . "A New Future for Wesley Studies: An Agenda for 'Phase III,'" in M. Douglas Meeks, ed. *The Future of the Methodist Theological Traditions* (Nashville: Abingdon Press, 1985), pp. 34–52.

_____ . *Theology in the Wesleyan Spirit*. Nashville: Tidings, 1975.

Palladius. *Palladius: The Lausiac History*. Translated by Robert J. Meyer. Westminster, Maryland: Newman Press, 1955.

Pearson, John. *An Exposition of the Creed*. New York: D. Appleton and Co., 1851.

_____ . *Vindiciae Epistolarum S. Ignatii*. 2 vols. Libary of Anglo-Catholic Theology. Oxford: John Henry Parker, 1852.

Pelikan, Jaroslav. *The Christian Tradition*, vol. 1, *The Emergence of the Catholic Tradition*. Chicago and London: University of Chicago Press.

Petry, Ray C. *Francis of Assisi: Apostle of Poverty*. Durham, North Carolina: Duke University Press, 1941.

Piette, Maximin. *John Wesley in the Evolution of Protestantism*. New York: Sheed and Ward, 1937.

Piggott, Stuart. *Ruins in a Landscape: Essays in Antiquarianism*. Edinburgh: Edinburgh University Press, 1976.

Pothorn, Herbert. *Architectural Styles*. New York: The Viking Press, 1971.

Quasten, Johannes. *Patrology*. 3 vols. Westminster, Maryland: Newman Press, 1960.

Rack, Henry. *Reasonable Enthusiast*. Philadelphia: Trinity Press International, 1989.

Reeves, William. *The Apologies of Justin Martyr, Tertullian, and Minucius Felix in Defence of the Christian Religion*. 2 vols. London: A. and J. Chiswell, 1709.

Reinhold, Meyer, ed. *The Classick Pages: Classical Reading of Eighteenth-Century Americans*. University Park, Pennsylvania: American Philological Association, 1975.

Rowe, Kenneth E., ed. *The Place of Wesley in the Christian Tradition*. Metuchen, New Jersey: The Scarecrow Press, 1976.

_____. "The Search for the Historical Wesley." In Kenneth E. Rowe, ed. *The Place of Wesley in the Christian Tradition* (Metuchen, New Jersey: The Scarecrow Press, 1976), pp. 1–10.

Runyon, Theodore M., ed. *Sanctification and Liberation*. Nashville: Abingdon Press, 1981.

Rupp, Gordon. "Son to Samuel: John Wesley, Church of England Man." In Kenneth E. Rowe, ed. *The Place of Wesley in the Christian Tradition* (Metuchen, New Jersey: The Scarecrow Press, 1976), pp. 39–66.

Sabatier, Paul. *Life of St. Francis of Assisi*. New York: Charles Scribner's Sons, 1922.

Schmidt, Martin. *John Wesley: A Theological Biography*. 2 vols. Translated by Norman Goldhawk. Nashville: Abingdon Press, 1963–1973.

_____. "John Wesley's Place in Church History." In Kenneth E. Rowe, ed. *The Place of Wesley in the Christian Tradition*. Metuchen, New Jersey: The Scarecrow Press, 1976.

Slater, William F. *Methodism in the Light of the Early Church*. London: T. Woolmer, 1885.

Snyder, Howard. *The Radical Wesley and Patterns for Church Renewal*. Downers Grove, Illinois: InterVarsity Press, 1980.

Spener, Philipp Jakob. *Pia Desideria*. Translated by Theodore G. Tappert. Philadelphia: Fortress Press, 1964.

Stephen, Leslie. *History of English Thought in the Eighteenth Century*. 2 vols. New York: Harcourt, Brace, and World, 1962.

Stephen, Leslie, and Sidney Lee, eds. *Dictionary of National Biography*. 28 vols. Oxford: Oxford University Press, 1921–1922.

Stillingfleet, Edward. *The Irenicum, or Pacificator: Being a Reconciler of Church Differences*. Philadelphia: M. Sorin, 1842.

Stoeffler, F. Ernest. *German Pietism during the Eighteenth Century*. Studies in the History of Religions, no. 24. Leiden: E. J. Brill, 1973.

_____. *The Rise of Evangelical Pietism*. Studies in the History of Religions, no. 9. Leiden: E. J. Brill, 1965.

_____. "Tradition and Renewal in the Ecclesiology of John Wesley." In Bernd Jaspert, ed. *Traditio, Krisis, Renovatio als theologischer Sicht: Festschrift Winfried Zeller*. Marburg, Elwert, 1976, pp. 298–316.

Sykes, Norman. *From Sheldon to Secker: Aspects of English Church History, 1660–1768*. Cambridge: Cambridge University Press, 1959.

_____. *William Wake, Archbishop of Canterbury, 1657–1737*. 2 vols. Cambridge: Cambridge University Press, 1957.

Temple, Sir William. *The Works of Sir William Temple, bart.* 4 vols. Edinburgh: G. Hamilton et al., 1754.

Thompson, Edgar W. *Wesley: Apostolic Man: Some Reflections on Wesley's Consecration of Dr. Thomas Coke*. London: The Epworth Press, 1957.

Turner, Victor. "Metaphors of Anti-Structure in Religious Culture." In Alan W. Eister, ed. *Changing Perspectives in the Scientific Study of Religion* (New York: John Wiley and Sons, 1974), pp. 63–84.

Tyerman, Luke. *The Life and Times of the Rev. Samuel Wesley, M. A.* London: Simpkin, Marshall, and Co., 1866.

Urlin, R. Denny. *The Churchman's Life of Wesley*. London: SPCK, revised edition, 1880.

_____. *John Wesley's Place in Church History*. London: Rivington's, 1870.

Vatro, Murvar. "Toward a Sociological Theory of Religious Movements." *Journal for the Scientific Study of Religion* 14 (September 1975): 229–256.

Vogt, Evon Z. "Culture Change." In David L. Sills, ed. *International Encyclopedia of the Social Sciences*. New York: The Macmillan Co. and the Free Press, 1968, 3:554–558.

Wake, William, trans. *The Genuine Epistles of the Apostolical Fathers*. London: Richard Sare, 1693.

Wakefield, Gordon S. "La Littérature du Désert chez John Wesley." *Irenikon* 51 (1978): 155–170.

Wakefield, Henry Offley. *An Introduction to the History of the Church in England.* London: Rivington's, revised edition, 1919.

Wallace, Anthony F. C. "Revitalization Movements." *American Anthropologist* 58 (1956): 264–281.

Ward, Benedicta, trans. *Sayings of the Desert Fathers [Apothegmata Patrum].* Oxford: Mowbrays, 1975.

Weinlick, John R. *Count Zinzendorf.* New York and Nashville: Abingdon Press, 1961.

Welsby, Paul A. *Lancelot Andrewes, 1555–1626.* London: SPCK, 1958.

Wesley, John, editor. *A Christian Library: Consisting of Extracts from and Abridgements of the Choicest Pieces of Practical Divinity which have been Published in the English Language.* 50 vols. Bristol: Felix Farley, 1749–1755.

_____, _____. 30 vols. London: 1819.

_____, and Charles Wesley. *Hymns and Sacred Poems.* London: William Strahan, 1739.

_____. *John Wesley's Forty-Four Sermons.* London: Epworth Press, 1944.

_____. *The Journal of the Reverend John Wesley, A.M.* Ed. Nehemiah Curnock. 8 vols. New York: Eaton and Mains, 1938.

_____. *Journal and Diaries.* Edited by W. Reginald Ward and Richard P. Heitzenrater. The Bicentennial Edition of the Works of John Wesley, vols. 18ff. Nashville: Abingdon Press, 1988.

_____. *Letters.* Edited by Frank Baker. The Bicentennial Edition of the Works of John Wesley, vols. 25ff. Oxford: Oxford University Press, 1980.

_____. *The Letters of the Reverend John Wesley, A.M.* Edited by John Telford. London: Epworth Press, 1931.

_____. ms. "Canons." A single sheet with 2 pages on each side, in the Methodist Archives, the John Rylands University Library, Manchester.

_____. ms. "Constitutions." A single sheet containing notes on the Apostolic Constitutions, in the Methodist Archives, the John Rylands University Library, Manchester.

_____. ms. diaries. Wesley's diaries are largely included in the mss. of the Colman collection, in the Methodist Archives, the John Rylands University Library, Manchester. I have cited the diaries in this work by date, then (in parentheses), by ms. name, volume, and page number(s).

_____. ms. "Different Views of Christianity." A 4–page ms. dated 25 January 1738 recounting the intellectual settings of Wesley's spiritual search, in the Wesley materials at Wesley College, Bristol.

_____. ms. "Of the Weekly Fasts of the Church." A ms. in the third Georgia diary (Ms. Colman 15), in the Methodist Archives, the John Rylands University Library, Manchester.

_____. *Sermons*. Edited by Albert C. Outler. 4 vols. The Bicentennial Edition of the Works of John Wesley, vols. 1–4. Nashville: Abingdon Press, 1984–1987.

_____. *The Sunday Service of the Methodists in North America*. London: [Strahan,] 1784.

_____, and Charles Wesley. *The Poetical Works of John and Charles Wesley*. Edited by George Osborn. 13 vols. London: Wesleyan Methodist Conference Office, 1868.

_____. *Wesley's Standard Sermons*. Edited by Edward H. Sugden. 2 vols. London: Epworth Press, third edition, 1951.

_____. *The Works of the Reverend John Wesley, A.M.* Edited by Thomas Jackson. 14 vols. London: Wesleyan Conference Office, 1872.

Wesley, Samuel. *Advice to a Young Clergyman, in a Letter to Him*. London: C. Rivington, 1735.

_____. *Dissertationes in Librum Jobi*. London: William Bowyer, 1736.

_____. *The Young Student's Library*. London: John Dunton, 1692.

Williams, Colin. *John Wesley's Theology Today*. New York and Nashville: Abingdon Press, 1960.

Williams, George Huntston. *The Radical Reformation*. Philadelphia: The Westminster Press, 1962.

Williams, Glanmor. *Reformation Views of Church History*. Ecumenical Studies in History, no. 11. Richmond, Virginia: John Knox Press, 1970.

Williams, John. *A Catechism truly Representing the Doctrines and Practices of the Church of Rome, with an Answer Thereunto*. London: R. Chiswell, 1686; reprint ed., University Microfilms International, "Early English Books, 1641–1700" series, reel 951.

Wood, Laurence W. *Pentecostal Grace*. Wilmore, Kentucky: Francis Asbury Press, 1980.

Workman, Herbert B. *The Place of Methodism in the Catholic Church.* London: Epworth Press, second edition, 1921.

_____ . *The Evolution of the Monastic Ideal.* Boston: Beacon Press, 1962.

Index